TOWARDS TRUE MONETARISM

TOWARDS TRUE MONETARISM

by
GEOFFREY GARDINER

Master of Arts, Cambridge
Fellow of the Institute of Chartered Secretaries and Administrators
Associate of the Chartered Institute of Bankers

THE DULWICH PRESS

First published 1993 by
THE DULWICH PRESS
Reg. Off. 3 Bedford Row, London, WC1R 4BU
Editorial: 59 Court Lane, Dulwich, London SE21 7DP

British Library Cataloguing in Publication Data

Gardiner, G. W.
  Towards True Monetarism
  1. Monetary Theory
  332.4

  ISBN 1-897657-01-3

Typeset by G. W. Gardiner in Monotype Plantin 11/13
Imagesetting by Print Co-ordination Ltd, Macclesfield

Production T · O · P West · Cornwall
Printed by Latimer Trend & Company Ltd, Plymouth

CONTENTS

CONTENTS

This book is dedicated with deepest sympathy to all those people throughout the world who have suffered from the folly of high interest rates.

Their suffering was quite needless. Sadly they may be the largest group of people ever to receive a dedication.

INTRODUCTION

'Every why hath a wherefore.'
WILLIAM SHAKESPEARE

A HISTORIC GENERAL ELECTION was held in the United Kingdom on Thursday third of May 1979. Future historians may even conclude that it was a turning point in the history of the world as well as in the history of the United Kingdom, for much of what was done by the new government elected that day was later imitated in other countries.

The election removed from power a government which reflected an uneasy compromise between intellectual middle class socialists, leaders of the working class, and arrogant trade union barons. More importantly a left-wing tradition which had been dominant throughout the twentieth century, infecting even nominally right-wing parties, was put into slow but steady retreat. That tradition had become too destructive, despite its good intentions.

By one of the greatest ironies of all political history, the radical policies of the incoming Conservative government were strongly reminiscent of those which the nineteenth century architect of the party, Benjamin Disraeli, had contested. In his day capitalism, free trade, the market economy, and non-intervention by government were all *left-wing* causes espoused by the Liberal party. Even the new government's views on social welfare tended towards the Malthusian principles of the Poor Law of the 1830s. It seems unlikely that many of the new leaders had read with enthusiasm

Disraeli's memorable political and social novel *Sybil: or The Two Nations*. That novel had highlighted the grim realities of the new industrial society, and preached the responsibilities of the rich and the government towards the poor. Three decades after writing the novel, Disraeli as prime minister led a government which ameliorated the evils of an unplanned economy by great public works intended to fulfil Disraeli's motto *Sanitas sanitatum*, which he humourously translated as '*Sanitation, all is sanitation*'.

The new Conservative government of May 1979 favoured the economic principles of Adam Smith, reasoning with considerable justification that intervention by the state in industry had proved in practice to have the opposite effect of what was intended. Naturally the new policies came to be known as *Thatcherism* After the new prime minister, Mrs. Margaret Thatcher, without whose inspiring leadership the changes might not have been effected.

The election therefore precipitated a chain of events which led to the toppling of communist and socialist dominance of political and economic theory worldwide. Many will see that decline as wholly good for the world. It also triggered important changes in the structure of the economy and the industry of the United Kingdom. The consequences of those changes were to be partly very good, and partly very damaging. The evaluation of whether the good outweighed the bad must be left to future economic historians, but what can now be proved is that many of the bad effects were wholly unnecessary. This book explains why that is so. Its further purpose is to show that the sound elements of Thatcherism, if they had been allied with *true* monetarism, might have been wholly beneficial.

A chilly start

General Election Day 1979 was very cold for early May. A long and severe winter seemed most reluctant to end. It had been made especially uncomfortable by a succession of strikes precipitated by leaders of public sector trade unions who were angry at the effect of inflation on the purchasing power of their members' wages. Journalists named it *The Winter of Discontent*. The considerable and longstanding ability of the trade unions to disrupt the economy had been strengthened by a minority Labour government which was unprepared to face reality.

Like most others who voted, I had not supported the existing Labour government, for I hoped that there could be some change in the post-war socialist consensus which had hampered British industrial growth, and had particularly damaged the private business sector. The success of numerous private companies, small and large, was very important to me in my role as manager of an office administering 8,000 private trusts. In some of those trusts we held controlling interests in private businesses, and were therefore entirely responsible for their future. Our trust administrators could be as emotionally involved in the businesses as if they had been their own, and we all knew well the damage governments could do, and had done, to industry. Indeed, for the previous 26 years I had experienced the full horror of a ringside seat at the destruction of British private industry. I desperately wished to see the destructive process brought to an end. For many years I had campaigned both politically and as part of my work for sensible economic and taxation policies which would both ensure the survival of small private businesses, and encourage them to grow.

After voting in the Cambridge constituency my wife and I set out on a motorcaravanning holiday in the Northwest Highlands of Scotland. A fierce northerly blizzard slowed our progress up the Great North Road, and by the time we reached our first night's stop-over the first election results were coming through on the radio. We stayed up to listen to them. Very late in the night it became clear that Mrs. Margaret Thatcher would be the new Prime Minister. We at last switched off the radio. A few stormy clouds were scudding across the clear cold Highland sky, occasionally concealing the stars which always seem so much bigger and brighter in northern latitudes. I lay awake wondering what storms lay ahead for the economy.

Contributing advice

For some years I had been contributing advice to the government on economic and legal topics through membership of committees and conferences. I had conducted economic research of my own, including, in 1971, an inflation accounting appraisal of the whole of the industrial sector of the British economy. I had to invent my own method of doing this as inflation accounting was not yet a settled technique. Fortunately the method I devised proved to be near to that later established in an official statement of accounting practice. My calculations convinced me that conventional historic cost accounting was disguising the fact that British industry was in long-term decline.

In 1973 I took part in a conference of economists at the Civil Service College, Sunningdale, on the problem of the control of inflation. It was organised by the head of economic training for the Civil Service, J. L. Carr. Primarily the conference was for Civil Service economists, but a few outsiders had been invited, two from clearing banks, one from the Bank of England, one from the American Embassy. The French Département de la Prévision sent a representative who especially impressed me with his knowledge and understanding. Speakers included the well-known economists Francis Cripps, Professor Geoffrey Maynard, and Professor Alan Walters. The College's own staff at the time included Alec Chrystal who later became a professor. One reason for Professor Alan Walters being there was to put the monetarist viewpoint, which was still something of a novelty, even though it had been strongly advocated for some years by Harold Wincott, leading columnist of *The Financial Times*, and by Enoch Powell M.P.

My own constructive contribution to the discussion at the conference seemed original but it found no favour. It was that since the capital base of the banks determines the amount of intermediated credit which can be created, the money supply could be readily controlled by restricting the banks' access to new capital, whether from the market or from accumulation of profits. The tool for effecting the restriction would be the Control of Borrowing legislation, supplemented by power to prevent banks from capitalising profits rather than distributing them to their shareholders as dividends.

There was plenty of discussion of monetarism and so my report on the conference included the following comment:-

> 'At the end of the seminar everyone present was agreed that an incomes policy was necessary. Although the monetarist view was appreciated there was no-one who agreed with Enoch Powell that the problem could be resolved by purely monetarist measures. The importance of the money supply was not under-rated but it was felt that a monetarist solution must in

*the present circumstances and given the present attitude of trade
unionists result in high unemployment.'*

Nevertheless my note went on to express the unhappiness of
the members of the conference with the idea of long-term physical
controls of incomes and prices. Certainly I did not have in mind
the sort of incomes policy then generally advocated. The last sentence of the quotation later proved to be an accurate prophecy.

I also became a member of *The Cambridge Policy Conference on
the Future of British Agriculture* which met in late 1976. Although
officially organised by Professor Sir Joseph Hutchinson (an emeritus Professor of Agriculture of Cambridge University), and
Dunstan Skilbeck, former principal of Wye College, the driving
force was undoubtedly Professor Sir Frank Engledow, also an
emeritus Professor of Agriculture, and one of the most important
scientists of the twentieth century. My part in the conference was
a dual role of taxation expert and economics adviser, though an
added qualification must have been that my office was normally
responsible in some degree, either as trustee or executor, for as
much as one thousand hectares of farmland.

Shortly before the 1979 election a working party of the
Conference, consisting of M. C. Thompson, of the Cambridge
University Department of Land Economy, F. R. Goodenough, a
director of Barclays Bank and a farmer, and myself, had published
a paper called *Tax and British Agriculture*. In it we had suggested
that the advent of North Sea oil raised a strong possibility that
sterling would become overvalued. We therefore suggested a
taxation régime which might counteract the detrimental effect of
overvaluation on the competitiveness of British industry. Our
views were repeated in a book, *Britain's Future in Farming*, edited
by Sir Frank Engledow and Leonard Amey, a former agricultural
correspondent of *The Times* newspaper, and financed by the
Nuffield Trust.

In October 1973 I had become a member of the Council of
the Institute of Chartered Secretaries and Administrators, a
professional body with 50,000 members scattered across countries
of the British Commonwealth and Ireland. My particular duties
included membership of the Law and Technical Services
Committee which formulated the Council's responses to all

government and European Commission discussion documents, and commented on draft legislation. Inflation accounting and company law reform were two lively topics then under consideration. I was also chairman of a working party considering a new legal structure for small businesses, and I had served on a working party which advised on the reform of the bankruptcy laws.

As I lay awake early that morning of the 4th May 1979 there was naturally a question in my mind: *'Will any of the policies and theories which I have instigated or campaigned for find favour with the new government?'* I had long been an advocate of a more market oriented economy when that was unpopular, and of neutral taxation when that too seemed a lost cause. On those two topics the answer to my question proved to be a qualified 'Yes!' Between 1964 and 1971, stimulated by lunchtime conversations with Professor James Meade and by discussions with another well-known economist, Dr. Malcolm R. Fisher, I had evolved my own answers to the main problems of monetary theory and policy. On those problems the answer to my question proved to be a firm 'No!' After 1971 I lost contact with Meade who went on to win the Nobel Prize and chair the Institute of Fiscal Studies' committee on *The Structure and Reform of Direct Taxation in Britain*. The *Meade Report*, as it was popularly known, was published not long before the 1979 general election.

Naturally I assumed that the deep flaws in monetary theory which I had detected would also be noted by the government's advisers. I did not therefore expect high interest rates to last long, especially as I regarded a permanently overvalued sterling to be the most damaging eventuality for the economy. That risk would be increased if interest rates stayed high. Perhaps a brief bout of severity would take place, just enough to frighten the unions into acquiescence. I underestimated both the crusading zeal of the new government and the intransigence of the trade unions. On the other hand I overestimated the government's ability to be tough towards organised labour. Mrs. Thatcher's first Minister of Labour, though highly respected for his knowledge and business experience, seemed to prefer persuasion to toughness. Effective action to deal with the unions was badly delayed. I also underestimated the importance of the need for privatisation. I would now acknowledge that detecting the importance of privatisation was

Mrs. Thatcher's greatest contribution to industrial efficiency. Across the world even socialist parties now acknowledge the principle is valid, though some stubborn dinosaurs, (of the species *tyrannosaurus burocraticus*), linger on in all British political parties. Mrs. Thatcher, by her determined action on privatisation helped Britain; and Britain's example helped the world. Overall, though, her gamut of economic policies was reminiscent of the legendary curate's egg - good and bad by parts. Indeed one must go further and say that it was very good, and very bad by parts.

The aim of this book is to reverse the bad parts. It advocates, above all, one clear and vital principle: that there is no need at all to use high interest rates as a weapon of economic policy, and certainly not of monetary policy.

The plan

First we shall review the monetary policies implemented by Mrs. Thatcher's first finance minister. Second we shall examine orthodox monetary theory. Third we shall examine all the techniques which have been used to attempt to control the money supply, and I shall try to demonstrate very clearly why they were wrong. Then we shall look at the history of the British economy from 1920 onwards giving particular attention to the credit supply and its relationship to economic growth.

The historical review will throw much light on the main influences on inflation and deflation. In these and later chapters many accepted economic theories will be challenged and there will be criticism of the misuse of scientific and mathematical techniques by economists. Some of the new arguments put forward in this book must challenge the basis of many economic textbooks and all of those devoted to conventional monetary theory. A chapter is included on the theory of saving in order to negate some illusions propagated by Lord Keynes. We shall also question the legitimacy of economic modelling.

How this book started

Since 1971 I have written many letters to the editor of the *Financial Times*, mostly on subjects to do with economic policy. The great majority have been published. Letters published in the *Financial Times* often provoke letters to the author from other readers, who quite commonly are also writers of letters to this wonderful newspaper. I have several files of letters, sometimes from overseas, and a mass of information acquired in this way. Some lasting friendships have been made.

On the 27th February 1988 a letter of mine received special prominence by being given a headline the width of five columns. The headline was a quotation from the letter and read, *'High interest rates are no better remedy for inflation than bloodletting was for fever.'* It provoked a letter from Christopher Meakin, who not only writes letters to the editor but had even started his working life as a writer on the *Financial Times.* We shared similar heretical views about monetary policy. A correspondence ensued which quickly led to a suggestion by Christopher that we should jointly write a new version of economic theory, and that I should take responsibility for the section on monetary theory. Unfortunately pressure of work prevented Christopher from completing the project, but the preliminary chapters on money were written.

The next event was in 1990 when Damon de Laszlo, Martin Cadman, and James Bourlet, Chairman and Secretaries of the Economic Research Council, asked me for a series of articles on monetary theory which could be combined to make a book. I started work on this difficult task, but in January 1991 I became so concerned about the effect of high interest rates on small businesses that I telephoned Stanley Mendham, director of the Forum of Private Business, and asked if his organisation would like to have the arguments which would prove that high interest rates were unnecessary. This offer was accepted and great help was also given in return.

The paper containing the arguments displaced the earlier project and was completed in September 1991. A few copies were distributed to sympathisers and their comments sought. One of them was not an economist, but an internationally eminent scientist, Dr. Jitendra Mehrishi, of the Department of Medicine at Cambridge University, and Fellow of the Royal College of Pathologists. He has long played Mentor to my Telemachus on scientific matters. He insisted that the paper must be published as a learned monograph, and proceeded to do everything in his power to try to ensure that happened. However Christopher Meakin had also received a copy and, free at last to undertake such work, urged a more popular format, and took over the final stages of publication, which have been the most onerous. He has given detailed guidance and help on the text itself and on sources, and helped determine the style of the book.

Acknowledgements

Most sincere thanks are therefore due to Christopher Meakin, Dr. Jitendra Mehrishi, Damon de Laszlo, Martin Cadman, and James Bourlet. My wife, Beryl, must be thanked for her outstanding help. She must be particularly thanked for accepting willingly the large financial sacrifice entailed in my switch from business to academic research, and for spending so many hours on checking.

Others to whom thanks are due include Michael Moore, who has provided a mass of essential information, and E. J. Quill, former member of the committee of the Economic Research Council, for both the pressure he kept upon me, and for important information culled from his varied collection of useful and occasionally quite seditious literature. A Swiss, Guido Dreier, is to be thanked for informing me about the Gesellians, and I also thank Gunnar Tomasson for showing me the scholarly papers with which he vainly tried to change attitudes among the economists of the International Monetary Fund. Finally I thank a valued old friend, Michael Watts, for acting as guineapig in a test to see if an intelligent non-economist could understand what I had written.

CHAPTER ONE

THE ASCENT OF MONETARISM

'There have been three great inventions since the beginning
of time: fire, the wheel, and central banking.'
WILL ROGERS

S IR GEOFFREY HOWE, a lawyer by training with little direct
business or industrial experience, was appointed Chancellor
of the Exchequer in the new Cabinet in May 1979. He put into
effect a tough policy for the control of the British economy. It was
a policy that would lay waste much of British industry, and especially manufacturing industry, though the Prime Minister and the
Chancellor believed that the purpose and achievement were to
revive the British economy. Great things were indeed done, which
were vitally necessary for industry and the economy, but the
aggregate net effect of all the measures taken was long-term
damage. That damage need not have happened.

Although the policies of the post 1979 Conservative governments are the main objects of criticism in the following chapters,
the criticism is in no way party political. Indeed one of the
continuing threats to the British economy is that the doctrines
which Sir Geoffrey Howe accepted and applied from 1979 are
also commonly accepted by opposing politicians and their advisers. For that very reason attacks on Conservative policy during the
period 1979-1992 were ineffective. All parties seem to have
accepted the same basic monetarist teaching. Other countries of
the European Community have also accepted it, and so have
many countries elsewhere in the world. It seems also to be the

basis of policies supported by the International Monetary Fund, whose client nations must therefore accept it as received wisdom.

The new economic policy

The policy was described as being monetarist, because its keystone was control of the money supply. There are however substantial differences among monetary theorists as to what are the correct measures to be applied in order to control the money supply. Chancellor Howe adopted the variant of monetarism which relies principally on the level of interest rates to control credit creation, and he supported it by the technique of overfunding. The principles behind these and other techniques will be described and discussed in Chapters Four to Seven. In adopting interest rates as the main weapon for the control of credit, the new government departed from the teaching of Professor Milton Friedman, who was accepted as the leading authority on monetarism. Friedman favoured more direct forms of control.

Shortly after taking office Sir Geoffrey Howe introduced a Budget. At the same time he raised the minimum lending rate (MLR) to 14 per cent, four percentage points above the rate imposed for seven days at the outbreak of the First World War in order to deal with a major banking crisis. The clearing banks responded to the rise in MLR by raising their base rates to 14 per cent on 15th June 1979, an increase of two per cent. On November 16th 1979 base rates rose by three per cent to 17 per cent, a record level and almost a record rise too.

Although the level of MLR set in June 1979 was not the highest ever known, the level of short-term nominal interest rates in 1979 was a record, soon to be broken, for the century. The average annual return on Treasury bills for 1978 was 8.06 per cent, for 1979 13.45 per cent, and for 1980 17.17 per cent, 34 times higher than the return in the period 1946 to 1948. Yet that period had included a grave crisis for sterling.

Market economics

Besides monetarism the new government was committed to the principle of a market oriented economy. The markets were to be left to decide what might be best for the economy, and the government intended not to intervene. In practice governments can never wholly resist the temptation to intervene, but the Prime Minister, Mrs. Margaret Thatcher, was strongly committed in principle to the philosophy of non-intervention.

She recognised that an economy is a complex living organism with its own natural balance, and that interference by government is usually based on too poor an understanding of the way the organism works for it to do anything but harm. There are occasionally good reasons for interfering, which will be looked at in Chapter Sixteen, but one must accept that in 1979 there was a very strong argument in favour of allowing market forces to have greater influence than had been permitted by any government since the end of the 1939-45 War. Many of Mrs. Thatcher's ministers, however, seemed less committed than she to the principle of non-intervention in the working of the economy.

Paradoxically Sir Geoffrey Howe's action in arbitrarily raising interest rates was an immediate contravention of the principles of market economics. There are those who think that in a free market for money market forces will set interest rates, and should be encouraged to do so. Sir Geoffrey Howe's action had the effect of confirming that a central bank can, within quite wide limits, fix the interest rate without regard to market forces. In economic jargon interest rates can be *administered*, though it may be much easier to administer short-term rates than long-term. (The influence of market forces on long-term rates of interest will be shown in Chapter Nine to have been significant from 1965 onwards.)

The flow of money

A bank may lend money it does not yet possess in the certain knowledge that the laws of double entry bookkeeping will ensure that the money must also exist as a credit balance somewhere around the banking system. It can therefore be retrieved as a deposit to provide the bank with the liability which will balance the asset resulting from its new lending. If one bank has fewer deposits than lendings, it is a logical and arithmetical certainty that some other bank will have fewer lendings than deposits. In a real time accounting system this would be immediately apparent.

If the money transfer system could operate electronically in real time a simple banking system which had no central bank might be operable. The problem of ironing out surpluses and deficits in the balances of individual banks would be solved by loans made direct from the one with a surplus of deposits to the one with excess lendings. But such a direct answer may not be practicable, and it is not favoured in a complex banking system such as that of Britain. Instead in Britain there is a sophisticated structure called *the Money Market* which irons out fluctuations in the need for funds of the various lending institutions. The final source of funds when a bank is desperate for deposits is the Bank of England. If the required funds cannot be found anywhere else in the money market, by elimination they must be in the books of the Bank of England. The Bank of England can set any price for its emergency lending, and the price it chooses, in the form of the rate of interest it charges, determines interest rates throughout the banking system.

The money transfer system does not operate entirely in real time. So there may also be time lags which could aggravate the problem of shortages of funds. For technical reasons, which are not relevant to the argument of this book, time lags are probably not a serious problem, but if they were, the central bank could neutralise them by creating and supplying funds. It could do this too at whatever interest rate it chose.

The central bank's power to influence interest rates is certainly not dependent only on the effect of time lags in the flow of money: it has the support of a much more important factor. The Bank of England also relieves banks' shortages of banknotes by swapping them for investments. The price which it elects to pay for investments, usually gilts, Treasury bills or bills of exchange, will establish the rate of interest on those investments also. In the 1970s an attempt was made to relate the Bank of England's minimum lending rate to market led criteria. It did not last. The government soon took effective control again.

Shortages of funds

Conventional textbook theory needs a slight clarification. Popular textbooks, even modern ones, seem to imply that there can be shortages of funds which the Bank of England can supply only by creating new money. Their authors may have somewhat misinterpreted the practicalities of the situation through incomplete mastery of the principles of double entry book-keeping. They have failed to see that all money is debt, and that if debt has been created by a bank, then money for a balancing deposit has inevitably been created too. Any funds needed to eliminate a shortage must already be on their way to the Bank of England, because any surplus must show up in its books once the system's brief time lag has been overcome. A permanent creation of new money should therefore never be necessary. Judging by their private statements, Bank treasurers well understand this principle.[1]

Between the Bank of England and the other banks stands a buffer in the form of the discount houses. When banks have surplus funds they may place them with a discount house, which will then lend them to the bank which is short of funds, or place them with the Bank of England. When a bank needs money it will borrow from a discount house, which in turn may have to borrow from the Bank of England. The banks do not normally deal directly with the Bank of England except with regard to Treasury bills. They generally keep their accounts at the Bank of England to a minimum. The discount house system is curious, and the necessity for its existence is not obvious.

Despite the inclusion of discount houses in the system so that some of the flow of funds between banks appears to be piped through them rather that through the Bank of England, there is no doubt that the Bank alone controls the valve which regulates the flow. Normally it will act to balance the pressures each side of the valve, but it can block the flow briefly, and thereby build up pressures which will have an effect on the level of interest rates.

The Treasury bill market

There is another curious custom. When the government wishes to borrow short-term money it offers a quantity of Treasury bills for sale, usually at regular weekly sales. The custom is that the discount houses are obliged to acquire any unwanted bills to ensure that the whole issue is sold. If the discount houses have insufficient money to complete the purchase, the shortage is covered by a loan from the Bank of England. This practice can only be described as farcical. On page 460 of his book *Money and Banking in the UK: A History*, Michael Collins, a sober historian, records the view that the bill tender contains an element of financial masquerade, and that it is a procedure akin to printing money.

---

[1]Superscript numbers refer to notes at the end of each Chapter.

The Bank of England, however, is satisfied there is a need for such a masquerade and has therefore ensured the survival of a redundant component of the money market, *the Discount Houses*. By insisting that the discount houses remain as a buffer between itself and the clearing banks, the Bank has compromised its ability to influence directly any particular bank which may be stepping out of line or acting imprudently. If all dealings were direct between the central bank and the commercial banks, the central bank would have much greater power, and the power could be much more specific in its effect on individual banks.

Category one money

The Bank of England's power to manage short-term interest rates rests also on its control of the supply of two special forms of money - (a) the common currency (banknotes), and (b) Bank of England deposits.

Professor Charles Goodhart tells us[2] that there is a natural tendency for the national stock of banknotes to flow towards the Bank of England. As he does not give a reason one can only guess, probably wrongly, that this flow might arise because public sector industries receive many payments in the common currency; perhaps the flow has diminished following privatisation. Although the balance sheets of the clearing banks show that they hold what appear to be gigantic sums in notes and coin, it is their practice to keep their stocks of banknotes as low as possible, as they earn no interest and cost a lot to store. Consequently, when banks' customers need to top up their own supplies of banknotes, the banks have to buy them from the Bank of England. The banknotes have to be paid for with the second special variety of money - Bank of England deposits. Perhaps we need a distinctive name for this special variety of money, and a simple yet flattering appellation would be *category one money*.

The clearing banks could pay for banknotes by running down their own balances on deposit at the Bank of England, but there is a limit to how far they can do this: each bank is obliged to keep a prescribed minimum amount on its account with the Bank of England. One would expect them to wish to keep no more than a working minimum credit balance on the account as deposits at the Bank of England are not remunerative. If the banks in the aggregate do not have enough category one money to satisfy the reserve requirement, they can acquire more only by selling investments, directly or indirectly, to the Bank of England. The Bank of England has the whip hand in dealing with these shortages. If only one bank has a shortage it might in theory be able to borrow category one money from another bank, but that is unlikely. The price demanded by the Bank of England for supplying either banknotes or category one money has repercussions throughout the whole financial system.

The textbooks seem to imply that the Bank of England could refuse to cooperate and decide not to make the money available. Perhaps even the Bank of England's own officials believe that could happen. Surely the rules of double entry bookkeeping must come into play; the notion must be wrong. The Bank of England *must* cooperate simply because it is the only way it can balance its own books. The only factor over which it has total discretion is the price it will pay for investments. If it buys them at a low price, it causes interest rates to rise. In the past it has been reluctant to do that because one of its policy objectives has been to support the price of gilts.

There are other special moneys

When one looks closely at the nature of money one discovers that there are many different varieties of money. Each could be given a different label: there is Midland Bank money, Barclays Bank money, Lloyds Bank money, and so on. Each bank's money is a special variety, because it represents its own debts. If a customer of the Midland Bank makes a payment to a customer of Barclays Bank, the Midland Bank then owes money to Barclays. Barclays, however, may not want to hold Midland Bank money - that is a debt from Midland - perhaps because it can get a better return elsewhere. The alternative is for Midland to pay over to Barclays in settlement of its debt some of the category one money on its account with the Bank of England. If the Midland Bank has insufficient money on that account, it can be sure that the Bank of England will be unwilling to hold Midland Bank money in return for supplies of category one money. That would make the two banks creditors of each other! So Midland must acquire some category one money by selling an investment to the Bank of

England, or to some other institution or bank which holds category one money. Or it may borrow from an institution which holds its money on an account at the Bank of England. A discount house is, of course, such an institution.

There appears to be a tendency for the Bank of England to be a net recipient of flows of money of all kinds, not merely banknotes. This gives the Bank of England a further lever on interest rates, for it is a monopoly supplier of last resort loans, and can dictate the terms on which the money returns to the other banks. Besides the reported natural flow of money towards the Bank of England, the government can cause additional money to flow from the banks (banks being widely defined to include building societies) by funding its own debt. The effect of the funding process will be looked at later in a discussion of overfunding. (See Chapter Seven.)

Formalised interest rates

At one time interest rates throughout Britain's banking system had a formal structure. This began in 1917, presumably to ensure stability in wartime. The justification for the formalisation, if there was any, must have been that since the Bank of England could determine rates of interest by market operations, everything could be simplified by relating all interest rates automatically to an announced *Bank Rate*, as the Bank of England's lending rate was then called. From 1917 to 1971, therefore, there existed a full cartel of clearing bank interest rates, and every clearing bank would set its interest rate on its lending in the form *Bank Rate plus 'x' per cent* (usually one per cent), *minimum five per cent*. Interest allowed on deposits was usually Bank Rate less two per cent, with a minimum of half of one per cent. Building society rates of interest were also subject to a cartel, being set for both borrowings and deposits by the Building Societies Association. A very few societies were not members of the Association and were therefore free to set their own rates. During the 1930s the banking cartel's lending rate was above the market rate of interest on bonds traded on the stockmarket, and this may have inhibited the creation of bank credit. If so, it would have been detrimental to the competitive position of those businesses which were too small to raise money through the stockmarket, for they would have had to pay a higher rate of interest on borrowings than their larger competitors who had the advantage of access to the bond market.

Since 1971 governments have preferred the pretence that market forces and competition determine interest rates. As a result each bank is expected to announce its own *base rate*, to which the rates of interest it charges and allows are related. No formal relationship is revealed between the level of base rates and the level of the Bank of England's minimum lending rate, but a fairly consistent relationship seems to exist. In practice MLR and most of the banks' base rates have been the same. Market forces also prevent one clearing bank's base rate from deviating from any other bank's base rate for more than the briefest period of time. Real cut-throat competition would destabilise the banking system.

Sir Geoffrey Howe, by succeeding in 1979 in fixing interest rates at an artificially high level, removed any remaining doubt about the ability of the government to control the trend of short-term interest rates. The government can control them so long as it controls the central bank. In Britain, unlike Germany or the United States, the central bank is under total government control, and has been since 1946.

Despite the events of 1979 many economists were for a while convinced that the market will ultimately determine interest rates. In the Institute of Economic Affairs Hobart Paper 90, *How to End the Monetarist Controversy*, in 1981 Samuel Brittan wrote,

> '*When the Vietnam War and the budget deficits of the late 1960s rendered conventional interest rates incompatible with stable United States monetary growth, the whole post-war monetary system exploded.*'

His opinion seemed well justified at the time he wrote, for U.S. interest rates had risen to a record level in the late 1970s. Later events proved however that government policy, not market forces, was responsible for the high rates. By 1992 the U.S. had returned to very low interest rates despite an even bigger budget deficit, coupled with an enormous trade deficit. There was no credit explosion. Provided it does not want use interest rates to bolster the exchange rate of its currency, a government can defeat the market and keep short-term interest rates low.

Economic vandalism after 1979

From 1979 the British government sought to limit its interference in the economy to the determination of interest rates, leaving the rest to market forces. Its action, however, in raising interest rates was crucial. The effects were far-reaching, and turned out to be different from what was intended. Many in British industry have since concluded that the raising of interest rates in 1979 was nothing less than an act of economic vandalism.

There have been other acts of economic vandalism in Britain. Perhaps the most famous was the repeal of the Corn Laws by Sir Robert Peel in the 1840s. That was done in response to famine, and in order to make food cheaper for urban industrial workers. The international competitiveness of Britain's manufacturing industry was thereby improved, but its farming industry was wrecked, causing very great suffering for farm-workers, suffering which was ignored by those who benefited from the policy. Two world wars taught the British people the frightening lesson that to leave agriculture unprotected was strategic suicide, and the policy toward agriculture was changed. Paradoxicaliy the effect of the ill-treatment on the farming industry was to make what was left of it very efficient. Sir Geoffrey Howe's punitive interest rates had the same effect on whatever manufacturing industry survived his bitter remedy, but the cost was horrifying.

Productivity certainly increased. It brought the revelation that the era of full employment after the 1939-45 War had been something of an illusion, and that Britain had almost certainly had much disguised underemployment, a common experience, it has since been learned, in countries where Marxist principles inspire government policy towards industry. Unfortunately the very high nominal interest rates of 1979 and after inhibited the provision of sufficient new productive employment for the labour shaken out of overmanned industries. A government has no right to boast loudly of increases in productivity caused by its policies if *total* manufacturing production has been savagely reduced in order to achieve the beneficial effect on productivity.

If it was high interest rates and not their intrinsic inefficiency which killed businesses, then their demise was an unnecessary calamity. Those businesses which relied on borrowed capital were more vulnerable than those whose capital was mainly of equity.

The death of a business could therefore be the fortuitous result of its capital structure, rather than of any operational weakness.

If the government hoped that manufacturing industry might somehow imitate the example of the farming industry, it failed to appreciate that agriculture had not been brought to efficiency and high productivity by market forces on their own, but had received much outside help. A cleverly executed campaign to restore farming had involved government, the universities, the chemical industry, and many others. Even the British Broadcasting Corporation played a significant teaching role through its daily radio programme, *The Archers*. No such campaign was put into effect to help manufacturing industry in 1979, though various ad hoc policies gradually emerged in the later years of the crisis. The resuscitation of the farming industry should have been a model for the restoration of other industries. Instead Britain's industrialists and workers were given a quick succession of palliatives administered by an equally quick succession of Secretaries of State for Trade and Industry.

Local government helped weaken industry

The agriculture industry had been given one useful competitive advantage in the 1920s: it had been freed from local taxation (the rating system). At the same time all other industry was given an abatement of three-quarters of its rate liability. Local rates are a non-wage cost of production, but most of the expenditure financed by the rates has no bearing whatsoever on the production of goods and services. They therefore inflate production costs for no good reason, and thereby damage competitiveness with foreign produced goods. This point was fully argued by the Confederation of British Industry (C.B.I.) in its paper, *Tax - Time for Change*, published in 1985, possibly influenced by an earlier paper on taxation prepared for the Cambridge Policy Conference on the Future of British Agriculture in 1978.[3]

The concession on rates made in the 1920s had been withdrawn long before 1979. Manufacturing industry in the 1980s not only suffered the full rating burden, but the rates grew faster than general inflation. It was a classic case of taxation without representation. The votes once exercised by businessmen in ·local elections had been removed soon after the Second World War.

There was no democratic voice to explain directly in local council chambers the drastic consequences of high rate burdens on local prosperity. Many councillors responsible for increasing the rate burden had been elected by inner city residents themselves exonerated from some or all local taxation. Some were employed in local government. Some were the tenants of housing subsidised by local taxation.

Following an ill-conceived campaign of political pressure, the exemption of unused buildings from rates was abolished. Local authorities were given discretion to charge half rates on them. The object was to discourage owners from leaving buildings idle. The change in the rating law owed its origin to the vacancy of one property, Centre Point, in Oxford Street, London, a new building which had remained unlet for many years after its completion. The owners were suspected of deliberately leaving it vacant in pursuit of some future profit. The strange notion that one could make a profit by foregoing rent made sense only to left-wing politicians who were eager to run a misguided hate campaign against commercial property developers. The truth seems to have been that the property was not easy to let profitably. By a curious irony, when a tenant was at last found, it was the Confederation of British Industry, whose members were to suffer terribly from the aftermath of that foolish campaign.

They suffered because local authorities in old manufacturing districts tended to be under the control of left-wing socialists who were prepared to exploit their discretionary powers to devastating effect. One real life example of this problem is no doubt typical of many. It concerned a fairly modern 800 square metre factory in an old district of Sheffield which was a mixture of factories and 19th century terrace housing. Because it was partly residential, the planners, under pressure from residents who included many university students, insisted that the property be used for warehousing only. There were many potential purchasers or tenants wanting it for light industrial use, but there was no demand for warehousing. After a four year search a prospective user was at last found, and planning permission for warehouse use was granted. In order to tempt the purchaser a price 95 per cent below building cost had to be conceded. The planning consent was then appealed against by the public transport authority which claimed that warehousing would lead to increased heavy traffic in a residential area, and suggested that the correct use would be light industrial, just what had always been wanted. By this time the rates levy had bankrupted the trust to which the property belonged. With the next rate demand came a circular letter from the Lord Mayor of Sheffield boasting of all that the City was doing to help small businesses! The incident was a very instructive but saddening example of the crippling effect of uncooperative bureaucracy and dogma-ridden municipal governments.

Because of the government-induced recession, many owners of factories were unable to sell or let them, however strong the financial incentive to do so. To avoid paying rates, they took the roofs off the buildings, after selling the machinery and equipment contained in them. In many districts it was financially impossible to mothball an unused factory and await better times. It was rumoured that the machinery, much of it out-of-date and therefore labour intensive, found a ready market in countries like South Africa, which had ample cheap labour.

A growing surplus of sites with industrial planning permission brought their value down below that of housing sites, and therefore many of the vacant sites were sold for housing. With no outlet for investment in industry, lenders used their funds to finance the purchase of houses, thereby creating a house price boom. In driving up the price of houses they increased the price of building plots by anything up to twenty times. The planning system introduced in 1947 had already pushed up house prices by creating an artificial scarcity of building plots. This effect was enhanced by the easy availability of mortgage finance for house purchase in an unregulated market for credit. The planning authorities were doubtless much more willing to grant planning permission for the conversion of old industrial sites to housing than to allow greenfield sites to be used. To them the dereliction of industry was a heaven-sent solution to the problem of vigorous protests against housing developments on greenfield sites.

Inflation uncured.

For sixty years before 1979, despite the best of intentions, a succession of governments had taken actions which had the effect of weakening the British economy, and Sir Geoffrey Howe continued the process. The efficiency which he encouraged was most necessary, but it was matched, and perhaps more than matched, by the destructiveness of his measures. He failed in his primary objective, the defeat of inflation. His failure resulted from defects in the monetary theory on which his policies were based. Unbeknown to him he was taking action which would not reduce, but actually stimulate and perpetuate inflation. Sir Geoffrey Howe added his name to the list of Chancellors of the Exchequer who have grievously, though inadvertently damaged the British economy. The most illustrious name on the list is Winston Churchill. For details of his action, see Chapter Eight.

From the beginning of 1979 to the end of 1983 inflation as measured by the Retail Prices Index was 67.87 per cent. This was less than the 108.17 per cent inflation of the preceding five years, but it still ranked as the second highest inflation of any other five year period. After 1983 inflation fell, but that was a result of the colossal unemployment which had been caused by high interest rates. The unemployment would have been even greater if the war in the South Atlantic had not precipitated the government into sanctioning some additional public expenditure which it might not otherwise have allowed. It also secured the government's re-election. Whether that was a good or a bad thing will never be known for sure. An alternative government might have resorted to even higher interest rates. Who knows?

Notes on Chapter One:-

1. In a lecture the head of treasury operations of a large clearing bank was most emphatic: *'If we are short of funds we know they have to be around somewhere: it is just a question of finding where they are and then paying the price to get them.'*

2. Lacking direct experience of working in the accounts department of the Bank of England one is must rely on the statements of Professor Charles Goodhart in his book *Money Information and Uncertainty*, (Second Edition, Macmillan, 1989.)

3. The paper was called *Tax and British Agriculture* by M.C.Thompson, F.R.Goodenough, and G.W.Gardiner.

CHAPTER TWO

TRUTHS ABOUT MONEY

'It is a truth universally acknowledged, that a single man in possession of a good fortune must be in want of a wife.'

JANE AUSTEN

JANE AUSTEN's first law of economics has long been accepted as valid. Other important truths are not so apparent and we are therefore compelled to declare:-

'It is a truth universally ignored by generations of economists that the ultimate determinant of the money supply is the capital base of the lending institutions.'

This is the first truth about money. To understand it, we must first have an understanding of that capital base. For the purpose of monetary theory the capital base of a bank consists of its shareholders' funds, plus its subordinated loan capital, minus any capital which is invested in intangible assets, such as goodwill, minus trade investments, such as shares in subsidiary or associated companies not involved in banking which may not be readily realisable, and minus any other asset which is difficult to sell.

In the published accounts of a bank the total of shareholders' funds is nowadays clearly identified, but it may also be broken down into several components. One of those components will always be the nominal value of the ordinary share capital in issue. Other items contributing to the total of shareholders' funds will be the nominal value of preference share capital, undistributed profit, share premium account, and possibly other reserves. Some reserves are not part of shareholders' funds: for instance a reserve for deferred taxation is not normally shown as belonging to the shareholders, even though it does not belong to anyone else.

Loan capital can also take a multiplicity of forms, but the common attribute is that in a liquidation of the bank, owners of the loan capital will not be repaid until the depositors have been paid in full, though they will be repaid before the shareholders get anything. Technically deposits are also loans to the bank, so in order to distinguish loan capital from deposits it is described as *subordinated loan capital*.[1]

The Basel Capital Accord

The capital base determines lending capacity in the following way. First, the risk value of the bank's assets is calculated in accordance with a scale of weightings decided by the Bank of England under the discretions given to it by an international agreement commonly known as *the Basel Capital Accord*). Most assets count in full, but mortgages by occupiers of residential property may be reduced by 50 per cent. The obligations of governments which are members of the O.E.C.D. may be ignored completely. After all reductions one arrives at the *risk-weighted value of assets*.

The Basel Capital Accord states that the capital base of the bank may not be less than eight per cent of the risk-weighted value of the assets. The percentage the capital bears to the risk-weighted value of the assets is known as the *capital adequacy ratio*, or just *capital ratio*. The Accord breaks the capital base down into two tiers: tier one is roughly shareholders' funds, and tier two is subordinated loans plus other assets. There are however some grey areas because some more exotic varieties of capital do not fit neatly into either category. Some forms of capital, such as convertible loan stocks, even have the capacity to change category. Initially tier two, on conversion into shares they become tier one. Unrealised profits on investments are not looked on with unqualified favour, and they may not necessarily be counted in full in the capital base. That has caused a problem for Japanese banks.

The year chosen for the implementation of the Basel Capital Accord was 1993, following the end of each bank's financial results for the accounting year ending in 1992, but for many years earlier the Bank of England had already enforced a similar system of control. The result in practice was that shareholders' funds in United Kingdom banks hovered at around five per cent of risk-weighted assets, slightly more than the internationally agreed minimum. That meant that the upper limit on a bank's risk-weighted lending capacity was twelve and a half times its capital base, and twenty times shareholders' funds, whichever was the less. With the sole exception of some government borrowing the intermediated credit supply is therefore strictly limited by the capital base of the banks.

A Loophole?

The nil risk-weighting allowed by the Convention for the obligations of O.E.C.D. governments looks like a huge loophole,[2] which might allow the infinite expansion of the credit supply by profligate governments, and could even lead to hyperinflation. In Chapter Seven we shall look at this possibility in more detail, and we shall find there is a limitation because of the effect of the credit multiplier. Banking prudence also plays a part: banks do not entirely trust government paper, and may not take full advantage of the weighting concessions. Nor has the Bank of England permitted the full exemption authorised by the Convention, and it appears that 10 and 20 per cent weightings are required for some gilts, the exact percentage depending on the length of maturity.

When the United States gave thought to the subject in the mid 1980s, it was decided that the weighting for government securities should be 30 per cent. The United States government appears to have been a late convert to the concept of weightings, for its original proposals ignored them. A fixed capital adequacy ratio of shareholders' funds to assets of 5.5 per cent was applied, regardless of the quality of the assets. Under such a régime the limitation of the money supply by the capital base is total. The fixed ratio did not take into account off balance sheet items; subsequent regulations did so. In January 1986 the United States Federal Reserve Board announced its proposals to apply risk-weighting, thereby adopting the line already taken by the Bank of England, and to keep the 5.5 per cent fixed ratio.

The proposal to allow the obligations of O.E.C.D. governments to be given, at national discretion, a nil risk-weighting has worried many commentators. One point which may however have escaped notice is that if there is no capital base needed in respect of bank lendings to governments, the return on assets for the bank is infinite provided it has some profit margin on the loans. A bank could use this profit to subsidise its other loans, or to pay for the money transfer system. It is possible that this took place in Britain during the period 1939-1960, when a huge proportion of bank lending was to the government.

Slow recognition

General recognition of our opening truth was a long time coming. Until the 1980s it was notable by its absence from the literature on monetary theory. The most famous book on monetary theory, the two-volume *Treatise on Money* by Lord Keynes, contains no suggestion that bank capital adequacy ratios set the upper limit of the money supply. Familiar textbooks on economics were also silent. A large number of the publications by the Institute of Economic Affairs has been searched in vain to find references to it. The Chartered Institute of Bankers recommends to students of monetary theory B. Kettel's book, *Monetary Economics,* published by Graham and Trotman in 1985. At page 69 Kettel mentions the discussion paper issued in 1975 by the Governor of the Bank of England on capital adequacy ratios, but he is silent about their significance in limiting the money supply.

Professor Charles Goodhart, once an adviser on monetary policy to the Bank of England, wrote two important books on monetary theory and practice. The earlier, *Money, Information and Uncertainty,* was first published in 1975. A second edition appeared in 1989. It has no reference in its index to the capital base of the banks. Nevertheless Goodhart must be given the credit for raising the subject, for in his other book, called *Monetary Theory and Practice* and published in 1984, the importance of capital adequacy ratios is discussed at pages 115, 167-169, and 179. One suspects that Professor Goodhart, in his role as adviser, may have originated the Governor's paper of 1975 on capital adequacy ratios. His discussion of them appears to be more concerned with banking prudence rather the control of the money supply, but it is implicit in his remarks that he is aware of the point, even though he may not have highlighted it to the extent one would wish.

In January 1992 the truth finally received proper recognition when Professor David Llewellyn of Loughborough University stated categorically in an article in *Banking World* (the journal of the Chartered Institute of Bankers) that the capital base of the banks is the ultimate determinant of their lending capacity. As money is created only by the process of granting loans, it follows that the banks' capital base is also the final limiting factor on the money supply. The only loophole is the one already mentioned, the generous treatment of loans to O.E.C.D.governments.[3]

Defining the money supply

The term *money supply* has several definitions. The broadest definition in use in the United Kingdom at the time this chapter was written was *M4*. It is collated by the Bank of England, and the updated figure is published every month by the Central Statistical Office (C.S.O.) in the Financial Statistics. The table number changes from time to time. As at 1992 it was Table 11.2, and column AUYM of that table contained the figures for M4. It is defined in the table as cash, plus the retail deposits of the banks and building societies, plus bank wholesale deposits (including certificates of deposit), plus building society wholesale deposits. According to the note put at the head of the table only private sector holdings of these items are counted, a very surprising and, it is suggested, quite unjustifiable limitation. M4 is therefore somewhat less than the total of all the items just listed as some holdings have been deducted. The heading does not state that the items included in M4 are all in pounds sterling. Table 11.7 gives the counterpart to M4, that is the bank and building society lending in pounds sterling. As these figures are specifically stated to be in sterling only, and as the M4 figure is repeated, one is left to deduce that Table 11.2 includes only sterling balances.

All money is debt

A close look at all things which are regarded as money in a modern society reveals a common characteristic: they are all transferable debts. The possessor of money is a creditor, though not necessarily of anyone in particular, for goods and services to the value of the money he owns. When he hands over money in return for goods or services, the recipient of the money takes his place as the creditor. So all money is debt, or credit, the two terms being the two opposite faces of the same concept. The concept of money is a creation of the human mind, and is implemented by means of a legal relationship, that of debtor and creditor. As money and credit are two aspects of the same thing, we could justifiably refer to the credit supply, rather than the money supply. However what is called *the money supply* is much less than the total credit supply. It is but a sector of it, and a rather ill-defined one. The word *money* is not a scientific term, and if it were not in such common use among monetary theorists one would replace it with an expression like *assignable debt*, or just *transferable debt*.

The credit supply: intermediated and non-intermediated

We call the total of loans made by banks *the intermediated credit supply*. The total credit supply extends of course far beyond the lendings of the banks. It includes bonds and mortgages, trade credit, shareholders' funds and all other forms of credit which do not involve a bank as an intermediary between the owner of the money and its borrower. Hence we may call all other credit *the non-intermediated (or disintermediated) credit supply*. The ugly word *intermediated* is always used to imply that between a saver and a borrower there is some middleman who takes prime responsibility for any loss resulting from the lending. It does not apply to lending arranged through any intermediary who does not take responsibility for loss. The middleman is a bank, for any financial institution which accepts deposits from savers and lends them out is by definition a bank, even though in popular parlance they may have other names such as building societies. Therefore the inter-mediated credit supply must also include credit provided by the Bank of England.

But for a technical detail economists might abandon the term *money supply* altogether and use instead the term *intermediated credit supply*. Unfortunately the figures which the government gathers to calculate the money supply are not correct for the inter-mediated credit supply, because they are taken from the wrong side of the balance sheets of the lending institutions. The money supply, as measured by the government and published in the official statistics, is the total of the deposits in banks, the external liabilities (i.e. not including shareholders' funds and loan capital) of the lending institutions. The intermediated credit supply, on the other hand, is the total of the lendings (including 'investments') which are the assets of those institutions. Their lendings are not wholly financed by deposits: the total lent includes some of the banking institutions' own capital as well. The intermediated credit supply can therefore be larger than the money supply.

Table 1. Comparison of M4 with sterling lending.		
Year	M4 (in £million)	Bank Lendings (in £million)
1985	225,293	233,459
1986	261,073	280,388
1987	303,662	333,557
1988	356,420	416,374
1989	423,485	504,694
1990	474,396	574,752
1991	501,854	604,564
		(Source: C.S.O.)

Combined figures for bank and building society lendings in the United Kingdom were not published until 1990, when Table 11.7 of the Financial Statistics was changed to include them. Retrospective figures to 1985 were made available. Table 1 sets out the totals for M4 and for bank lendings for the period 1985 to 1991. Foreign currency deposits and public sector deposits are not included, so the figures are not an accurate indication of the total intermediated credit supply. Nor does the difference between the two columns indicate exactly the amount of bankers' capital that is being lent. This is due to the unsatisfactory way the figures are collated, and to the deductions referred to earlier. But the table does make it clear that lending is greater than deposits.

It is sad that this statistic was not published until nearly fifty years after the C.S.O came into being. Lendings, rather than deposits, are significant in any properly scientific study of money, as it is lendings which create money.

Figures for the total assets and liabilities, including foreign currency deposits and loans, of banks alone (excluding building societies) are also published. Some of the foreign currency deposits and lendings are of doubtful relevance to the money supply of the British economy. Table 2 shows the figures for total liabilities to the public of the United Kingdom banks for the years 1981 to 1991. Unlike the published figures for M4, public sector deposits appear to be included. Table 2 quotes also the figures for non-deposit liabilities, which presumably reflect shareholders' funds and subordinated loan capital.

Table 2. Total bank deposits and bank capital.

Year	Bank Deposits (in £million.)	Non-deposit liabilities: Capital &c. (in £million.)
1981	331,705	13,783
1982	410,634	16,156
1983	479,442	19,315
1984	604,477	25,082
1985	589,880	33,482
1986	704,158	36,955
1987	728,649	43,718
1988	816,606	52,826
1989	1014,344	68,048
1990	1031,241	70,182
1991	999,076	71,525
		(Source: C.S.O.)

The second truth: money is not all

Both the intermediated *and* the non-intermediated supplies of credit are important for the progress of an economy and for the growth of inflation. They are of *equal* importance for the control of inflation. If only one is controlled, there will inevitably be pressure to expand the other.

The two markets for credit are interrelated. Credit is first created in the intermediated sector, that is in the banking system, from which it then leaks through into the bond and equity markets as a result of new issues. A new issue of bonds or shares on the stockmarket reduces both the deposits *and* the loans of the banks, and thereby releases part of the capital resources of the banks to act as a base for the creation of yet more intermediated credit. The cycle can then be repeated indefinitely.

There are four significant scenarios: the first is an increasing supply of intermediated credit, coupled with a reducing supply of non-intermediated credit; the second significant scenario is a reducing supply of intermediated credit, coupled with an increasing supply of non-intermediated credit; the third and fourth scenarios are an increasing supply in both sectors, and a reducing supply in both sectors. Of course, two other scenarios are in theory possible, but in practice never occur: they are that one or both supplies should remain completely invariable.

What matters for an economy is whether the overall credit supply is increasing or decreasing. It is perfectly possible for the intermediated credit supply to remain nearly constant in either nominal or real terms, and yet for there to be an increasing supply of credit which will keep the economy expanding. This was a common scenario in Britain during the first sixty years of the twentieth century. For instance, during the fifteen years 1948 to 1963 the nominal deposits of the London clearing banks grew at only two per cent a year. Nevertheless the Gross National Product more than doubled. Adjusted for inflation the money supply fell sharply while economic growth increased. This growth seems to have been financed in the main by the retained earnings of companies. Retained earnings are in effect an increase in the amount of credit supplied by shareholders to companies. They should therefore be added to the amounts raised by direct new issues of bonds and shares to determine the true figure for credit provided through the capital markets. During the period reviewed real capital formation ran at a very high rate. This was in no way reflected by the increase in the total of bank deposits.

Therefore monetarists who look at only the progress of the money supply, ignoring the rest of the credit supply, are missing a very large part of the picture. Their diagnosis of the situation is bound to be mistaken, and their prescription inappropriate.

The third truth: the importance of the demand for credit

As money is created by the granting of credit, it follows that the size of the money supply is determined by the demand for credit. Too many economists, including Lord Keynes, have assumed that the demand for money, meaning the willingness to maintain deposits, is a determining factor. It cannot be so. If a loan is granted, and drawn down by the borrower making a payment with it, then a deposit is automatically created when the recipient of the payment places it into his bank account. Someone *has* to hold that money on deposit. That is an inescapable law of arithmetic as reflected in the rules of double entry bookkeeping.

Keynes and others talked of *liquidity preferences* as if the decision to switch from holding cash to holding bonds was an option available to all wealth owners at the same time. It is not. If one wealth owner decides to use his cash to buy an existing bond, then there must be a seller somewhere whose holding of cash will rise as the bond purchase takes place. Any general switch from cash to bonds would require the issue of *new* bonds, an action which would reduce intermediated borrowing. The decision to replace a bank loan with a bond issue is primarily a decision of the borrower and secondarily of his banker. It is not a decision for wealth owners, though the borrower's choice may be influenced by their preferences, for they will be reflected in the relative yields on bonds and cash deposits. If the wealthy prefer bonds because their interest yield is fixed for a long period, the interest rate on bonds will tend to fall, tempting the borrower to issue a bond.

The fourth truth is about savings and investment

Savings equals borrowing. Savings are not equal to investment, as so many economists, including Keynes seem to have assumed. Savings can be used to finance loans for the purchase of short-lived consumer items just as readily as they can finance productive capital formation. See Chapter Thirteen for a fuller discussion of the general theory of saving.

Stability in the value of money

For over a hundred years until 1914 the purchasing power of the British currency was almost stable. Inflation was temporary and slightly more than balanced by periods of deflation so that the secular trend was deflation. Perhaps it is wrong to call nineteenth century fluctuations in prices *inflation* and *deflation* in the modern sense, for it seems that they were, in the main, genuine increases or decreases in real costs. It would be more appropriate to restrict the terms inflation and deflation to alterations in prices which are in some way irrational, perhaps resulting from an increase or decrease in the credit supply, or from inflationary wage rises which are not a reflection of increased productivity.[4] Since 1945 the people of Britain has experienced inflation of retail prices even when real production costs were falling, and even during periods of recession. They therefore come to regard inflation as the norm, whereas deflation, a potentially more damaging phenomenon, is the true norm, for in an age of technical innovation and capital investment real production costs are bound to decline.

Nevertheless we must bear in mind that any fall in prices, for whatever technical reason, can start a true deflationary spiral because of the problem it causes for debtors in servicing their borrowings. The fall in prices in the United Kingdom in the 1920s may have been caused by productivity improvements by overseas suppliers, and true deflation was thereby triggered. More recently we have seen dramatic falls in the prices of some goods such as computers, due to technical innovation leading to lowered production costs. This phenomenon has caused many retailers of such goods, despite huge increases in the volume of sales, to run into losses or bankruptcy, with knock-on effects throughout the banking and insurance systems.

Should the money supply be controlled?

It is now commonly accepted that every government should seek to control the rate at which money is created. It is accepted that the creation of credit, and the resulting creation of money, is a fundamental requisite for the controlled expansion of the economy. Some people however demand that the control of the money supply should be exercised by a body which is independent of government. There are a few governments which do delegate the task of controlling credit to an independent central bank.

Some commentators claim that for a period during the first half of the twentieth century economists and governments tended to disregard the duty to control the money supply. In the 1950s

Professor Milton Friedman fought to re-establish its importance in applied economics, and as a consequence he was awarded the Nobel Prize for Economics. Professor Friedman, like any scholar who wishes to be truly scientific, has emphasised the importance of ensuring that economic theory is fully supported by the empirical evidence. The opening paragraphs of his 1976 Alfred Nobel Memorial Lecture assert his strong commitment to the scientific method.

> *'Do not the social sciences, in which scholars are analysing the behaviour of themselves and their fellow men, who are in turn observing and reacting to what the scholars say, require fundamentally different methods of investigation than the physical and biological sciences? Should they not be judged by different criteria? I have never accepted this view.'*

Earlier, in his 1970 Harold Wincott Memorial Lecture, he appears to imply that the followers of Lord Keynes, the most influential twentieth century economist, had ceased to take proper note of all the relevant empirical evidence, and had therefore fallen into error. In particular they were accused of disregarding that evidence which proves the importance of monetary control. Because they emphasise the primary importance of controlling the quantity of money, Friedman's followers are called *monetarists*. Sincere monetarists will not wish to be accused in their turn of disregarding some significant empirical evidence. Since Professor Friedman's views were first published important new empirical evidence has appeared about the effects of applying a variety of methods of controlling the money supply. The new evidence needs careful interpretation, but one can already see that it casts some considerable doubt on earlier theories.

New evidence and new analyses suggest that drastic revisions are needed to standard monetary theory. The intention of succeeding chapters is to demonstrate where monetarists have failed, perhaps inadvertently, to take proper account of some significant, indeed crucial, empirical evidence. Also many past explanations of the operation of the monetary system have relied on reasoning which now appears flawed.

Hindrances to the truth

Mark Twain said, *'There are three kinds of lies: lies, damned lies, and statistics'*, but he could have honestly replaced the word statistics with *'bank balance sheets'*. A succession of British Companies Acts have granted recognised banks the right to conceal their true financial position, though latterly in the United Kingdom only merchant banks take advantage of the concession. The truth, it was thought, might cause panic. Banking profits can fluctuate wildly, and it was better to allow the banks to smooth out the wilder fluctuations from year to year for fear that the public would overreact. This smoothing was achieved by transferring undisclosed profits or losses to secret inner reserves. Popular opinion credited the banks with huge inner reserves. Even if that opinion was an illusion, no banker dared challenge it publicly. The erroneous and misleading myths about the past irked the chief accountant of a large clearing bank so much that in the late 1960s, having looked at the old records, he revealed privately that his bank was experiencing very poor profitability for some years after the 1939-45 War.

Keynes often complained about the quality of economic data. Monetary theorists too must have been handicapped by faulty data. It is impossible to assess correctly what effect circumstances and events in the banking system had on economic progress if one does not know the vital facts, its true profitability and the true strength of its capital base. A number of universities have been provided with departments of banking and finance which are sponsored by major banks. The sponsoring banks should further support them by revealing the true profitability and capital resources of the banks during the important five decades from 1920 for which such information is not published.

Error is a hardy plant; academic error can be a poisonous one. It has been the cause of many destructive policies in twentieth century economic history. Many of the economists who have shared the guilt have been famous and very worthy; they have, without doubt, made useful contributions to economic thought, Keynes especially, but at some stage they have gone awry. The mistakes which are set out in later chapters, both those of Keynes and of the monetarists, may share a common origin. That origin is a less than perfect ability to understand the principles of double entry bookkeeping, mastery of which should be a basic skill of every economist. This failing seems to indicate that the study of bookkeeping and accounts does not receive sufficient emphasis in university courses in economics. Perhaps the time has come to insist that a qualification in bookkeeping should be a mandatory requirement for every prospective student of economics.

The development of double entry bookkeeping was a very important step in the history of commerce, and perhaps even in the progress of civilisation. Many practitioners of double entry bookkeeping do not have a full grasp of the concept behind it, even though they apply its principles every day. Economists lack experience in using it, and for them there is an even greater barrier to understanding. They suffer from a major handicap.

Statistics

Bookkeeping is not the only source of error for economists. Another is the application of statistical techniques. Economists resort to sophisticated statistical techniques because it is not possible for them to make use of the standard technique which physical scientists use to discover the truth, that is the technique of observation, hypothesis, and experiment. Human sciences, of which economics is one, suffer this problem to varying degrees, economics probably having the worst difficulty. Anthropologists also have to use statistical techniques, but they claim that they do not regard a hypothesis as proved on the basis of statistical evidence alone: they wait until they have ascertained the actual link of physical cause and effect.[5] Elaborate statistical techniques can predicate constant functional relationships where common-sense suggests that none is likely to exist. The functions of economics can rarely have true constants. They continually shift, quite unpredictably and often very rapidly, and so do the values of the variables. Professor Friedrich von Hayek was a pungent critic of the use of constants by the followers of Keynes. In his Institute of Economic Affairs Hobart Paperback, *A Tiger by the Tail*, published in 1978 he says at page 101:-

> '*His (Keynes') final conception rests entirely on the belief that there exist relatively simple and constant functional relationships between such "measurable" aggregates as total*

*demand, investment and output, and that empirically estab-
lished values of these presumed "constants" would enable us to
make valid predictions.*

*'There seems to me, however, not only to exist no reason
whatever to assume that these "functions" will remain constant,
but I believe that micro-theory had demonstrated long before
Keynes that they cannot be constant but will change over time
not only in quantity, but even in sign.'*

The willingness of economists to employ statistical techniques
which have been successful in physical sciences, but are inappropriate in a human science, has attracted critical attention from
some scientists, and in one case the criticism was both very well
informed and savage. It came from the late Professor Sir Frank
Engledow, Drapers' Professor of Agriculture in the University of
Cambridge. Sir Frank masterminded Britain's agriculture and
food policy during the 1939-45 War and his efforts were remarkably successful. His status as one of Britain's most influential
scientists was confirmed by his appointment to be one of the first
trustees of the Nuffield Trust when it was established by Lord
Nuffield in order to promote scientific research. Sir Frank had in
the course of his own research work in plant breeding developed
sophisticated statistical techniques, and he used them to increase
the yield of wheat five times. He made the following comment
about their use by mathematical economists:-

*'Economists use multilinear regression analyses, every
parameter in which is an assumption.'*

The scathing tone of voice in which he spoke these words
made it clear that this was a scientific way of saying they were
indulging in quackery. They should take Sir Frank's authoritative
criticism to heart and look hard at their methods with a view to
eliminating the causes of such fierce condemnation. In the process
a vast amount of work carried out in the name of economic
research would regrettably be downgraded in its significance; it
would still have some use as a pointer, but no longer as proof.

Notes on Chapter Two:-

1. For a detailed discussion of bank capital see *Bank Capital and Risk* by Bernard Wesson, Institute of Bankers, 1985, ISBN 0-85297-134-6. This is a very useful source book for information which illustrates our arguments, but it covers only the period 1976-1983. Mr. Wesson's study, which was undertaken as the Centenary Research Fellow of the Institute, needs to be extended to cover the period from 1920 to the present.

2. Professor Milton Friedman has blamed excessive government borrowing as the prime cause of the credit explosion which has tended to fuel inflation during the second half of the twentieth century. This may be thought to be an oversimplification, but the effect of government borrowing must have been significant for inflation for at least part of the time. His followers will not be enamoured of the way the Basel Capital Accord appears to open the floodgates.

Anglo-Saxon readers may be surprised at the use of the spelling Basel, and not Basle as appears in all the official documentation in English. Surely this German-speaking Swiss city deserves in an age of Europeanism to have its name spelt as the inhabitants now spell it, and not as Anglo-Saxons imagine the French spell it. The French spelling is actually Bâle, and even that may be replaced by Bale if the French implement the proposal to abolish unnecessary accents. But even Michelin uses the German spelling on its road maps of France, the current French spelling being noted in a very light type-face.

3. One of the United Kingdom Treasury secretaries in the early 1970s expressed the opinion that he could not see that bank shareholders served any useful purpose. That was almost true in the days when the majority of bank lending was to the government, and the capital base became negligible. It was not true in later decades when the capital base became vital, and shareholders had to provide additional capital in large amounts. He may also have been misled by the fact that the Bank of England operates without any obvious capital base. Superficially it would seem to break the Basel Capital Accord. Its true capital base is no doubt the aggregate wealth of the British people.

4. Keynes seems to use the same definition of true inflation. See pages 119 and 303 of his *General Theory of Employment Interest and Money* (Macmillan).

5. The remarks made here derive from a discussion of statistical techniques with a leading anthropologist.

CHAPTER THREE

THE THEORY OF MONETARISM

'Money should circulate like rainwater.'
THORNTON WILDER

MONETARY THEORISTS, such as Professor Milton Friedman,[1] believe that inflation will more readily take place if there is an excessive creation of credit (money). Professor Sir Alan Walters put the point cogently in the Eighth Wincott Memorial Lecture (at page 11 of the version published by the Institute of Economic Affairs as Occasional Paper 54):

> *'The essence is very simple: if the quantity of money is increased by a substantial amount, the "Price" of money (in terms of goods exchanged per unit of money) is likely eventually to fall. In other words, the general level of prices must rise.*
> *'It is, of course merely an illustration, but a very famous one, of the laws of supply and demand.'*

Sir Alan may be going too far in saying that an increase in credit causes inflation. This is not necessarily true. It may be more accurate to say that the creation of credit provides the *fodder* for inflation, which may have another primary cause or other causes. The cause of inflation, indeed, seems to be rooted in human greed: it may be an original sin of mankind. Moreover, inflation cannot take full hold unless there is an increase in money incomes. An increase in the money supply facilitates such an increase, but it is perhaps not merely a quibble to query whether it actually causes it? More fuel in the tank of the car will enable it to go further, but not cause it to do so.

Money is debt

All money is debt. If one holds money it means that one is owed goods and services to the value of that money. In its guise as a medium of exchange money could be defined, as suggested earlier, as *assignable debt*. As all money is debt, additional money can be created only by the creation of additional debt.

Of course, debt, or *credit,* if one prefers the complementary terminology, is readily created by a lending institution such as a bank simply by lending money to someone. The ordinary person assumes that money cannot be lent until it has already been created, but that cannot be true as money itself is debt. A bank allows a customer to make a payment which overdraws his account, thus putting it into debit. The credit balance which is needed to match the debit on the loan account is provided by the account into which the payment is deposited by the person to whom it is made. An additional deposit therefore comes into being *only* when it has already come into being as an additional lending. The time gap between the two creations - lending and deposit - can be momentary or even non-existent, but the one creation is dependent on the other, and it is the *deposit* which is the dependent creation, not the lending. A bank which lends an existing deposit is lending money which has already been created by a previous grant of credit. Only a lending which is as yet unmatched by an existing deposit can create new money.

To the ordinary person this statement may appear to be contrary to commonsense, but it is impossible to understand monetary theory until this basic principle is grasped. A bank's balance sheet can be increased by the dual process of making loans, and then borrowing back the money it has itself thus created. In this way the bank establishes a liability upon itself (that is, a deposit) to balance the loan. A loan is an asset: a deposit is a liability, a debt. Thus the assets and liabilities sides of the bank's balance sheet are kept equal. It is of course a formal requirement for all banks that they should always be equal, in accordance with the normal principles of bookkeeping.

When a bank accepts new deposits (that is money created by some other bank) which bring its deposits above the level of its existing lendings, naturally it must lend the new deposit immediately. The totals of both the debit and credit sides of its balance sheet are thus increased. If the deposit originates from a drawing down of a loan granted by another bank, the balance sheet totals of *both* banks are increased. The true origin, however, of *both* balance sheet increases is the first of the two loans.

A loan granted by one bank can thus cause the intermediated credit supply to increase by *more* than the amount first lent. This is one form of the *multiplier effect*.

An increase in the money supply can arise *only* from an increase in the level of debt. Of course this statement becomes obvious - even a tautology - if for the word *money* we substitute *credit*. In the study of monetary theory perhaps we should do so.

It also follows that the intermediated credit (money) supply can be reduced only by a payment which reduces *both* the deposits *and* the lendings of the same bank.

The money supply

One customary definition of the money supply is that it is the total of all the debts (deposits and other borrowings) of the lending institutions. Money in this definition is confined to debt which is intermediated by lending institutions.

Money which is to be used solely as a medium of exchange could be differently defined as *assignable debt* or *transferable debt*. The money supply would then include some non-intermediated debts, such as bills of exchange and Treasury bills, but would exclude non-assignable intermediated debts, such as fixed term deposits. But the inclusion of some non-intermediated debts in the definition does not affect the argument that money is created by the lending of money. What we have called *the money supply* in the last paragraph, we should, in the interests of clarity, call *the intermediated money supply* when we want to distinguish it from assignable but non-intermediated debt which may sometimes be used as money.

The process of creating intermediated debt can be more readily seen if the loan agreement between banker and customer is immediately put into effect by debiting a loan account in the customer's name, and then crediting the money to the same customer's current account. At this stage the two accounts, one with an increased credit balance, and one overdrawn by the same amount, are still in the same person's name at the same bank. The credit creation process has taken place nevertheless. The intermediated money supply has already been increased. When the customer draws a cheque to draw down the balance on his current account he is not destroying the money, for the cheque will have to be paid into another account, owned by the recipient of the cheque. As a result, the total of debit balances *and* the total of credit balances within the banking system remain in balance.

In the aggregate all the debit balances of the whole banking system will exactly balance all the credit balances. This is virtually a natural law even though the rules of double entry bookkeeping are the creation of man, not of nature. Though it looks like a conjuring trick, money is created in the very simple way described above, but there are still very many people who cannot accept that it is true. Some of them are bankers! One was a former President of the Institute of Bankers in Scotland. The argument ought to have been settled by the evidence of the Bank of England and the Treasury to the Radcliffe Committee on Credit and Currency which reported in 1959. The Bank of England summed the matter up as follows:-

'Because an entry in the books of a bank has come to be generally accepted in place of cash it is possible for the banks to create the equivalent of cash [i.e. credit]. Thus a bank may pay for a security purchased from a customer merely by making an entry in its books to the credit of the customer's account; or it may make an advance by means of a similar entry. In either case, an increase in its deposits will occur.'

How to create money electronically

It is easy to overlook an example which clearly shows the money creation process, and which happens at regular, fixed intervals. It is initiated by the touch of a button on the computer. What happens is that every quarter most clearing banks charge and allow interest. Those customers who owe money have their accounts debited with the interest which has accrued. Thus an additional debt may be created if there is no credit account against which the interest due can be charged. At the same time the owners of interest bearing deposits are credited with the interest which has accrued on their behalf. The difference between the amounts charged and allowed will be transferred to the bank's profit and loss account. If the bank has run its business correctly the amount transferred to profit and loss will be a credit.

This operation initiates credits and debits which will, as is the rule in double entry bookkeeping, be equal. If the debiting of interest increases the debit balances of some overdrawn accounts, the bank's balance sheet total will increase. The two sides of the bank's balance sheet will rise by identical amounts, and when the Bank of England collates the figures for the total deposits in the banking system on the next third Wednesday of the month, it will be able to announce that there has been an increase in the money supply. Some of those who regularly watch the monthly figures of M4, and comment in the press about the rate of increase in the money supply, seem to be quite unaware of the fact that the crediting and debiting of interest can put spikes in the graphs which illustrate the growth or growth rate of the money supply, or of its complement, the credit supply.

Without any intention of sounding unkind or malicious we can say that banks routinely use their computers to print both money, and their profits, four times a year!

Inflation

It is axiomatic that if a large quantity of money is created (by encouraging borrowing), the public's demand for goods and services is stimulated. The demand may be stimulated beyond the ability of industry to provide them immediately. In that case the excess money will tend to bid up prices, and inflation will be triggered. But a permanent increase in retail price inflation is unlikely unless at some stage the increase in the money supply is used to pay higher wages or to make higher profits. The possibility of permanent inflation of prices must therefore rest on whether the struggle for increased wages or profits is favoured by the existence of appropriate environmental factors.[2]

If nominal profits and wages do not increase, then there has to be a downturn in demand until the level of debt has reduced.

Thus a cycle of boom and recession is initiated unless wage and profit inflation continues. A higher money supply enables it to continue. But we also know from experience that wage and price inflation can take place without a higher money supply. When that happens inflation leads to high unemployment, because there is no longer enough money to sustain the previous quantity of production of goods and services; the recession therefore deepens.

Attempts to control wage inflation directly have tended to fail since 1945. Mrs. Margaret Thatcher's government preferred to believe that the control of the money supply would indirectly control inflation of wages, profits, and prices. They believed this despite warnings that the pressure for wage increases was too strong, and that the trade unions would continue to demand and get wage increases at a rate always greater than the increase in production. Therefore high unemployment would result from an exclusively monetarist policy as there would be insufficient money to finance the same physical volume, but higher nominal value, of production and sales.

Monetarists having decided that the increase in the money supply is the cause of inflation, and having also decided that inflation must be controlled, are faced with the problem of how to control the growth of the money supply. They have recommended and used a number of methods. It is now our task to examine the effectiveness of the methods and the validity of those recommendations. The examination leads to results which may surprise readers who are conversant with current dogma.

Notes on Chapter Three:-

1. See page 16 *Monetarist Economics* by Milton Friedman, Basil Blackwell Ltd. 1991.

2. Inflation will often increase nominal profits but it is more likely to decrease real profits, unless the business is highly geared (leveraged).

CHAPTER FOUR

CREDIT CONTROL
BY INTEREST RATES

'The modern world is filled with men who hold dogmas
so strongly that they do not even know they are dogmas.'

G.K.CHESTERTON

MONETARY THEORISTS believe that people will be more inclined to borrow money if the interest rate is low.[1] This is an acceptable proposition, for no-one could sensibly deny that

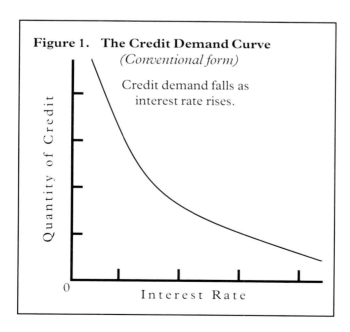

Figure 1. The Credit Demand Curve
(Conventional form)

Credit demand falls as
interest rate rises.

Quantity of Credit

Interest Rate

0

the demand for credit would probably be infinite if the nominal interest rate were nil and no repayments were required. The proposition is usually illustrated in textbooks by a conventional graph such as that in Figure 1 on page 37.

The theorists also firmly believe that banks and other lending institutions will be more willing to create money if interest rates are high. Lending is a risky business and the risks are more acceptable if the rewards are high. Economists therefore assume that the supply curve for money is one which rises as interest rates rise. This proposition too is perfectly acceptable. It is usually illustrated in the textbooks by the graph in Figure 2. Note that there would still be some supply of credit even at a zero rate of interest. This is because there is always a need for money as a store of wealth, regardless of the income it earns. Therefore there will always be people prepared to lend their savings regardless of whether there is any return on them. Indeed experience proves that there will still be a demand for a store of wealth even if interest rates are negative, though the graph in Figure 2. does not illustrate that fact.

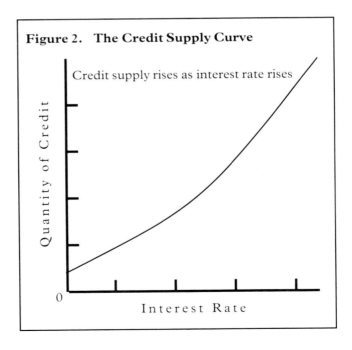

Figure 2.   The Credit Supply Curve

Credit supply rises as interest rate rises

Quantity of Credit

0

Interest Rate

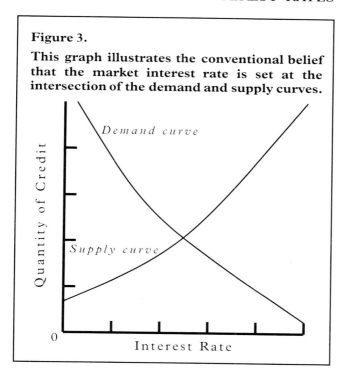

Figure 3.

This graph illustrates the conventional belief that the market interest rate is set at the intersection of the demand and supply curves.

With the two graphs combined, as in Figure 3, one can claim that the point of intersection of the curves determines the market rate of interest. The composite graph provides an elegant, simple, logical, and readily comprehensible example of the operation of the laws of supply and demand. Nevertheless it cannot be correct because, as we have already decided, interest rates - and especially the short-term interest rate - can be administered: the government can fix them, unless there is some extreme crisis which is beyond the government's control. If the government can fix interest rates it should follow that, provided the government's economists can discover the mathematical function which determines the relation of the supply of credit to demand for credit, it can determine the amount of credit to be created. The government does this by choosing an interest rate at whatever point on the supply curve relates to the quantity of credit it wishes to have created. If that quantity is also under the demand curve of the graph, its determination should, in theory, be effective.

Discovering the mathematical function which determines the position of the supply curve on the graph is not an easy task. Nor is there any reason why the function should be a constant, never varying. Unfortunately the numerical value of the function can never be ascertained with a precision that is better than a vague assumption. The ascertainment can only be completed long after the event, by which time the value will undoubtedly have changed.

An untenable theory

Unless the function is variable over an extremely wide spectrum, a phenomenon which would make any attempt to use it quite hopeless, the empirical evidence of two separate twelve-year periods leads one to the firm conclusion that the theory does not work.

During the twelve years following 1948 the Bank Rate was never higher than seven per cent. During the twelve years succeeding 1979 the MLR never fell below 7.5 per cent. If the theory were correct there would have been lower inflation in the later period than in the earlier, and a slower growth of the money supply. The opposite was true: *both inflation and the level of bank deposits grew more slowly in the first period than in the second.* Clearly influences must have been at work which over-rode the supposed effect of interest rates, or alternatively, there were factors which caused the supply and demand functions which pertained in the two periods to be very different from one another.

In the twelve years which followed Sir Geoffrey Howe's action in 1979, the Retail Prices Index (RPI) showed about 150 per cent inflation. In the twelve year period which commenced in 1948 the RPI registered 46 per cent inflation, and London clearing bank deposits grew by no more than an average of two per cent per annum. Their growth was lowest when interest rates were lowest. Two per cent was well below the growth rate of the Gross National Product. In the period 1979-91 the popular measure of the money supply was corrected to include building society deposits, for they had come to constitute a vast share of the money supply. We have already noted with some regret that the new measure, known as M4, was recorded by the Central Statistical Office from 1985 only. Its growth in the three years ending the 31st December 1990 was very large. A growth rate of 18 per cent per annum of this, or earlier, monetary indicators was quite common throughout the whole period of comparison. That rate was several times greater than the growth rate of the economy (GNP), quite the reverse of what happened from 1948 to 1960.

Thus the empirical evidence suggests that the measures which were supposed to stop the intermediated money supply from increasing rapidly were causing it to grow very fast, thus providing the fodder for inflation. Unfortunately some supporters of the policy adopted by Sir Geoffrey Howe reject this interpretation of the empirical evidence. They are firmly convinced of the truth of their theory, no matter how much it is discredited by real events. They will not look for the reasons for their errors. We must therefore do it for them.

The real demand for credit

The theorists had neglected to take into account the interaction between the separate influences which determine the supply and demand curves; the supply function and the demand function are not independent of one another. The public's willingness to take up credit is not an inbuilt, genetically determined instinct,

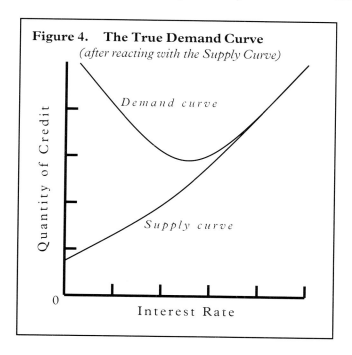

Figure 4.   The True Demand Curve
(after reacting with the Supply Curve)

unaffected by the environment. On the contrary the public's desire for credit can be strongly influenced by an environment of good salesmanship, and effective advertising and marketing. As was clearly seen in the late 1980s, whenever high interest rates make lending very profitable, lenders do not wait for the borrowers to appear. They go out and find them. The pressure they bring upon potential borrowers clearly tilts the demand curve around so that it goes up as interest rates rise, not down. The true graph may look very roughly as in Figure 4, and certainly not as in Figure 3. In Chapter Twelve we shall describe how banks were easily able to cause a volcano of credit in the three years from 1988 despite very high interest rates.

It may well be that it is only lack of capacity to service a debt which eventually discourages borrowing, rather than a high rate of interest itself. Admittedly a high rate of interest will lower the borrower's capacity to service loans, but the empirical evidence is that the propensity to borrow seems to resist the influence of high rates of interest for much longer than the theorists expected, and for much longer than is safe.

Gibson's Paradox

The suggestion that, contrary to standard doctrine, there is a historical correlation between rising prices and rising interest rates, the latter being caused by the former, and that lower interest rates lead to lower prices, appears to have been first publicised by A. H. Gibson in an article in the January 1923 issue of the *Bankers Magazine*. Gibson's revelation is not mentioned in the popular textbooks. In 1930, after five years work, Lord Keynes published his *Treatise on Money* in two volumes. It is a work with failings, some of which he appears to have later acknowledged, but in the second volume Keynes makes up a little for its faults, not only by publishing Gibson's discovery, but also by expanding the evidence for it. On page 178 of the second volume Keynes makes this fascinating comment on Gibson's theory,

> *'The Gibson paradox - as we may fairly call it - is one of the most completely established empirical facts within the whole field of quantitative economics though theoretical economists have mostly ignored it.'*

Expanding Gibson's own figures Keynes prints a comparison of the yield on Consols with the wholesale price index for the period 1791 to 1928. The two sets of data march in step. It is more than likely that the data could be extended up to the present day with the same high correlation that Keynes revealed except for the unusual wartime period, 1939 to 1946; but even during five of those seven years, throughout which Bank Rate was two per cent, the rate of price increases was remarkably low by the standard of the 1980s. As the level of interest rates between 1940 and 1946 was influenced by Keynes, he must have kept in mind Gibson's Paradox. He cannot be accused of ignoring it himself.

It is long-term interest rates which the Gibson Paradox correlates with prices. The correlation, which is very high, is not quite so strong for short-term rates of interest, but, according to Keynes, it is still highly significant. One interesting thing about Gibson's data is that it clearly shows that the rise in interest rates follows the rise in prices, not the other way around. This is surprising as one would expect rising interest rates to push up prices. The much higher interest rates of more recent times certainly pushed up both costs *and* prices.

Gibson would have found the modern theory of the relationship of interest rates and inflation rather curious. He would have suggested that low interest rates on gilts encourage the application of savings to real investment in the hope of a better return. Real investment (plant, machinery, and other productive assets) if effective, should reduce real prices because it should lower production costs. Gibson's reason for the fall in the prices of basic commodities at the time he was writing was the big investment made in food and raw material producing countries in the period 1907-1913. He states,

> *'All economic history proves that the cost of foodstuffs, for man and beast, regulates, directly or indirectly, the ultimate costs of commodities in general consumption.'*

In the later decades of the twentieth century it has perhaps been more correct to say that the cost of energy, and especially oil, is the ultimate regulator of costs (if indeed there is one).

Price variations which arise from natural variations in costs of production, such as the variation brought about by investment in more efficient machinery, are quite a different thing from what we now know as inflation and deflation. Inflation, which has been the main bugbear of the second half of the twentieth century, is not necessarily a rational phenomenon. It may have very little to do with underlying costs. Instead it may have as one of its main causes[2] excess demand arising from the unregulated creation of credit. One can see a dilemma: even if it were true that high interest rates discourage the creation of credit, it would still be true also that they discourage the investment which might reduce real costs of production, and expand the economy. Surely the latter objective is more important than the former? If, however, the monetary economists are wrong, and high interest rates cause both inflationary and real price rises, and they also lower the rate of investment, one threatens the economy with a triple jeopardy whenever one raises interest rates in pursuance of an erroneous monetary theory.

Keynes and the Paradox

Keynes' reference to Gibsons's Paradox is in the second volume of his *Treatise on Money*. Volume one, which is the least satisfactory part of the work, reveals little evidence that he was yet taking note of Gibson's Paradox. It could be argued that what is bad in modern monetary theory has its origin in volume one of the *Treatise on Money*, except that Keynes is, very wisely, much more cautious than later theorists have been. At page 132 he writes,

> '*It is even conceivable that the cash deposits may remain the same, the velocities of circulation may remain the same, and the volume of output may remain the same: yet the fundamental price levels may change.*'

On page 194 he states,

> '*There is no simple or invariable relation between the effect of an alteration of Bank Rate on the price level, whether of liquid consumption goods or of output as a whole, and the associated alteration in the quantity of bank money.*'[3]

Yet if Figure 4, shown on page 41, is the *correct* graphical representation of the interrelation of the credit supply and demand curves with the interest rate, the theory of credit control by interest rates is untenable. As all the empirical evidence tends very strongly to support our graph, there is a strong case for revising, or refining, the theory of credit control. Also we must look for an alternative method of control which does the job without the need to resort to absurdly high rates of interest. The next step, therefore, is to examine whether there is greater virtue in the method which uses reserve assets as a means of controlling credit creation.

Notes on Chapter Four:-

1.   The standard theory of interest rates can be found in (among many other places) Chapter 5 of B. Kettel's *Monetary Economics*.

2.   Another main cause of inflation is of course high wage demands. We shall analyse later the motivation for such demands. At this stage it may help if we state that neither *cost push* nor *demand pull* is preferred as the principal explanation of inflation; usually both were involved in most of the period after the 1939-45 War.

See also the remarks about the causes of inflation on page 33 above.

3.   How many computerised emulations (models) of the economy accord with Keynes' view? An error in this functional relationship might perhaps act like a Lorenz Attractor in any equation which included it and cause totally spurious results. Lorenz had only three equations in his original model of the weather system, yet a tiny difference in a figure altered his long-term results completely. Mathematical models of the economy contain hundreds of equations and therefore an infinite ability to produce errors. Surely an economy is almost as much a chaotic system as is the weather. Chaos theory must be applicable to all mathematical economics, and so-called *Butterfly Effects* must abound.

46

CHAPTER FIVE

CREDIT CONTROL
BY RESERVE ASSETS

*'Money is like a sixth sense without which
you cannot make use of the other five.'*
W. SOMERSET MAUGHAN

T HE BEST KNOWN advocate of the policy of the control of
the money supply by government is Professor Milton
Friedman. He does not favour the use of interest rates as the
means to achieve control. The method he prefers is to insist that a
fixed part of a bank's assets be invested in a particular form of
security whose supply should be firmly under the control of the
government. Among those who support this doctrine a common
choice of security for the purpose is Treasury bills. These bills are
securities for debts owed by the government. They are a promise
by the Treasury to pay a fixed sum of money three months
(usually) from the date of issue. They are an excellent example of
non-intermediated transferable debt. Because of their short maturity it is very easy to alter the supply of the bills. The supply may
also be regulated more directly by sales and purchases of the bills
by government agencies.

If all banks and lending institutions were forced to keep at
least 10 per cent of their assets in the form of Treasury bills, the
money supply could never be more than ten times the amount of
Treasury bills currently in issue. This would appear to be a perfect
way to control the intermediated money supply, and one would
think that control is so easy that the only real problem - the
ultimate and most difficult one - would be to decide the most

effective level for the intermediated money supply. Ideally banks alone should be permitted to hold whatever asset is chosen to be the reserve asset. If it were available to any investor there might not then be sufficient for the banks. On the other hand, if owner-ship were limited to banks, the asset would not be freely mar-ketable. Yet that is usually considered to be an essential character-istic of any reserve asset. It could be objected that unless an asset is marketable, it is not a suitable reserve asset at all. The objection, if indeed it matters, could be overcome if the Bank of England were required to be prepared to purchase any reserve assets ten-dered to it, in much the same way that it was obliged to buy and sell gold in the days of the full Gold Standard. By such reasoning have we perhaps deduced a modern and improved successor for the discipline of the Gold Standard?

So far no such interesting tactic has been tried. It would be logical to try it, though only experimentally in view of the virtual impossibility of prophesying either its success or its failure with any great confidence. It would only be feasible to use Treasury bills as the sole reserve asset so long as they were issued exclu-sively to banks, and to no-one else.

The reserve asset system

In the past reserve asset ratios have been imposed upon British banks for long periods, yet B. Kettel in his textbook, *Monetary Economics*, states, rather surprisingly, that reserve ratio changes were not designed to control monetary growth. In the 1950s and 1960s liquidity ratios of two levels were imposed, one tranche of assets to be in cash and deposits at the Bank of England, and another, and bigger, tranche to be in easily realisable investments such as Treasury bills and short-dated gilts. *The Radcliffe Report* of 1959, which described the functioning of the money markets in the 1950s, also denied that these ratios were intended to control the money supply. Throughout the period when such liquidity ratios were imposed, M3 grew less violently than under later control systems. But the matter is so complex that there could be many explanations of that phenomenon.

At the time the reserve asset system was coming to an end the clearing banks were under an obligation to keep 28 per cent of their *eligible liabilities* in liquid assets. That meant that 28 per cent of the assets of the banks were forced loans to the government, and that proportion of clearing bank deposits was consequently unavailable for the financing of industry. Unfortunately a parallel requirement to maintain such a high level of liquid assets was not imposed on other lending institutions, such as building societies. As a result the dam of regulations, which should have held back the flood of credit, became increasingly leaky.

In 1971 a much more elaborate system of credit control was instituted to replace the former 28 per cent liquidity rule. The manner in which the new system was applied made it totally unsuccessful in controlling the growth of intermediated money, even though the theory behind it may have been sound. The new form of control was related to some of the banks' deposits, but not all. Those deposits which were affected were also referred to as *eligible liabilities*. A reserve ratio was imposed which was related to the total of eligible liabilities. The reserve had to be invested in a range of specific securities, some of which were capable of being kept in short supply, but none were investments which were exclusively for banks. They were:-

> Balances at the Bank of England (special deposits coin and notes held as till money were excluded),
>
> Treasury bills, tax reserve certificates,
>
> Money at call with the London money market,
>
> Local authority and British commercial bills eligible for rediscount at the Bank of England, but subject to a limitation of commercial bills to two per cent of eligible liabilities,
>
> British government securities with one year or less to maturity.

The clearing banks were required to keep 12.5 per cent of their eligible liabilities in these reserve assets, and finance houses (effectively the hire purchase companies) had to keep 10 per cent of their eligible liabilities in reserve assets. It was intended to subject all the other banks or near-banks, often referred to at that time as *fringe banks*, to reserve requirements. But at the time of the introduction of the system there were still many deposit-taking companies which were not required to hold reserve assets. The legislation covering banks and deposit-taking companies was very complicated. Some fringe banks were covered by the Protection of Depositors Act of 1963, and others were exempt. Some qualified under the Companies Acts for exemption from publishing true accounts, while others had to send copies of their accounts to depositors. Experts on the classification of banks bandied around cryptic expressions such as *section 127 banks, section 123 banks, section 25 banks.* What these titles meant exactly is now merely ancient history as they were swept away by later legislation. If memory of these statutory complexities is accurate, the crucial classification was *section 123 banks*, referring to a section of the Protection of Depositors Act 1963. *Section 123 banks* seemed to be able to get away with financial mayhem.

The Bank of England's intention to control all banks was slow to come into effect. Questioned as to the current position in September 1973 the Bank of England answered that the reserve system would soon be applied to *section 123 banks*, but in the following May further enquiry revealed that nothing had yet been done.[1] Academic writers on banking history may not be aware of this divergence of practice from announced intention. Certainly one otherwise excellent history of banking states that the 1971 system was applied to all banks, but enquiries at the time indicate that this did not take place for at least three years.

A large bubble of credit was inflated. By 1974 the bubble had burst and the Bank of England had a major banking crisis on its hands. The Bank had probably delayed the implementation of the reserve requirements in order to avoid precipitating a crisis, but it came anyway. Some fringe banks had used short-term deposits to finance long-term projects such as the construction of large office blocks. Catastrophe was inevitable at the first down-turn in confidence in any of the fringe banks.

The Failure of the system

The system of reserve assets which was started in October 1971 never worked properly. It was not allowed to work! The clearing banks found useful loopholes in the system, but perhaps the most important reason for the failure of the credit control system in the 1970s was that despite its superficial sophistication, a section of the banking system which was growing very rapidly was not sub-jected to all its rules. The fault lay with government officials and the technical experts of the Bank of England. They were using a very narrow definition of what was a bank. Logically a bank is any institution which takes deposits and makes loans. The government had not followed that logic. On the other hand the clearing banks were too stringently controlled. If their interest bearing liabilities rose above a predetermined level they had to make additional deposits, called *special deposits*, at the Bank of England. This strin-gency encouraged them to exploit the loopholes in the system.

It may seem odd that the system of special deposits was used to control the banks' interest bearing eligible liabilities (IBELS) more strictly than non-interest bearing liabilities. It is possible, though not likely, that the United States' experience in doing the opposite in the 1920s provided the reason. Because they required much smaller reserves, banks in the U.S. greatly expanded their interest bearing liabilities in the late 1920s. The expansion was helped by a convenient linking with a corresponding increase in loans to stockmarket speculators. In 1929 the U.S. stockmarket crashed. That was followed by the crash of many thousands of banks. The experience may have persuaded British banking super-visors that it was particularly important to control the expansion of interest bearing deposits. Certainly from 1971 special deposits were applied for that purpose. Britain did not thereby succeed in avoiding a stockmarket catastrophe. It struck in 1974/5.

The interest bearing liabilities which were affected by special deposits included only those which were repayable within two years; later maturing liabilities were excluded. Any attempt to exploit this loophole was ineffective as there was no worthwhile incentive for depositors to tie their money up for more than two years. In fact the opposite incentive existed. Consequently long-term loans could not be prudently made by banks because they lacked long-term deposits.

The growth of the fringe banks

The many deposit-taking institutions which were unrestricted grew very fast. They included the building societies, which were becoming a truly major force in the monetary system. Building societies were beginning to allow depositors to operate, often semi-officially, what were truly interest bearing current accounts. The building societies were ignored by the monetary authorities because there was a quaint assumption that their balances represented permanent savings having a low frequency of circulation.[2] They were totally exempted from the provisions of the Control (Borrowing and Guarantees) Act 1946 by a Statutory Instrument issued in 1958. This was the legislation which should have been used, as was originally intended, to keep control of the whole of the credit creation process.

The building societies were in the habit of reporting the turnover on their accounts, something the banks have never done, and the figures began to look very impressive. Indeed, the turnover was equivalent to about 10 per cent of GNP by the end of the 1970s, when the total liabilities of the building societies had risen to a level no less than 80 per cent of the liabilities of the banks as measured by £M3. By 1991 the turnover on building society accounts was equal to 20 per cent of GNP, despite the conversion of Abbey National, a major society, into a true bank, so that its turnover figures were no longer included. Withdrawals from building societies are probably used in the main to pay for major items of consumer expenditure. They are therefore very significant for the economy.

A host of other deposit taking institutions escaped the effect of credit control regulations. They did not have to make special deposits and were operating without prudent free capital ratios or liquid asset ratios. They did not accept that there was any need to balance the maturity of assets and liabilities, although what were effectively long-term lendings, financed by short-term deposits, may have been deliberately window-dressed to look like short-term loans. They were only taking to its logical extreme the established but unacknowledged practice of the big banks.

The lack of any requirement to hold officially denominated reserve assets (which tended to give a low return as they were scarce) gave the fringe banks a competitive advantage over the clearing banks in seeking deposits. Inevitably they could afford to pay a higher rate of interest on deposits than the recognised banks which were subjected to reserve asset requirements, because their assets were on average earning them a higher yield. The result was that the fringe banks enjoyed mushroom-like growth.

If you cannot beat them, join them

Eventually the clearing banks had to fight back. They set up their own subsidiaries which were not officially recognised as banks and were effectively exempt from the reserve asset rules. Some may have been taxed as investment institutions instead of as banks. This meant that their profits on gilts were free of tax. The consequence, rather fortuitously, was a big change in the character of the deposit-taking business of the clearing banks. Up to that time the bulk of their deposits had been obtained direct from the public, and were therefore called retail deposits, as distinct from wholesale deposits obtained through the London money market. Of the two, retail deposits were much cheaper, and it was a profitable privilege of the clearing banks to have ready access to them. In the early 1950s as much as 67 per cent of clearing bank deposits were on current accounts and therefore cost free, no interest being payable. The clearing banks' new subsidiaries began to accept wholesale deposits, even though long-serving and experienced staff of the banks considered the margins obtainable to be ridiculously low. Some senior officials of the clearing banks were savagely contemptuous. Nevertheless the change was to become a permanent one, with far-reaching consequences for the role of the clearing banks in capital markets.

A strange mood of optimism gripped many of the fringe banks and they happily ignored prudence, borrowed short, and lent very heavily on big construction projects to property developers. A senior employee of an American bank which was active in the same market later admitted privately that they were even careless about obtaining formal security for their loans, due to overoptimism about their customers' financial status. Some of the deposits of the fringe banks came from the treasuries of the clearing banks themselves and of their subsidiaries. If the fringe banks had any conscious philosophy behind their policy, it must have rested on the belief that they would always be able to pay the top rate of interest, and would, therefore, never be short of deposits. Perhaps it was for that reason that they did not worry about the need to keep a prudent level of liquidity, or about preserving a balance between the maturity dates of assets and liabilities. It is more likely, however, that no deep thought was ever given to such important issues.

The government sinks the fringe banks

It appears to be a peculiarly British assumption that the purpose of a bank is to convert short-term deposits into long-term loans. A more prudent view is that the government's banking regulations should encourage a closer matching of the maturity dates of assets and liabilities. It is true that if no-one foolishly rocks the boat, the practice of mismatching the maturity dates of assets and liabilities can continue for a long time quite harmlessly, but what happens if the government itself rocks the boat suddenly and violently?

In the early 1970s the government began to pursue yet more firmly the traditional British practice of trying to keep the pound overvalued. In order to succeed in this objective it engineered high interest rates. Then in 1973 the price of oil leapt five-fold, causing a panic. British interest rates were pushed up to unprecedented levels. The fringe banks were plunged into disastrous trouble since many of the property developers to whom they had lent money were unable to afford such high interest payments.

It was very regrettable that this should happen because their lending, though technically injudicious in terms of prudent banking, was nevertheless promoting the construction of buildings and other forms of real capital formation. It thereby expanded British industrial activity, whereas some other expansions of the money supply have tended to finance imports, aiding thereby the expansion of foreign economies instead. Expansion of building society lending simply increased house prices at a rate faster than the general level of inflation, thereby creating some serious social problems, besides making overnight multi-millionaires of those who sold building land.

The fiction of short-term lending

At that time the clearing banks were still maintaining the fiction that they were following the dogma, which was preached in banking textbooks, that banks should provide only short-term loans. Indeed up to the First World War bill-broking was the clearing banks' preferred activity. They experienced pressure from the 1920s onwards to make medium term loans to industry but lacked medium term liabilities with which to finance them. The Macmillan Committee of 1928, of which Lord Keynes was a member, reported accordingly:-

'There is substance in the view that the British financial organisations concentrated in the City of London might with advantage be more clearly coordinated with British industry, particularly large scale industry, than is now the case; and in some respects the City is more highly organised to provide capital to foreign countries than to British industry.' [3]

In 1932 Lloyds Bank advanced £3,000,000 to Stewarts and Lloyds to start the Corby steel plant. This is reckoned to be the first example of industrial participation by a British bank.

Otherwise the banks did nothing of any significance except that they formed one of the institutions which later became the 3i's Group. The Macmillan Committee was wrong in saying *'particularly large scale industry'*, for a more urgent need was finance for small scale industry, which normally lacks access to market sources of capital which big business can tap. That problem was addressed in 1946 by the founding by the clearing banks of the Industrial and Commercial Finance Corporation, which also in due course became part of the 3i's Group, but the supply of long-term finance for industry from banks remained weak.

Pressure was renewed in the early 1970s. Some clever person at National Westminster Bank suggested that the most solid deposits held by banks were the bottom tranches of their current accounts, because customers rarely ran their current account balances down to nil. A proportion of the balance on most current accounts has no frequency of circulation at all, so the bottom tranches of the balances are in practice, though not in theory, long-term deposits. The more incautious but persuasively clever people in banking therefore argued that the banks could quite safely lend these deposits long-term.

It is an attractive proposal and has a large element of truth in it. It is dangerous nevertheless. That the proposal was put forward reveals just how frustrating and injurious was the banks' lack of long-term liabilities.

The fringe banks simply went ahead regardless of risk. But for the oil crisis they might have escaped danger for much longer. But why were they not restrained? That is the mystery. What went on at the Treasury and the Bank of England? What discussions took place? Was there any relevant discussion at all? [4]

The efficacy of the reserve asset system

Whether or not a reserve asset system can control the intermediated money supply has not yet been established in Britain. No conclusion should be drawn from an experiment such as that described above because of the incomplete way in which it was implemented. The contribution of academics commenting on the problem has been woolly in certain details. In a lecture in 1980 on the British situation even Professor Milton Friedman showed concern only for M3 as a measure of the money supply. That

---

Table 3.   Official Measures of the Money Supply

Abbreviated definitions

M0   = Notes and coin in circulation outside the Bank of England plus bankers' operational deposits with the Banking Department of the Bank of England.(C.S.O. table VQKT)

M1   = M0 plus private sector current account balances. (M1 is not published by the C.S.O. but its components are. They are C.S.O. tables VQKT and AUYA.)

M2   = M1 plus some short term and smaller retail sight deposits at banks and building societies. (C.S.O. table AUYC)

£M3 = M0 plus all sterling bank deposits, whether on current or interest bearing accounts, (but not building society accounts) of UK residents in the private sector. (No table published.)

M3   = £M3 plus the foreign currency bank deposits by UK private sector residents. (No table published.)

M4   = £M3 plus building society deposits less deposits by building societies in banks. (C.S.O. table AUYM)

M4c = M4 plus bank and building society deposits in foreign currencies. (No table published.)

M5   = M4 plus certificates of tax deposit, sterling Treasury bills, bank bills, deposits with local authorities, and National Savings deposits and securities. (No table published as at 1992.)

---

attitude came to look very silly in the late 1980s when the Central Statistical Office ceased to print M3 in the official statistics. M4 came to be looked on as the correct measure of the intermediated money supply, for it includes the liabilities of building societies.

We have an insight into what the discussions were like at the Bank of England at that time as Professor Charles Goodhart, then a monetary adviser to the Bank, has written about them, and published discussion papers which he presented to the Bank. His account provokes the irreverent thought that many of those involved were trying to play a complex computer game without realising that they had acquired the wrong instruction manual. Take the following quotation from page 206 of Goodhart's book *Monetary Theory and Practice* as a very simple example:-

> *'If banks have to maintain a minimum ratio of cash to deposits and if the central bank exercises sufficiently vigorously its undoubted potential power as "the" source of cash, then clearly the size of the high-powered money base imposes a ceiling on the level of bank deposits and thus, indirectly, on the stock of money, however defined.'*

Cash has many meanings, but in this context Goodhart means currency, that is banknotes and coin. The amount of currency required by an economy is determined by market forces of supply and demand. Any attempt to diminish the supply provokes the market to find a substitute. Otherwise a situation will arise in which banknotes have a premium value over bank deposits of the same nominal value. In the present era an attempt to limit the currency supply would increase the use of plastic money. It is therefore somewhat doubtful whether Goodhart is wholly correct in ascribing so much influence to the power to limit the supply of high-powered money. Market forces may over-rule that power.

Exogenous forces

Professor Goodhart and others talk constantly of *exogenous forces*, that is forces which affect an economy, but are not themselves affected in return because they are external to the system being studied. Exogenous forces in economics are largely a figment of academic imagination, mere wishful thinking. In real life there is probably no such thing as a completely exogenous factor. Any computer model which postulates an exogenous variable is likely to be nonsense. The factors which some economists are proposing as exogenous are, on close examination, not truly so. They are really endogenous, and therefore subject to the natural law that for every action there is a reaction.

What happened to the money supply control system of the 1970s is a perfect example. The controls imposed were thought to be exogenous, but the reaction of the lending institutions in exploiting loopholes defeated their purpose and expanded the credit supply. This book proposes that the intermediated credit supply be controlled by physically limiting the capital base of the banks. Obviously a reaction to that limitation would be an expansion of the non-intermediated credit supply, and consequently that too has to be controlled, and so on.

It may be argued that we are defining *exogenous* too strictly. Maybe so, but the point is that any attempt to control human beings must take into account that there are reactions from those controlled. They are at least as clever as those who attempt to do the controlling. Some are cleverer.

The other capital market

So what about the non-intermediated capital market? The reserve asset system makes no attempt whatever to control it. Surely it must play a part in promoting inflation? One cannot assume that disintermediated capital does not have a capability to circulate. Stockmarket securities are readily convertible into cash when needed, provided every holder does not attempt to make the conversion at the same time! The turnover on the stockmarket is over £1,500billion a year. There are forms of cash balances which have a *lower* frequency of circulation than wealth held in the form of securities which are readily and frequently traded. As will emerge shortly, it is the combined effect of the intermediated and non-intermediated capital markets which determines the effective credit supply, and therefore decides the expansion or contraction of the economy.

There would be a very serious problem with a truly effective system of monetary control: it would have to be expertly operated. The damage which imprudent or inexpert manipulation could wreak is immense. Judging by past performance there is as yet no convincing evidence that any government department or the Governor of the Bank of England would manage the control with sufficient finesse. Nor are the necessary techniques yet available for determining what is an ideal level of credit supply. Nor would Professor Friedman's ideal, a steady year by year, month by month, increase in the money supply as the economy grew be appropriate. It is a dangerous, and arguably ridiculous, proposition. It would however appeal to the tidy-minded planners and perfectionists he despised, rather than to the pragmatic believers in the market economy whom he claimed to favour.

A need to increase the intermediated money supply can arise quite suddenly. An illustration would be the decision to build the Channel Tunnel using largely borrowed capital. To enable that project to reduce unemployment and be an addition to real capital formation, a substantial and out-of-the-ordinary increase in the intermediated credit supply was required. It is wrong, of course, to finance such a risky project with variable-rate intermediated loan capital, but the days are regrettably long gone when such a project could be financed with debentures paying a fixed rate of interest, as was the Manchester Ship Canal earlier in the century. One must hope that the Channel Tunnel proves to be more profitable than the Manchester Ship Canal; arguably the Channel Tunnel is a project of such long-term benefit that an assessment of its financial viability using the standard techniques of investment appraisal is not appropriate.

The Institute of Economic Affairs has published a small book as *Occasional Paper 86* called *Monetarism and Monetary Policy* by Friedman's close collaborator, Anna J. Schwarz. At page 19 she makes the following recommendation:-

> *'The monetary policy recommendation that follows is that to combat inflation, a central bank should limit the growth rate of a monetary aggregate to the long-term growth rate of the economy.'*

The reference to *'a monetary aggregate'* seems more than somewhat vague. The recommendation would suit those people who take the first chocolate from the box without looking at the key to help them make a choice of filling. The British government changed its choice of monetary aggregate during the 1980s whenever it discovered that the monetary weevils had fouled a particular chocolate filling.

The recommendation is based, like so much unsuccessful economic theory, on wishful thinking. The wish might be to achieve an 'x' per cent rate of growth of GNP. Applying the function, a 'y' per cent growth of the money supply is calculated to be correct to achieve 'x' per cent growth. One could aim for it, provided one knows how. Then the gremlins take over, probably in the form of a batch of aggressive trade union leaders who are trying to justify their existence. One then finds that one's nicely planned growth in the money supply is absorbed entirely by wage inflation and no economic growth takes place at all. Any expansion of the money supply affects the future, not the present, and somehow one has to find out what expansion of the real economy is about to take place. The only way one can come near to being sure what growth will take place is to plan it ruthlessly. That takes Friedmanism full circle, right back to the Keynesian fully-planned economy, something to which Professor Friedman is, quite rightly, wholly opposed.

To reconcile strict and planned monetary control with an unplanned, or market, economy, is very difficult, if not, indeed, a logical impossibility.

The two themes of Friedman's policy are from different and independent philosophies. He is an ardent and persuasive advocate of the market economy, but he is also a convinced interventionist in monetary matters. The only way to reconcile the two attitudes is by means of a compromise, albeit an uneasy one. That is what the long struggle between Friedmanism and Keynesianism is all about. It is what the doctrinal conflict between socialism and capitalism is about. At what point does one compromise between freedom and intervention? We shall be commenting further on this point in Chapter Sixteen. There we shall show that compromise between planning and freedom is essential, and indeed inevitable.

Notes on this Chapter are overleaf.

Notes on Chapter Five:-

1.   I recorded the result of these enquiries of the Bank of England in notes which I retained. The details of the legislation covering lending institutions were very complicated. Few bank officials knew them, and those who did were not senior directors but back-room advisers. My recollections of those details may not be accurate. I decided not to repeat the research I had to do in 1973-4 as it took a great deal of time, and the legislation is now of academic interest only.

2.   The use of the term *frequency of circulation* in place of the normal *velocity of circulation* is explained in Chapter Fourteen.

3.   The system of currency boards used in British Colonies seems to have had the effect of draining colonial capital to the London money market, and it was therefore essential for the colonies that the London market should recycle funds back to them. For a full expanation see *Do Currency Boards Have a Future*, the twenty-second *Harold Wincott Memorial Lecture* given by Anna J. Schwarz in October 1992 and published by The Institute of Economic Affairs (ISBN 0-255 36312-5).

4.   A week spent in discussion with Civil Service and Bank of England officials at the Civil Service College left me with an impression of unfocussed prolixity and lack of professionalism. Of course the Civil Service had a policy of discouraging its staff from studying for professional examinations (unlike the Armed Services, whose policy is exactly the opposite), as it relied on its own internal courses at the College. My impression was that the reliance was somewhat misplaced. Because I was then a member of the Council of the Institute of Chartered Secretaries and Administrators, an examining and qualifying body for high level executives, I shall be accused of prejudice. My opinion was, however, shared by others with experience both inside and outside the Civil Service.

CHAPTER SIX

CREDIT CONTROL
BY SPECIAL DEPOSITS

'Sound finance may be right psychologically: but
economically it is very depressing.'

LORD KEYNES

A THIRD TECHNIQUE for controlling the money supply is the use of *special deposits*. It was applied in the 1960s and 1970s. In 1990 the Labour Party announced that this was the control technique which it would use if it ever gained power.

The services of central banks, such as the Bank of England, are available only to a very few customers. The principal ones are the government, government departments, important financial institutions such as discount houses, the clearing banks, market-makers in government stocks, and the Guardian Royal Exchange Assurance which has a historical connection. A clearing bank's deposit at the Bank of England is conventionally regarded as its most liquid financial asset after cash, and it is the deposit on which it may need to draw in order to make a remittance to another clearing bank.

There is no point in any bank drawing a cheque upon itself in order to pay money to another party, for that cheque could only be honoured if the recipient were to use it to open an account with the bank on which it was drawn, a procedure which does nothing at all to change the initial creditor-debtor relationship. Therefore a payment from a bank must be by a cheque, or other form of remittance, which is drawn on an account with some third party, preferably one with the Bank of England.

The Banking Department of the Bank of England, like any other financial institution, must balance its books. If it holds a bank's deposit, it must either make a loan to match it, or buy an investment (an investment is just another form of lending), or else it must hold some form of currency. The currency can be its own, in which case it becomes a creditor of its own Issue Department, which, in turn, holds investments to balance the liability created by the issue of currency. Fortunately the government is usually a ready borrower from the Bank, whether from the Banking Department or the Issue Department, and it is usually not only willing but eager to mop up surplus funds. Consequently in normal times much of the lending made by the Bank of England is to the central government.

When inflation began to be a cause for special concern in the 1960s, the prevalent idea that it was attributable to an excess of money caused economists to apply their minds towards the possibility of reducing the supply of money by artificial means. One fashionable method for doing this was to force the banks to deposit more money with the Bank of England than they might otherwise prefer. These additional deposits were called *special deposits*, and they were to be fixed and frozen: the banks could use them neither for their ordinary business nor as reserves. The size of the special deposits was fixed at a stated percentage of the banks' own deposits, though the percentages might differ with regard to each class of deposits, long term deposits tending to be totally exempt. In order to make special deposits into a kind of punishment or discipline they commonly earn less than a market rate of interest, and sometimes earn no interest at all. Unless special deposits are required from every deposit taking/lending institution they can be discriminatory and grossly unfair.

Negative feedback from banks

It is worth noting the reaction of the banks to special deposits; it is an example of the reactive relationship between economic planners and those subjected to planning. The banks examined all their accounts, and eliminated every possible offset account, so that the special deposit was levied on the smallest possible sum. As a result of their action, there is a small but incalculable discontinuity in the published statistics of the money supply.

A close look at the detailed bookkeeping of special deposits reveals that the only way a bank can make a deposit at the Bank of England is to obtain, directly or indirectly, some form of financial instrument drawn on the Bank of England. That financial instrument could be banknotes, but they are an unlikely payment medium because, as currency does not earn interest, the banks keep only sufficient to enable them to cover their customers' day by day demands for it. As already explained, it is pointless for a bank to give to the Bank of England a cheque drawn on itself: that can only force the Bank of England to lend the money back to the originating bank. If the bank has money owing to it by another bank, it can draw on that bank instead. This would cause the second bank to draw on its own balance at the Bank of England at the very time when the Bank is probably requiring it also to make special deposits.

Therefore the only practicable way in which the banks can increase their aggregate deposits at the Bank of England is to pay into the Bank cheques, or other forms of payment, drawn on the Bank (i) by the government, (ii) by some other customer of the Bank of England, or (iii) by the Bank on itself. The process might well be a little more roundabout than that. The money markets have a traditional but not wholly necessary ritual for moving money and investments around the banks themselves, and between the banks and the Bank of England. That ritual requires the involvement of the discount houses, which make some of their profits by borrowing from the Bank of England and lending the money on to the other banks.

When the banks increase their deposits at the Bank of England, the Bank lends or invests the deposited money. It has the usual options, (i) to lend to the government, (ii) to buy gilts, (iii) to buy bills of exchange. Sometimes it will lend money to the government which will itself use it to buy investments. It is, of course, likely, if not inevitable, that the investments bought either by the Bank or by the government will be the same ones as those which have been sold by the banks in the first place. The procedure begins to look ridiculous. It is ridiculous! Put at its simplest the procedure is, (i) the Bank of England lends money to the government which (ii) uses it to buy government stocks or bills of exchange from the banks. With the money received (iii) the clearing banks make special deposits at the Bank of England. The effect of special deposits is (iv) to transfer lendings (government stocks or bills of exchange), from the commercial banks to the Bank of England. All that has happened is that there has been a change of lender. Nothing more significant has taken place.

The special deposit procedure, so highly prized by 1960s economists, is at best a zero sum game. As a control technique it is useless, and can even cause inflation if it raises interest rates and therefore costs. Whether it raises interest rates will depend on the price at which investments are bought by the government. If the purchase of stock is direct from the banks, the liabilities side of their balance sheets, that is their customers' deposits, remains unaltered. The assets side total also remains the same, but the make-up of the assets is now slightly different. The figure for government stocks has fallen, and the figure for deposits at the Bank of England has risen. Meanwhile the Bank of England's deposits and liabilities have both increased. Therefore, if one chooses to include the Bank of England's balances in the money supply figures, something the government is careful not to do, *the money supply will have gone up!* Since the purpose of the exercise was to bring the money supply *down*, the whole mechanism has failed. Monetarist economists who subscribe to the efficacy of the special deposits fudge must disguise their illusion by refusing to include the totals from the Bank of England's balance sheet in the calculation of the money supply. That is neither sensible nor logical: the assets (loans) of the Bank of England *are* part of the credit supply.

A bank could always acquire some of the special Bank of England money by another route. Someone is bound to suggest it. The government or the Bank of England could purchase stock from an investor other than a bank. The purchase price would be deposited by the seller in his own bank, and that would increase that bank's deposits. The bank could then make its special deposit at the Bank of England because it would have received from its customer a cheque drawn on the Bank of England. In other words it would have acquired some *category one money*, that is Bank of England money. The money the bank received from its depositor would have increased the money supply further. That arises solely because the Bank of England has provoked an increase in intermediation in the capital market, and simultaneously reduced non-intermediated investment.

In this scenario the Bank of England would have precipitated two increases in the money supply, one in its own books, and one in the books of the bank at which the vendor of the stock holds his account. Thus a technique has been used which has had exactly the opposite effect of that intended. *The intermediated money supply has been expanded, not contracted.*

Unpredictable effects

However, the additional deposit created in the banking system may do more than just increase further the amount of special deposit required. It could also prevent the bank concerned from using its capital base to support the creation of further credit. The bank might even need to reduce some other lending, probably by encouraging a customer to fund his debt by raising finance in the non-intermediated capital market. That might appear to achieve the government's objective, but it is rather hit and miss. The consequent limitation of credit growth, if any, will be difficult to predict as it depends to what extent the borrower can resort to the bond market. If the result is merely to replace intermediated with disintermediated credit, surely nothing of significance for the economy has taken place.

One would expect that a person who sells an investment to the Bank of England might want to spend the proceeds, in which case the Bank of England has helped create some money with a higher frequency of circulation. The procedure does not therefore seem to be a reliable way of controlling the money supply or inflation.

There is yet another defect. Special deposits do not necessarily pay the banks as high a rate of interest as the assets which they have been obliged to sell. Indeed, when *supplementary* special deposits were invented in 1973, they were made interest free. The banks, therefore, must charge higher rates of interest for other loans in order to cover the interest payable on their deposits. These higher rates may be determined partly by market forces. The banks cannot dictate them absolutely. But they will try to raise the margin on their variable rate lendings. This margin is the difference between their base rates and the actual rate of interest charged. If the result is that a higher interest rate has to be charged to producers of goods and services, costs will be raised, and, therefore, there will be price inflation.

If market circumstances allowed the banks to reduce the rates of interest paid on deposit accounts in order to effect a widening of margins, what would be the effect? It could further encourage wealth owners to disintermediate in order to get higher yields in the bond market. If that were to happen, it would free some of the banks' capital base to support the creation of additional credit.

One can, therefore, envisage a wide variety of possible effects from special deposits, each tending to have a different effect on inflation. All the effects are generally unpredictable, a common result of trying to override market forces. The argument embraced by A. H. Gibson was that any fall in deposit interest rates caused wealth owners to contemplate real investment in order to achieve a higher yield. A fall in interest rates also causes bond prices to rise, which may increase the capital base of the banks if that base is invested in bonds. If bond prices rise investors feel wealthier and are inclined to spend.

For special deposits to have any success in stifling an over-heated economy it is therefore essential that they do not cause the interest rate on deposit accounts to be lowered. On the other hand, if the technique of special deposits is implemented in such a way that it reduces demand, that too can increase producers' unit costs, and thereby give rise to price inflation.

Did special deposits cause inflation?

Special deposits were introduced from 1960 onwards as a means to control inflation. In the years thereafter inflation increased from 1.8 per cent in 1960 to a peak of 24.9 per cent in 1975. The five years 1974 to 1979 saw the highest ever inflation, but before one rushes to conclude that special deposits cause inflation rather than cure it, it would be as well to note that other factors were at work also. They will be described in Chapter Nine. Special deposits were used twice in 1960, then again in 1964, 1966, and 1970. Between 1973 and 1980 the punitive scheme of supplementary special deposits, also known as *The Corset*, was used several times.

The period 1965 to 1973 is very interesting. The total deposits of the clearing banks rose in that period from a nominal £9.4 billion to £21.1 billion. However, the inflation-adjusted figure was unchanged, a strikingly neutral result. By coincidence or otherwise the whole increase is equal to the additional loans made to industrial and commercial companies. About £5billion of the increase in loans was covered by increases in deposits by similar companies, the money coming in the main, no doubt, out of the £39billion of savings of the corporate sector. The main source of disintermediated credit was in shareholders' funds as a result of ploughing back profits. New issues of disintermediated credit through the stockmarket were unimportant by comparison. Building societies were of course unaffected by special deposits. Their annual level of lending quintupled during the same period with the inevitable result that house price inflation was 200 per cent, well ahead of retail price inflation.

A significant occurrence which coincided with the use of special deposits was the reappearance of unemployment as a serious problem at the same time that inflation was increasing, a phenomenon which was given the name *stagflation*.

It is more than possible that special deposits had exactly the opposite effect of what they were intended to achieve. It would not have been the first - or the last time - that an anti-inflationary device promoted inflation rather than cured it.

No money is taken out of the system

Special deposits do not, cannot, never have, and never will take money out of the system. The technique of special deposits was abandoned after 1980. It had been in fashion for twenty years - two decades during which inflation went soaring. One might reasonably expect its demise to be permanent. But not so, for 13 years later it was resurrected by Mr. John Smith, MP who appeared to have adopted it as Labour Party policy. In a long televised interview with the redoubtable and respected Mary Goldring he seemed to imply that he favoured the reintroduction of special deposits as a weapon of monetary policy, '....*so that the money cannot be lent*.' Since all money is debt anyway such a statement is nonsense. All present day money is lent. Money is created only by lending it. It is more than time that all prominent politicians grasped that concept. It has been public knowledge for over a hundred years.

CHAPTER SEVEN

CREDIT CONTROL
BY OVERFUNDING

'The debits are on the side nearest the window.'
BANKER'S AIDE MEMOIRE

T HE LAST CHAPTER has demonstrated that a purchase of
stock by the government or the Bank of England from the
public can cause a problem for the banks. It brings about an
increase in their deposits, and as a consequence the banks may
have to increase their reserves. This limits the banks' ability to
expand further the amount of credit given to the public. Surprisingly, the monetary theorists are under the impression that it is
better to do the opposite if the government wishes to restrict the
money supply. Indeed, they advocate that the government should
overfund, by *selling* government stocks to the public rather than
purchasing them; overfunding simply means that the government
borrows money it does not need.

The theory behind their policy is this:- A member of the
public buys a newly issued gilt and makes out a cheque in payment to the Bank of England. The bank on which the cheque is
drawn can only honour that cheque by acquiring some Bank of
England money. It does this by selling a gilt or other investment
(directly or indirectly) to the Bank of England.

The resulting bookkeeping when the overfunding takes place
is as follows:- The Bank of England's liabilities increase, because
the government's cash balance in the Bank's books rises. Its assets
also rise, because it has acquired investments from a bank. The

bank which holds the account of the customer who has bought gilts sees its deposits and its assets fall by exactly the same amount by which the Bank of England's deposits and assets have risen.

Is this a reduction in the money supply? Only if balances at the Bank of England are ignored when measuring the money supply. How can it be justifiable to ignore them when the Bank of England's deposits are being used to finance investments which are active components of the credit supply, and indeed are probably identical with the investments removed from the banks? Therefore balances of the Bank of England *ought* to be included in the total of intermediated money supply. It is nothing short of ridiculous to ignore the Bank of England's own banking activities.

Money used to buy gilts is likely to have been previously kept as an investment and therefore had no frequency of circulation. Nor would it have circulated in its debit form on the other side of the bank's balance sheet if it was represented by a static holding of gilts in the bank's name. Has anything worthwhile been achieved by the manoeuvre of selling gilts to the public? No, it may have achieved nothing of significance to economic activity.

It may, however, have increased the banks' capital adequacy ratio, unless all the investments sold by the bank are those government obligations, against which it may not have to hold a capital reserve. The capital ratio has to be at least eight per cent of risk-weighted assets in accordance with the Basel Capital Accord. The bank's capital base earns interest by being lent, but it does much more than that: as has already been explained in Chapter Two, it sets the effective limit on the amount of deposits which the bank can accept, and the amount of money it can lend.

How banks make profits

Because the rate of interest a bank charges on loans is more than it pays to its depositors, a profit is earned on its own capital over and above the interest earned by that capital itself. Suppose the following parameters apply: the difference between income on unsecured loans and borrowing costs, after deducting overheads and bad debts, is a quarter of one per cent; the capital ratio is eight per cent; the interest rate is 10 per cent; the risk-weighting is 100 per cent. The calculation of the resultant profit on a loan of £1000 should be as set out in the box on the next page. Our calculation assumes that for the purpose of profit planning it is correct to have first set off all non-interest earning assets, (cash and infra-structure) against non-interest bearing deposits.

Profit on a bank's capital

Bank's capital   £80   x   10.00 per cent =   £8.00
Deposits   £920   x   0.25 per cent =   £2.30
Total income after expenses   = £10.30

Return on capital   = $\dfrac{£10.30 \times 100}{£80}$ =   12.88 per cent

---

With a trivial margin of a quarter of one per cent the basic return on the shareholders' capital is increased by over a quarter, from £8 to £10.30. If, as is now permitted by international convention, only £40 of the £80 capital is shareholders' capital, the other £40 being subordinated loan capital, the return on capital rises to over 25 per cent (because £10.30 is 25.6 per cent of £40).

In 1991 Lloyds Bank achieved a net interest margin on its domestic banking of 5.33 per cent.[1] In 1987 it was even higher at 5.84 per cent. This percentage sounds huge, but it does not take into account the writing off of bad debts which makes the true net margin far smaller. Historically a true net margin of one per cent is high. Assuming a gross yield on loans of 10 per cent, a one per cent net margin raises the target net yield on the bank's capital base to 21.5 per cent. In the unlikely event that all loans were mortages to occupiers of houses, and therefore qualify for a 50 per cent risk-weighting, a maximum return on shareholders' funds of 59 per cent is possible with a one per cent true net margin.

The directors of some clearing banks have set a target of 20 per cent as the return they aim for on any investment of shareholders' funds. Clearly when interest rates are low it is more difficult to achieve such a target than when they are high. Achieving it is helped by raising subordinated loan capital to provide some of the capital base, for that helps to gear up the return on shareholders' funds. A typical balance sheet of a bank in 1990 showed shareholders' funds at five per cent of unweighted liabilities, the rest of the capital base being derived from subordinated loans. Ignoring any margin earned by lending loan capital, the effect is that a net margin of a quarter of one per cent earned by lending depositors' money should be multiplied 18.4 times, not 11.5 times, in order to calculate the addition to the interest earned by lending shareholders' capital (because deposits are 18.4 times shareholders' funds).

Naturally those banks whose capital adequacy ratio is lower than eight per cent can make do with lower interest margins, because the multiplier is higher. This may explain the aggressively priced loans which Japanese banks were able to offer in Europe before they had to increase their capital adequacy ratios to comply with the Basel Capital Accord.

A bank's capital base must fully earn its keep

The purpose of this explanation is to show why the directors of a bank cannot afford to waste the earning power of their shareholders' capital. They must keep the capital adequacy ratio as low as possible if profit per share is to be maximised. Therefore when overfunding of government debt has the effect of increasing a bank's capital adequacy ratio, as it will if the bank has to sell assets such as bills of exchange which have a high risk-weighting, its directors will be most anxious to reduce the ratio by increasing lending. So when a government funds or overfunds its debt the effect can be to stimulate the banks very strongly to create more credit. In that case the money supply is fully maintained, and the overall credit supply is increased. The policies pursued since 1979 in the name of controlling inflation, which for a while included overfunding, were effectively sabotaging that objective.

There is evidence that the bankers of Britain have never been prepared to waste the earning power of their capital bases by leaving them idle for any lengthy period. On the contrary the history of capital bases is one of increasing risk being taken. It has been reckoned that in the early 19th century the average capital ratio was 35 per cent. In reality it was higher, for until 1858 shareholders in banks risked unlimited liability, and therefore the reported capital base was only that part of their capital which was employed in the business. The total amount at risk then included all the personal fortunes of the bankers.

The capital base gradually fell to 20 per cent in 1880, to 13 per cent in 1914 and six per cent in the 1920s. The lowest ratio was around two per cent in the 1950s. That does not mean that bankers were then taking exceptional risks since only about 20 per cent of their assets consisted of advances to private sector borrowers. Most of their loans were to the government and therefore deemed risk free. Measured as a percentage of advances to non-government borrowers the capital base in the 1950s was more than adequate. Around 1959 banks began to increase the proportion of their assets invested in advances and, as a result, found it necessary to raise additional capital.

The published balance sheets and profit and loss accounts of banks for the period before full disclosure began in the early 1970s may not give a true picture. If the banks wished to mislead, it would surely be with intent to exaggerate the strength of their capital bases. Popular myth at the time was probably foolish to credit them with the opposite attitude. In the light of the evidence that no bank has ever done other than make the shareholders' funds earn their keep, and that except for brief interludes the capital base has been fully employed, it must be apparent that an economic stratagem which depends for its success on the willingness of directors of banks to forego profit on their shareholders' capital must be ineffective.

The results of overfunding

Overfunding was pursued in the period 1980 to 1984. In his book, *Money, Information and Uncertainty,*[2] Professor Charles Goodhart states that '*the overfunding exercise (of 1980-84) was remarkably successful.*' This claim seems to be belied by his next sentence: '*Although bank lending to the private sector surged ahead over the years 1980-84 at an annual rate of no less than 19.6 per cent.*' Thirty years earlier that rate must have been nearer three per cent.

This is precisely the result the analysis outlined in this chapter leads one to predict. The phenomenon Goodhart reports offers persuasive evidence that overfunding leads to an *increase* in lending to the private sector because opportunity to lend to the government is blocked. It *increases* the overall credit supply, and it may also replace money having a low frequency of circulation with money of a higher frequency of circulation. That the ploy had the opposite effect of that intended may have been a godsend to the British people. It may have caused some inflation, but it helped end the recession of the early 1980s. That was far more important except to those for whom an inflation-free pound is a sacrament.

The sad story does not end there. By the end of 1990 the gilt holdings of Barclays Bank were down to a half of one per cent of its assets! The overfunding exercise so stripped the clearing banks of gilts that the Bank of England could persist with the overfunding policy only by using the money it received from successive gilt issues to buy commercial bills from the banks, no gilts being available for it to buy. Thus it was buying investments for which the banks selling them had to have a full eight per cent capital adequacy ratio. Therefore the government was freeing the banks' capital base for further credit creation. Perhaps the banks instructed their staff to foster the use of bills of exchange as a lending medium so that they always had plenty of bills available to sell to the Bank of England. Professor Goodhart states that the overfunding policy put so much money into the bill market that it had the effect of reducing discount rates on bills of exchange. That means that, among other things, it cheapened the financing of imports, which are often paid for with bills of exchange!

Would underfunding be better?

If overfunding can have the opposite effect of what is intended, could that also be true of underfunding? Underfunding has been suggested as a way of expanding the money supply. That would seem logical, for if the government does not fund its debt by selling gilts it must borrow from the banks. That must increase the supply of intermediated credit and also increase cash holdings with the power to circulate. If the government monopolises the intermediated credit supply, which is limited in size by the required capital adequacy ratio, then surely private sector borrowers are squeezed out?

Not necessarily, for government borrowing can be zero risk-weighted for the purpose of the Basel Capital Accord, and no capital base is therefore required. Admittedly the United Kingdom is not taking advantage of the authorisation of a nil risk-weighting for all government debt. Gilts appear to have been given 10 or 20 per cent risk-weightings.

The underfunding would therefore have to take the form of those borrowings for which no capital base is required under British regulations. If this is done, and the required capital ratio of the banks is calculated on lendings other than those to the government, underfunding would not reduce the supply of credit to the private sector. Nor would it increase it. The hope of those who have advocated some underfunding seems to be that the increased deposits which would be created would circulate freely, and have a multiplier effect on the money supply. Unfortunately, for a credit multiplier effect to take place there *has* to be an increase in the capital base of the banks as it is bound to mean increases in loans which attract a full risk-weighting. So we are back to square one!

But is there really all that much difference for money control purposes between a cash deposit and a holding of gilts when the latter can be traded for cash in minutes? Any competent investor knows that gilts are as good as cash. That is why gilt turnover on the stockmarket sometimes tops a trillion pounds a year.

Another form of money control

The analysis in this Chapter has made it apparent that there is another technique for controlling the money supply. That is the direct limitation of the capital bases of the lending institutions. Provided it is coupled with control of new issues so that the whole credit creation process is under government supervision, this technique could be very effective in controlling private sector borrowing. We can attempt to assess the technique's possible effectiveness by looking at the history of monetary policy from 1920 onwards. Such a review begins to reveal that directly controlling the credit base, that is the banks' capital base, can be highly effective. A clear understanding of how the monetary mechanism operates is the powerful tool which will open up the road towards a truer monetarism. Other very important lessons also emerge from the history of the 70 years after 1920 which will now be reviewed.

Notes on Chapter Seven:-

1. The source is page 16 of the directors' report for 1991.

2. At page 232, second edition, 1989, Macmillan.

CHAPTER EIGHT

GOING FROM GOLD

'He [Churchill] is often right, but
when he is wrong - my God!'

F. E. SMITH (Lord Birkenhead)

TO CHOOSE 1920 as a commencing date for a review of British monetary policy is perhaps arbitrary for monetary problems did not start then. 1920, however, marks the start of a long period, still continuing, during which there has been greater government interference in monetary matters. That interference became intensely damaging to the British economy, and led to its long-term decline.

During the 1914-18 war Britain had spent much of its accumulated wealth. It had incurred a colossal addition to the national debt of some £6,000,000,000. It had, however, also developed its industrial potential. The urgent postwar task was to find a peace-time use for the massive factories which had been built to supply armaments and other war provisions.

One example illustrates the history of the British engineering industry through 60 years. It was the Birmingham Small Arms Company's factory at Armoury Road, Small Heath, Birmingham. The factory was half a mile long and several storeys high. The business had been founded in 1692 for the production of personal fire-arms, *small arms* as they were then called. Its largest factory had been hugely extended in 1915 to accommodate the production line for a Belgian-designed light machine-gun called the Lewis Gun. To encourage workers to go into the armaments

industry Winston Churchill provided for them a special weekly
bonus which came to be known as *The Churchill Award*.[1] Women
who worked an eleven-and-a-half hour night shift for six nights a
week had been able to earn £8 or £9 a week while their menfolk
received a few shillings a week for enduring the Flanders' mud.
After the war the giant factory was converted to motorcycle and
bicycle production using continuous assembly lines. It was a very
remarkable example of how the stimulus of war can create a valuable capital asset. The returning men replaced the women, but the
wages were more than halved.

Seventeen years later the factory had to be reconverted to
arms production. It housed the production lines for the Bren gun,
another light machine-gun, this time of Czech origin, and the
Browning gun, the American-designed machine-gun with which
aircraft such as the Spitfire and Hurricane were armed. In
November 1940 the original gun-barrel mill was destroyed and
the assembly line damaged by bombing. After 1945 the damage
was repaired and for a while the factory thrived on motorcycle
production. Then competition from the wartime enemies, Italy,
Germany and Japan, coupled with the damaging effect of silly
monetary policies, destroyed it more effectively than any wartime
bombing. In 1992 local unemployment was unofficially estimated
to be 35 per cent.

Deflation

In our starting year of 1920 inflation was 20 per cent. Bank Rate
was pushed to seven per cent, higher than it had been during the
war. The national workforce fell by 2,000,000. In 1921 the previous year's inflation of 20 per cent was fully reversed by an equal
deflation. Its effect was to increase to at least 28 per cent the real
rate of interest charged to commercial borrowers. Although Bank
Rate was down again to five per cent by the end of 1921, the
economy contracted with a massive fall in the Gross Domestic
Product. An exactly opposite policy was to be followed after the
1939-45 War. The distress which followed the 1914-18 War was
thereby avoided as the real rate of interest for the post-1945 period was around two per cent at the highest.

From 1922 until 1925 the British economy advanced steadily.
The advance was accompanied by falls in Bank Rate to the three

to four per cent range. The advance was made despite being accompanied by an initial fall in the intermediated money supply, but from 1922 to 1925 bank deposits were stable in nominal terms. In real terms, that is after adjusting for the deflation which was taking place, the money supply increased quite considerably. The frequency of circulation of bank balances also increased. Whether that was significant is impossible to say, as there is no data to reveal what proportion of the cheque clearings related to purely financial transactions. It could easily be true that after deducting financial transactions (that is transactions which did not relate to sales and purchases of goods and services but to movements of financial assets) the circulation of money was slowing: that would be normal in a period of deflation when debts tend to remain outstanding for longer.

Although deflation can cause great distress to borrowers it also makes money go further; a given nominal value of money can finance a greater physical volume of transactions. This is a very important phenomenon. It means that the money supply, though nominally constant, can finance a higher level of economic activity. Consequently the banks do not have to increase their capital bases or their reserve assets, as would be necessary if the nominal as well as the real money supply had to be increased. It is not necessary for the banks to be highly profitable in a period of deflation since they do not face the same need to attract additional capital as a base for increased nominal lendings.

Reserve assets

Under the system of monetary control practised at that time, reserve asset ratios were very important. These ratios were the prescribed proportions of a bank's assets which were to be held in liquid or near liquid form. That usually meant deposits at the Bank of England, or investment in short-term government paper such as Treasury bills. Whether the supervising authorities paid any attention to free capital bases or capital adequacy ratios is less clear. Academic economists paid no attention at all to capital adequacy ratios. Perhaps the ratio of shareholders' funds to lendings was regarded as unimportant by officialdom. Capital adequacy ratios might not, therefore, have been an official limiting factor on monetary growth, but it is difficult to accept that cautious bankers took no notice of them. Indeed the evidence is that they kept sensible ratios. However the calculation of what level of capital adequacy was maintained is complicated and confused by the practice of some banks at that time of having a capital structure which included reserve capital. Some banks' shares were only partly paid-up, and the unpaid capital, known as *reserve capital*, could be called up in the event of a liquidation.

The advance falls short

Despite the increase in production of goods and services from 1920, according to figures quoted by Keynes the volume of production in 1925 was still about 10 per cent lower than in 1913. The rate of unemployment fell from over 11 per cent in 1921 to seven per cent in 1923, but then began to rise again. The rise in unemployment seems to have reflected a fall in the real money supply. It may also have reflected greater productivity resulting from an increase in capital investment which had gone forward quite strongly after 1922. The data for this period is contained in the Bank of England's *Panel Paper No. 23*, written by the Bank's panel of academic consultants in 1984. Unfortunately the item of data the Panel never mentions is the level of banks' capital bases. Even when the Panel Paper was published, half a century after the events it describes, the importance of the capital adequacy ratio was still not appreciated by leading academic economists. They remained, it would seem, impervious to all attempts to interest them in its significance.[2] Lacking hard evidence one can only deduce tentatively that the credit supply in the period 1922-1925 was adequate to finance capital formation, but perhaps not consumer finance as well. Both are needed if an economy is to grow.[3]

During that period no truly adequate statistical data was collected. Therefore all conclusions are of necessity tentative. It may however be legitimate to suspect that economic growth could have been much faster if there had been a better growth in the credit supply, and if the circulation of the existing money supply had not been slowed down, as it very likely was, by deflation.

A media campaign for gold

Economic policies are widely debated in the information media and thereby become the victims of fashion.[4] In the 1920s the restoration of the Gold Standard became a fashionable policy. The nation was urged by the media to look forward to the rebuilding of Britain's economic glory, of which the outward and obvious symbol was to be a stable, respected, and highly valued currency. Germany's experience in 1923 of hyperinflation helped to encourage this attitude. There was a great agitation to prove Britain's European, and indeed global, superiority by going back to the Gold Standard, which the government had been forced to abandon during the 1914-18 War.

A huge mythology has always surrounded gold. Many people believe that its value is somehow sacred and immutable. That is not a rational attitude as gold is a commodity like any other. If it ever has a stable value it is only because governments choose to give it that quality - in so far as they are able to do so. When gold serves as currency it needs ideally to be given an exchange value in terms of all other goods and services which is far above its market value as a commodity, otherwise its value becomes subject to all the vagaries of the demand for gold for industrial and other purposes, and also subject to the effect of variations in the supply of newly mined gold. There is evidence of these effects on the level of prices during the 19th century, a period in which the value of the currency was firmly linked to the price of gold. Gold does not automatically give stability.

To avoid these influences gold as a currency should be given an artificial and very high exchange value, far ahead of its value as a commodity, just as happens with brass coins. Its exchange value should never be related exactly to its commodity, or intrinsic value, in other words to its price for utilitarian purposes. The supply of new-mined gold is far more than is needed for industrial uses, and there are also vast stocks in existence. Such an excess of supply over demand would quickly reduce its price dramatically, were that ever to be determined solely by industrial demand.

Reality and stability

The public's sentimental yet wholly irrational attitude was to be expected. Such is the mystique of gold it needed little encouragement, though it is surprising that financiers and economists were also infected with gold fever. Gold has the power of a secular religion in distorting reality, and those who have blind faith in gold are very like religious fundamentalists. They are the victims of an obsessional neurosis which occupies an area of the brain that is not amenable to reason. A gold-based currency was believed to be a *reality* which gave *stability*. The pressure for a return to the Gold Standard became greater and greater as people yearned for a lost stability. Psychologically they had not had long enough to adjust to the new experience of living with a currency whose buying power had become unstable. The extent of that instability was illustrated by Lord Keynes, who showed the wholesale price index rising from a base of 100 in 1913 to 308 in our starting year, 1920, and then falling back down to 159 by 1925.

A universal Gold Standard is a way of expressing the relationship between the currencies of nations which adopt the standard. The Bank of England before the 1914-18 War had stated that it would supply gold on demand at a fixed price in pounds sterling, and that it would always buy back gold at that price. When other countries' central banks did the same for their currencies, a price relationship among national currencies was established as each was related to a fixed quantity of gold. The system proposed in 1925 for the return to the Gold Standard was less extreme than the prewar version, for a high minimum value was prescribed for any sale or purchase of gold by the Bank of England. This served to exclude the ordinary person from dealing in gold. Nevertheless, with regard to every matter which had any international aspect a very tight discipline was imposed on the British economy by setting a fixed international price for the pound in terms of gold.

In any system of fixed exchange rates, whether it be the Gold Standard, the Bretton Woods variable peg system agreed in 1944, or the latest, the European Monetary System's *Exchange Rate Mechanism* (ERM), the effect is always the same: every other economic objective is subordinated to the need to maintain the exchange rates of the currencies in the system at a fixed level. Even full employment becomes a lower priority.

The Economic Consequences of Mr. Churchill

A fixed exchange rate does no great immediate harm if it is set at a sensible level. Unfortunately the choice of rate in 1925 for Britain's return to the Gold Standard was more idealistic than practical. The rate was chosen for one reason only: it was the same as the prewar rate. Nothing could have been less scientific. It reflected the romantic ideals of the more articulate section of the British people, nowadays often referred to as *the chattering classes*. The one man who dared to expose this foolish nonsense was John Maynard Keynes (Lord Keynes). He stated his arguments in three telling newspaper articles which were later published in a small 32 page book by his friends Leonard and Virginia Woolf at their Hogarth Press. The book was called *The Economic Consequences of Mr. Churchill*, after the Chancellor of the Exchequer who had, rather reluctantly, taken the decision to return to the Gold Standard at the prewar exchange rate.

To facilitate the return to the Gold Standard the exchange rate of the pound was bolstered by an increase in interest rates. The purpose was to make it an attractive currency to hold, and to encourage deflation by discouraging the creation of credit. Bank Rate was fixed at five per cent on 5th March 1925.

Keynes' arguments were expressed with great vigour in his little book which was published that same year:-

> '*The object of credit restriction......is to withdraw from employers the financial means to employ labour at the existing level of prices and wages. The policy can only attain its end by intensifying unemployment without limit, until workers are ready to accept the necessary reduction of money-wages under the pressure of hard facts.*'

> '*It is a policy, nevertheless, from which any humane or judicious person must shrink.*'

> '*Credit restriction is an incredibly powerful instrument, and even a little of it goes a long way.*'

> '*No section of labour will readily accept lower wages merely in response to sentimental speeches by Mr. Baldwin. We are depending for the reduction of wages on the pressure of unemployment and of strikes and lock-outs; and in order to make sure of this result we are deliberately intensifying unemployment.*'

'We want to encourage businessmen to enter on new enterprises not, as we are doing, to discourage them. Deflation does
not reduce wages "automatically." It reduces them by causing
unemployment. The proper object of dear money is to check an
incipient boom. Woe to those whose faith leads them to use it to
aggravate a depression.'

'It is a question of relative price here and abroad. The
prices of our exports in the international market are too
high......Why are they too high? The orthodox answer is to
blame it on the working man for working too little and getting
too much. In some industries and in some grades of labour,
particularly the unskilled, this is true; and other industries, for
example the railways, are overstaffed......it is not true in those
export industries where unemployment is greatest.'

'By maintaining discount rates in London at a sufficient
margin above discount rates in New York, it can induce the
New York money market to lend a sufficient sum to the London
money market to balance both our trade deficit and the foreign
investments which British investors are still buying despite the
embargo. Besides when once we have offered high rates of
interest to attract funds from the New York short loan market,
we have to continue them, even though we have no need to
increase our borrowings, in order to retain what we have
already borrowed.'

Keynes also demonstrated that Britain's major export, coal,
could not compete in foreign markets while sterling was deliberately and severely overpriced.

In order to maintain the new fixed exchange rate at its
excessive level wages had to fall, and they did fall, despite bitter
opposition from the trade unions. The unions lost their battles to
stop wage reductions, including the General Strike of 1926, but
they remembered their defeat with bitterness, and it brought a
determination to exact revenge. The opportunity to do so came
twenty years later. Trade union militancy in the post-1945 years
flowed directly from the painful defeats in the 1920s.

A history lesson for all time

Those who ignore the lessons written in the pages of history are condemned to learn them from painful experience. There is a chilling similarity between the debates and decisions of 1925-26 and those of 1990-92. The chill is rendered even icier by the fact that Britain in 1992 was not the world economic power it was in 1925. It was no consolation that it had less to lose because it had already lost much of its manufacturing industry. Keynes' words in his little book still make impressive and instructive reading. They are much clearer in their message than in his later, less well-written books. *The Economic Consequences of Mr. Churchill* should be compulsory reading for every student of economics.

Deflation continued until 1934. But Keynes had inadvertently laid the foundation of a powerful delusion: that high interest rates could cause deflation (or reduce inflation). His own reasoning at the time was not in serious error: he makes clear that lower wages would result from higher unemployment caused, in its turn, by high interest rates and a consequently overvalued currency. The delusion from which others later suffered was that high interest rates could cure inflation just by the reduction in the demand for credit. Very high unemployment was not seen as an inescapable stage in the inflation-curing process. But in Britain it *is* an inescapable stage. The attitude of the trade unions ensures that that is so. While a trade union still retains sufficient power to get a wage increase by using the threat of strike action, and is still motivated to do so, control of inflation by restriction of the credit supply will bring about high unemployment. The history of the 1980s proves that is so.

Academic economists and the Treasury's theoreticians, both remote from the real action, deluded themselves about the progression statement which describes the process of curing inflation. The true statement is, as Keynes knew, (A) High interest rates lead to (B) Unemployment leading to (C) Reduced inflation - provided the wind is fair. By the 1980s that progression statement had been altered into the very different statement that (A) leads to (C), (B) now being redundant. Since (A) is easy, and (C) is considered pleasant, the body politic preferred to draw a convenient veil over (B), which is very unpleasant. Many millions of people in Britain, and in other countries which have pursued similar policies, have discovered very painfully that (B) means unemployment, and is inescapably part of the progression. They are being asked to pay the price of the simplistic and forgetful understanding of Keynes' theories by the economic establishment of the United Kingdom, by the International Monetary Fund, and by many governments throughout the world, especially that of Germany. Keynes would be horrified at the foolish accretions which have become attached to his careful analysis, and at the unnecessary human suffering which is being inflicted as a result.

Keynes was not wholly correct

But even Keynes was not entirely right in his expectation that unemployment would cure inflation. The 1980s demonstrated that if workers and their leaders were intransigent, unemployment and inflation would both grow simultaneously, the phenomenon known as *stagflation*. His mechanism does not always work, and when it does work it may take a decade or more to have any effect.

There was, admittedly, a difference between the 1920s and the post 1945 era. It was deflation that took place in the 1920s, not a reduction in inflation which became the quite different objective after 1945. Deflation is a far more horrifying thing than inflation, and its horrors are magnified by its effect on the exchange rate. A deflating currency is popular with foreigners, and especially with those whose own currencies are inflating rapidly. There were many such currencies in the 1920s, not least the German Mark. The deflated pound became sought after internationally, intensifying the problems of British exporting industries even further. No worse fate can befall a national currency than to become a reserve currency which foreigners wish to hold; it inevitably leads to a huge trade deficit, as the United States also later discovered.

No capital issues

In his book Keynes implies that, concurrently with the high interest rates, there were also embargoes on capital issues at the time of Britain's return to the Gold Standard. Thus not only was the growth of the intermediated credit supply attacked by high interest rates, but there was also an attack on the expansion of the non-intermediated credit market. Of the two the attack on the latter was the more important. Besides having a direct effect on the creation of credit, it also stopped any attempt by the banks to increase their capital bases, a primary requirement if the banks were to create credit. Without new issues of capital to supplement their capital bases there was no hope of the banks increasing the nominal intermediated credit supply.

Figures quoted by Keynes in his *Treatise on Money* indicate that the deposits of the London clearing banks fell slightly, from £2,023,000,000 in 1921 to £1,843,000,000 in 1925, and then rose to £1,940,000,000 in 1929. In real terms (adjusted for inflation) deposits rose sharply in value. The real meaning of the deflation-adjusted increase is difficult to interpret, but at least it saved the necessity for a capital injection into the banks, for deflation, as we have already noted, makes bank capital stretch further in real terms. Keynes also noted that during the same period bank deposits in the United States grew in *nominal* value and that the volume of industrial production increased, whereas in the United Kingdom production was slightly less in 1927 than in 1907, a depressing indication of Britain's industrial decline.

Deflation is self-perpetuating

Positive nominal interest rates, that is rates above zero, can be raised or reduced. Real interest rates, the nominal rate less the rate of inflation or plus the rate of deflation, cannot be reduced once the nominal rate is down to zero. Britain has never tried a mechanism to apply a negative nominal interest rate, when the depositor pays interest instead of receiving it. The Swiss federal government, by contrast, has on occasion ordered the application of negative nominal interest rates to foreigners' deposits.

If deflation is running at five per cent, then even if the nominal rate of interest is zero, the real (deflation-adjusted) rate of interest is also five per cent. The lowest nominal rate of interest ever charged in Britain by the Bank of England is two per cent. This may well be the lowest practicable level for Bank Rate. Once that level is reached there is no longer an interest weapon available with which to stop the recessionary effect of high real interest rates. How does one break out of a downward recessionary spiral once nominal rates of interest are too low to allow the central bank to reduce the real rate of interest any further?

Heretics at large

Ways out of the downward recessionary spiral were suggested by two very controversial but influential amateur economists called Silvio Gesell and Major C. H. Douglas. Gesell, who was born in Belgium in 1862, started writing in the 1890s. *Die Natürliche Wirtshaftsordnung durch Freiland und Freigeld* is his major work. *The International Association for a Natural Economic Order*, which was founded to spread his teaching, is still active, and his memory is kept well alive in Switzerland where his theories are respected. Douglas, a Canadian, was the founder in the 1920s of a somewhat similar movement called *Social Credit*, and he too still has many devoted followers. He disturbed many professional economists, as can be seen from references to him in Sir Roy Harrod's life of Lord Keynes, and in Keynes' own writings.

Gesell and Douglas both made proposals which might have been effective in reducing unemployment and curing deflation, even though the reasoning behind them is faulty. Gesell, like many moralists before him, realised that the build-up of wealth implies the build-up of debt, as the two are opposite faces of the same phenomenon. He therefore wanted to reduce the propensity to save, and the consequent necessity for borrowing. In order to encourage people to spend their money rather than save, he suggested that the state should make money lose its purchasing power by a fixed percentage each year. His theory as it stood was quite unworkable as it was only the value of banknotes which he proposed to depreciate, and that left bank balances untouched. A system could certainly have been devised to achieve his purpose in respect of the whole money supply. The oddity in Gesell's views is that he was strongly against inflation, and yet moderate inflation has precisely the effect he was trying to achieve.

As Gesell is the inspiration of the Swiss National Bank it is appropriate that the recent history of the Swiss franc reflects the nearly perfect implementation of Gesell's wishes, but not by the method he proposed. Switzerland has experienced moderate inflation, so that in the twenty years from 1971 the purchasing power of the Swiss currency depreciated about fifty per cent. Its inflation rate was the lowest in Europe, which has tended to obscure the fact that it was, nevertheless, subject to inflation. When the rate of inflation was very low the growth of the Swiss economy faltered;

when the inflation rate increased so did the rate of growth of the Swiss economy.

The buying power 'Gap'

Douglas's proposals were based on the theory that the costs of production are not matched by an equivalent buying power, and there is therefore a gap which has to be bridged. No modern accountant would accept his reasoning. His proposal was that the gap be closed by the state giving everyone some money, a sure way to get out of a deflationary spiral and into an inflationary one!

Would their proposals have been more effective than Keynes proposals? Or do they in pure essence amount to the same thing? Keynes could not accept the theories of either Gesell or Douglas. Nevertheless he wrote about them with sympathy even though he also linked them with Karl Marx as belonging to an 'underworld' of economic theorists. He also refers to them as 'brave heretics'. Present day admirers of both Gesell and Douglas claim that Keynes was finally converted to their views. Such claims merely demonstrate their great anxiety to earn the approval, even post-humously, of the century's best known economist.

Effects of the Gold Standard

The worst effect of the return to the Gold Standard was the sacrifice of future economic growth, rather than any actual decline. For a year or so there was a dip in both fixed capital formation and in output, with a two per cent dip in employment. Average earnings had been falling since 1920 and they bottomed in 1924. They then rose slightly until 1929. There was a slight dip in 1931, and then an upward trend until 1938. Once the 1926 strikes were over, output rose sharply until the 1929 crash.

In the years immediately following the abandonment of the Gold Standard in 1931 there were some important realignments of relative currency values. Most significant was the rise of the British pound against the American dollar, partly as a result of a deliberate devaluation of the dollar by Roosevelt, who may have seen a truth to which the British government was still blind. British deflation was all too effective in making sterling an alternative popular currency for foreigners to hold. Ultra low interest rates in the 1930s may have lessened the tendency of deflation to push up sterling's exchange value, but by 1937 its appreciation was enough to bring a modest economic recovery to a halt.

The danger of averaging

Such statistics as there are of wages for the 1920s and 1930s are difficult to reconcile with the anecdotal evidence of industrial workers of the time. The difference between data and recollection may be caused by the reliance of the economists on averages. Although averaging is perhaps the simplest of all the arithmetical techniques used in statistics, it is probably the most dangerous, and it constantly leads people away from the truth, not towards it. In this case averaging concealed the fact that producers of goods were much the worst affected. Public employees, by contrast, fared exceptionally well in the 36 per cent deflation which took place between 1920 and 1934. By 1935 the treasured jobs in the community were in central and local government. Teachers and bus drivers were envied people. Bank clerks too were lucky: they lost one pay increment in 1931; otherwise their salaries remained as they were.

The economists' averages disguise the fact that manufacturing industry in the 1930s paid very little to its workers: that low pay level must have been determined by the exigencies and realities of foreign competition in an era when sterling was overvalued. The worst effect was between 1929 and 1932 when exports fell by a third and unemployment rose to 23 per cent of insured workers. The problem is put succinctly by Sir Roy Harrod in his book *Policy Against Inflation*, published in 1960. He writes at page 60,

> '..he [Franklin Roosevelt, the U.S. President] was given power to devalue a further 10 per cent without reference to Congress. The "gold bloc" currencies had been left high and dry by the devaluation of sterling and the dollar, and everyone believed that they would in due course be devalued also, as in fact they were. Germany had declared a moratorium, the mark had been brought under a new system of Exchange Control, including multiple currency arrangements, and was by no means a suitable refuge for money in search of safety. What other important currency was there? For the period from 1931 to 1939 sterling appeared the safest bet.'

In 1925 Keynes had foreseen this inequality of suffering. In his book, *The Economic Consequences of Mr. Churchill,* he stated in several places that the burden of the necessary cut in nominal wages would be borne by the export industries, and the strong would benefit at the expense of the weak. He said on page nine,

> *'...there is no machinery for effecting a simultaneous reduction. Deliberately to raise the value of sterling money in England means, therefore, engaging in a struggle with each separate group [of workers] in turn, with no prospect that the final result will be fair, and no guarantee that the stronger group will not gain at the expense of the weaker.'*

The result was not at all fair. The real life examples of the Birmingham Small Arms Company (B.S.A.), and of banking, (*'a sheltered industry'*, to use Keynes' term,) illustrates the inequality in experience. In 1937 the B.S.A. prepared a management plan to centralise the buying of materials for all its dozens of factories which at that time were very deeply involved in the rearmament programme as well as in consumer production. The manpower of the department was fixed at 279. The basic pay of the head of this vital department was set at £5..10..0 a week, £5.50 in decimal money. His deputy earned £3..15..0. At that time a bank clerk commenced at the age of 16 with pay of £1 a week. At age 31, if he had been given no promotion to a responsible post, his pay reached £400 a year. In addition he received child allowances, had his income tax paid for him, and was in a non-contributory pension scheme. The ordinary bank clerk's responsibilities came nowhere near those of a foreman at B.S.A., upon whose efficiency depended the well-being of many thousands of other workers.

The low value of the dollar and the intricate system of exchange control in Germany, which was designed to keep export prices low, helped to depress British export industries. By the time war began in 1939 German consumer industries were in fine fettle compared with those in Britain. Even high tariffs failed to keep German products out of the British market. Adolf Hitler's finance minister, Hjalmar Schacht, seems to have laid the foundation for the German post-1945 success in production of consumer goods, to judge from remarks made by Albert Speer in his book *Inside the*

Third Reich. The British worship of a strong pound proved to be a profound economic tragedy. Perhaps the most deeply depressed industry between the two wars was not an export industry at all. It was British farming, which could not compete with cheap foreign produce, especially from North America.

Churchill confesses

In the budget debate in Parliament in 1932 Winston Churchill who had by then been out of office for three years, made his sincere and emotion-charged apology for his action in 1925.

> *'When I was moved by many arguments and forces in 1925 to return to the Gold Standard I was assured by the highest experts, and our experts are men of great ability and indisputable integrity and sincerity, that we were anchoring ourselves to reality and stability; and I accepted their advice. I take for myself and my colleagues of other days whatever degree of blame and burden there may be for having accepted their advice.*
>
> *'But what has happened? We have had no reality, no stability......'*

The quotation shows Churchill honourably defending the capability and sincerity of his advisers. This he no doubt did because Keynes on page 10 of *The Economic Consequences of Mr. Churchill* had attacked the advisers. In answer to his own question, *'Why did he do such a silly thing?'*, Keynes had explained,

> *'Partly, perhaps, because he has no instinctive judgment to prevent him from making mistakes; partly because, lacking this instinctive judgment, he was deafened by the clamorous voices of conventional finance; and, most of all, because he was gravely misled by his experts.'*

Churchill also observed that it had become much more expensive in real terms to pay off a loan because of the deflation. The greatest debt was that incurred for fighting the war of 1914-18. Of the £6billion borrowed to pay for that war one third took the form of an issue of gilt-edged stock called 5 per cent War Loan, with a nominal value of very nearly £2billion. The postwar deflation, triggered by the return to the Gold Standard and intensified by the 1929 crash, made the real cost of servicing the loan about 50 per cent greater. In 1931 the problem was partly resolved by replacing the original 5 per cent War Loan with a new 3.5 per cent War Stock, thus restoring the interest cost of the stock to its original level in real terms. Luckily for the government the capital was not yet repayable. One of the bits of trickery involved in the conversion of 5 per cent War Loan to 3.5 per cent War Stock was that the original obligation of the government to redeem the Loan by 1946 at the latest was replaced by a government option to repay it, but only in 1952 *or after*. It never has been repaid, and because of inflation its real value has become comparatively trivial. By March 1991 the original £2billion had grown in real terms to more than £58billion. To get the effect of 1920s deflation in perspective we must imagine what it would have been like if the 1992 National Debt were increased by £29billion without any money actually being borrowed, and therefore without any benefit to the government. For a heavily indebted government to cause deflation is an act of unbelievable incompetence. That the British people allowed it shows Quixotic idealism - or grievous ignorance!

Inflation on the other hand is an arbitrary tax on every wealth owner. By inflating the currency, Governments get their wars on the cheap. When the Premier and Chancellor of the Exchequer in the 1980s and 1990s repeatedly placed *curing inflation* at the top of their priorities, they were reversing the historical self-interest of governments down the ages. Governments can either pay off their debts or they can wash them away altogether by inflating the currency. Every widow who has had her nest egg of 'safe' government stock or her building society deposit inflated to nothing has been doing her indebted government and other borrowers a huge favour. She has paid for wars; she paid for the nationalisation of *'the commanding heights of the economy'* by the postwar Labour government; she paid for roads, schools, hospitals, the running of the coal mines and the railways; she has paid for all the governments' money wasting schemes as well as their sensible ones; she has repaid the mortgages of a legion of postwar house buyers. She has handed over the greater part of her life savings without even being half-aware that she was doing so.

Inflation has forced savers to pay for everything for which money is borrowed. Some it has beggared; some - the borrowers - it has made wealthy for no effort. The millions who are robbed by inflation, and they include every owner of a building society deposit, of a bank deposit, or of a non-indexed National Savings Certificate, lead their lives seemingly unconscious of their loss, even though they complain of rising prices! A government which practises taxation by inflation can be accused of having the low morality of a loan shark. Significantly, National Savings were invented in the 1920s after the swindler, Horatio Bottomley M.P., had shown how easy it was to get hold of the citizen's savings by playing up to his patriotism.

But what is the alternative to taxation by inflation? Higher tax rates? The problem is that such a huge proportion of total national expenditure is in the hands of the state that to finance it without inflation necessitates high tax rates which are strongly resisted. Inflation is the easy way out, and the voter supports it. So who is the true shark? Is it the government or the voter? The very government which proclaimed its opposition to inflation won the 1992 election by its stance against higher taxation!

There is a consolation. Inflation does not destroy an economy as does deflation, though the vain methods used to try to cure inflation may do so. Many economists have claimed that inflation causes unemployment, including the respected Samuel Brittan. Have they truly got the progression statement right? It is surely not '*Inflation leads to unemployment*', but, '*Inflation leads to foolish counter-inflationary measures which lead to unemployment*'.

Ultra low interest rates

The 1925 policy of high interest rates and a fixed exchange rate having proved disastrous, a policy of ultra-low interest rates was adopted in its stead. From June 1932 to 1951, with only a brief break at the outbreak of war in 1939, Bank Rate remained at two per cent. Traditional monetary theory predicts that such a low interest rate will precipitate a vast increase in the intermediated money supply, an over-heated economy, and very high inflation. It did none of these things. Indeed, deflation continued for another four years. Unemployment halved but remained high at 1,400,000 (though total employment rose by 2,600,000 in five years). There was a small boom in manufacturing. By 1937 Gross Domestic Product was 33 per cent above the 1907 level, having been a little below it in 1925. The growth rate of manufacturing averaged about two per cent annually. The long period of deflation ended only when rearmament was started. Then inflation reappeared. That was five years after the reduction of Bank Rate to two per cent. In the meantime the real value of bank deposits had increased. It was not low interest rates which were responsible for ending deflation. The heretical question is therefore prompted: *'Were low interest rates then causing **deflation**, not inflation?'*

The main effect of the switch to low interest rates was to alter the proportions which cash, non-interest bearing and interest bearing deposits bore to one another. When interest rates are low there is little incentive to switch one's money to interest bearing deposits. So cash holdings and current accounts rose sharply. The total of cash and bank deposits (not officially known as M3 until much later) surged initially, fell back again, surged briefly when deflation ended, and then resumed a slow rate of growth. A fifth of the increase in the money supply was banknotes. That is interesting as M0 (currency) requires no capital base, and therefore lack of new capital does not restrain its growth at all in the way it does for bank money.

Were there restraining factors at work, hindering the rapidity of the growth of the nominal money supply? Was such a factor the lack of growth in the capital base of the banks? Initially there was ground to be recovered because in 1931 bank deposits were 10 per cent below their 1920 level. The growth in bank deposits petered out when they reached 10 per cent above the 1920 level. The required capital base was presumably already in place at the clearing banks for the restoration of lending to its 1920 level, unless the banks had made secret losses during the period 1920 - 1931, and concealed them, as was then permitted. Nor would it have required much of a decline in the capital ratio to enable the growth in lending which took place after 1931. But would the capital base have supported any further growth? There is a very slight possibility that from 1932 it would have done so. The clue to what might have happened beneath the veil of banking secrecy may lie in a prophecy made in A. H. Gibson's article in the *Bankers Magazine* of January 1923. That article not only included the data for the famous *Gibson's Paradox*, but also a prophecy that if the price of 2.5 per cent Consols rose to 77 per cent, the banks would make enough profit out of capital gains to cover their dividends for ten years. With the fall in general interest rates after the reduction in Bank Rate to two per cent, Consols duly rose in price to 77 per cent. Did the banks make a paper profit so that their capital bases were sharply, but secretly, increased? Was this the support for the initial surge in the money supply?

Since the 1939-45 War banks have held only shorter-dated gilts, which cannot appreciate as dramatically when interest rates fall as the 'longs' or the undated gilts. But earlier in the century short-dated gilts were uncommon. On the basis of 19th century experience it would not have seemed risky to hold undated gilts. Did Gibson know the make-up of the banks' investments in 1923? If he was right then, had the make-up of the banks' portfolios changed by 1932? This is an intriguing mystery, the answer to which could prove to be significant to monetary theory. The banks should delve into their archives and reveal the true state of their balance sheets and profit and loss accounts for that era. Much might be explained. Information about the true capital base at that time would be most welcome.

What financed the little boom of 1932-1937?

Because the growth of bank loans in the 1930s was slow, and advances to the private sector actually fell slightly in nominal terms, the credit supply had to be strongly supplemented through the non-intermediated market for credit. Between 1931 and 1936 domestic new issues of stocks and shares quintupled and must have provided the fuel for the economic growth of the period. The cost of borrowing by way of debentures and preference shares fell by a quarter. In total such issues nearly equalled the growth in bank deposits. The Treasury too funded large amounts of debt.

The banks all paid the same low rate of interest on deposit accounts, probably because the oligopolies which controlled deposit banking had a propensity to suppress price competition. The expansion of the clearing banks was consequently retarded. But in view of the high level of funding, new credit must have been regularly created by the banks to replace the large sums lost through disintermediation. The overall level of bank lending reveals nothing about the rapidity of the turnover of debt. The importance of the close interrelation between intermediated and disintermediated credit is once again highlighted. Regular supplies of disintermediated debt were available, but there can have been only a very limited supply of credit for companies too small to use the disintermediated credit provided through the stockmarket.

In the view of economists there was an economic recovery during the 1930s. It was even the subject of a report in 1984 by a Bank of England Panel of Academic Consultants, to which reference has already been made. (Panel Paper No 23). The paper admits that the growth in manufacturing output was *'unexceptional'* at two per cent annually! That is trivial compared with growth rates of countries which have not been handicapped by overvalued currencies or the sundry other impediments to the forward progress of Britain's industrial complex.

We must observe that the very low interest rate of 1931 onwards did *not* lead to any great expansion of the nominal intermediated credit supply; between 1932 and 1937 its growth was nowhere near the level of the increase achieved in later decades when nominal interest rates were higher. Indeed in the later 1930s the earlier growth in the credit supply petered out even though Bank Rate was lower than the inflation rate; in 1937 even the long-term real interest rate fell below zero. The root of the problem was almost certainly that the benefit of the 1931 devaluation had been completely eroded by the appreciation of the exchange rate of the pound, measured against a basket of currencies, to the pre-1931 level.

The expansion of both the intermediated and the non-intermediated credit supplies during the period lends support to the contention that studying the intermediated credit supply in isolation is an unsatisfactory way to fathom the depths of monetary theory. A somewhat older example which illustrates the combined effect is provided by Lord Keynes in his *Treatise on Money.* It concerns the period 1894 to 1896. In 1894, as official gold holdings had recently doubled, Bank Rate was lowered to two per cent. Although bank deposits increased by 20 per cent Keynes noted that trade during the two years was stagnant, employment figures bad, and prices were falling. The reason for this paradox must have been that new issues of stocks and shares were low, and the rise in the intermediated credit supply was not sufficient to compensate for a slowing down of the rate of increase of non-intermediated credit.

War and its aftermath

War is the most catastrophic event an economy can undergo; it can normally be expected to bring both a financial crisis and high interest rates. Yet throughout the 1939-45 War nominal interest rates were as low as they have ever been. Churchill now made good use of the ingenuity of Keynes, the economist who in 1925 had so savagely criticised him. Keynes had an office in the British Treasury from 1940. Over the five years from the time he went to the Treasury in 1940 until 1945, official inflation totalled 9.5 per cent. A rather more realistic unofficial calculation puts the rate of inflation at a little over five per cent per annum, still a remarkable achievement in such destabilising war-time circumstances. By the end of the war Keynes and his ideas had achieved supremacy in the world of economics. He did not live very long to enjoy his success. He died in the Spring of 1946.

What people *assumed* would have been Keynes' policies, had he lived, continued to develop. The old mistakes which Keynes had criticised so vehemently in the 1920s were brought back into fashion, even by his self-styled 'successors'. The pound was seriously overvalued. British determination to keep it high caused an increase in interest rates from two per cent in 1945 to 4.5 per cent in 1955. Inflation averaged 3.9 per cent during the same decade. Some temporary inflation was inevitable in a period of recovery and rebuilding after such a devastatingly destructive war, and following the lifting of so many wartime price controls. Subsidies were also gradually reduced though not abolished. The inflation worried people, even though by comparison with later decades it was trivial. A nation which had become used in the interwar period to prices going down found it difficult to adjust to the novel experience of prices going up, and wanted inflation stopped. Inflation is indeed an aberration, though it would be difficult for anyone born after 1940 to accept a statement which sounds so heretical. In an era of high investment, constant technical innovation, and consequently of increasing productivity, falling prices ought to be the norm, as indeed they were until 1937.

Inflation was to continue, becoming endemic in the British economy, though it declined to an average rate of three per cent in the decade ending in 1965. The reason it continued was very simple: it was the practice of regular annual pay claims by trade unions which always won very nearly what they asked for in un-equal battles with weakened employers, and automatic rises for executive staff who can be relied on to look after themselves. After the war the general public was very sympathetic to claims by workers for *cost of living increases*, not understanding that such increases could not compensate for the rise in the cost of living when the economy was already at full stretch. Politicians gave in to popular opinion. Trade unions which had lost their battles of the 1920s to avoid wage cuts, won their battles in the 1930s to preserve jobs, and brought so much underemployment into the economy that there was apparently a shortage of labour. From 1945 onwards the cards were stacked in favour of Britain's trade unions by history, by circumstances and by the actions of its first-ever majority Labour government. The leaders of the trade unions, and many members of the government, were those who had endured the harsh sufferings of the great deflation and were embittered by it. In their determination to avoid a return of the depression they went too far in the other direction. The Labour movement was a victim of its own legends in which the demons were always the employers, but never the foolish politicians of all parties, never the mistaken economic advisers, and certainly never their own leaders.

The great socialist experiment

The immediate postwar government was ultra-socialist, even by world standards. Its brave attempts at socialist planning held the economy in check when they did not actually drag it backwards. The government persisted despite all set-backs with that blind fervour which is the characteristic of idealistic do-gooders of all eras. The aim was to bring all key or basic industries, the so-called *commanding heights of the economy*, into public ownership. *Public ownership* meant, in truth, the de facto ownership by civil service barons assisted by cohorts of bureaucrats who paid danegeld to buy off trade unions whose behaviour differed little from that of protection racketeers. The industries made losses, an inevitable consequence, it was later discovered, of socialisation, but whose truth was then a lesson still painfully to be learnt. The capital needs of state industries had to be met either by taxes or as part of the public sector borrowing requirement. High taxes became a further stimulus for inflationary wage claims.

It was a most frustrating time for those who saw that Britain had an opportunity to become one of the two leading industrial powers of the world. Small private businesses, which are commonly the growth points of industry, were especially handicapped. With a top rate of income tax of 95 per cent a businessman who started a successful new venture might receive only five per cent of his profit, but he suffered 100 per cent of any loss if it was unsuccessful. Success created another hazard, the possibility of an estate duty charge of up to 80 per cent on the death of the owner. Very few businesses can sustain the loss of 80 per cent of their capital once in every generation. The only answer to the threat of estate duty was to become a public quoted company, and suffer the loss of that freedom to manoeuvre which is the virtue of the private business. Fancy techniques of avoiding destructive taxes were developed, but they too often had the injurious side effect of reducing the businessman's ability to manoeuvre quickly.

The early postwar governments all ignored the essential life truth which is that human beings are willing to provide whatever goods or services the community wants provided it is made worth their while to do so. The businessman's frustrations were not only financial. Many essential resources were allocated by the planning bureaucrats, and the small businessman lacked the clout to compete with the big organisations in the scramble for scarce resources. Without the planning controls it is likely that many of the shortages would have disappeared: such shortages are a feature of the planned economy which truly causes them.

The wartime controls on prices had the opposite effect of what was intended when peace came: they kept prices up. The new Conservative government which came to power in 1951 saw this and took action. Price controls were abolished on many raw materials including lead and zinc. The controlled prices of these two materials had been about £117 and £120 a ton respectively. The planners and the socialists screamed that prices would soar and that it was folly to end the controls. By 1956 both metals were selling at around £60 to £65 a ton. This had an odd effect. At Avonmouth near Bristol the Imperial Smelting Company was producing zinc by three processes. The first was the method of horizontal distillation used by the ancient Egyptians. The second, the vertical distillation method, was considerably more modern and produced purer zinc. Thirdly there was a brand new plant using the improved vertical distillation method. Because of the slump in prices it was not economic to run all three processes and one was temporarily closed. Which one? Oddly it was not the ancient Egyptian, labour intensive method, but the ultra-modern one. Perhaps it was too clever to work! The explanation actually given was that the old plant had been written off and was costing nothing in depreciation. If the same thing had happened in the 1980s the company would have been tempted to destroy the new plant in order to avoid a charge for local taxation.

For 'Keynesian' read 'Socialist'

Because the postwar Labour government adopted those economic policies which were commonly thought to be derived from Lord Keynes' theories, their right-wing opponents gradually came to identify incompetent interventionist socialism with Lord Keynes. Keynes' statement on page 145 of the *Treatise on Money* rather encouraged this misleading belief. It reads,

> *'Perhaps the ultimate solution lies in the rate of capital development becoming more largely an affair of state, determined by collective wisdom and long views.'*

Some governments have, rather miraculously, followed that solution effectively. One such is Japan, not normally classified as left-wing. In Britain even Conservative governments pursued for many years policies inspired by Keynes' dictum, though their enthusiasm was sometimes attenuated.

Keynes might well have resented the identification of his ecnomic philosophy with any political system. His political allegiance was to the Liberal Party. He was called a radical, but his brother-in-law, a Conservative Member of Parliament,[5] maintained that Keynes grew less radical as he grew older. Though a radical he was clearly a pragmatist and also a supremely successful speculator. He made a great fortune from financial speculation which secured his total academic independence. Many of his close acquaintances were progressive in their views, and appeared deca-dent. A son of two close friends was an intimate associate of the future traitors, Blunt, Burgess, and Maclean, and later died in the Spanish Civil War. Any malevolent but misguided right-winger who wished to damn Keynes from his associations had ample ammunition available. Professor A. V. Hill may be right in his statement that at the end of his life Keynes was less of a radical. Can one speculate that he had lost faith in the *ultimate solution* he had proposed in 1928, and would not have supported the policy of the postwar socialist government? He had cynical moments and a journalistic turn of phrase, journalism being one of his professions, and if he had lived, one can imagine him commenting in the privacy of the Senior Combination Room at King's College, Cambridge, that the fault in postwar British planning was that the collective stupidity, not the collective wisdom, of the British electorate was dictating the planning of capital development.[6] In the history of postwar monetary policy one can see the short view predominating in Britain rather than the long views advocated by Keynes, and which have been followed with some success in other countries. Keynes would have been more willing to face reality than were postwar governments.

Keynes died in April 1946 and was therefore unable to tell his followers that many of the circumstances of the postwar era were sufficiently different from those in the 1920s and 1930s to require policies which were also different from some of those with which his name had become firmly associated. Despite his oft-quoted phrase '*in the long run we are all dead*', it is most unlikely he would have approved the short-termist manoeuvres which were to be a feature of postwar monetary policy.

One wonders too if he would have approved of the attempt, so seriously pursued, of turning his illustrative algebraical equations into computerised emulations of the economy, with real numbers inserted in the place of his mathematical symbols. That many economists were anxious to make use of mathematics is entirely understandable. Powerful mathematical tools were available and many of them would know the famous dictum of the great scientist, Lord Kelvin, which goes as follows:-

> *'When you can measure what you are speaking about and express it in numbers, you know something about it, but when you cannot measure it, when you cannot express it in numbers, your knowledge is of a meagre and unsatisfactory kind.'*

Few economists are prepared to be content with meagre and unsatisfactory knowledge, and admit that truly that is all that is available. Moreover, hidden in the obscuring recesses of faculties of economics are serious scholars with great mathematical skills for which they desperately wish to find a practical use. They do not drink to the traditional toast of mathematicians, *'Here's to higher mathematics; may they never be of any use to anyone!'* Such is their desperation that they are prepared to use their skilled techniques in the complex manipulation of spurious data, in spurious formulae, with spurious results.

The science of economics

It was Keynes more than anyone else who had made economics respectable as a science. That was the firm opinion of his brother-in-law, Professor A. V. Hill, whose own status as a scientist - Director of the National Physical Laboratory, Nobel Prizewinner, and a President of the Royal Society - was unassailable.[7] Many socialists of those days prided themselves on being scientific, and believed all their pet policies to be based on science. Economists of that generation adopted scientific procedures, especially statistical techniques, which were appropriate to the physical sciences, but which were not valid for a human science. They rejected the stricter methods considered correct by other human scientists, and ignored the scathing protests by the physical scientists against their flagrant misuse of statistical techniques.

Not surprisingly the British economy did not function as well as pseudo-scientists and academic socialists expected. The British are believed by many foreigners to be perfectionists who are always seeking the ideal. The ideal was not being attained, and therefore the post-Keynesian establishment in economics came under increasingly sceptical scrutiny, particularly by those on the political right. They inspired a penetrating inquisitor and effective publicist in the form of the best-known columnist of the Financial Times, Harold Wincott. A most effective writer, he expressed views which appealed to many businessmen, who found him easy to understand. Wincott argued his case very well and targeted his attacks with precision, even if his line of argument was sometimes rather simplistic. It helped him that Keynesianism had indeed been corrupted, making it an easy target. Keynes himself shortly before his death talked of an economics *'turned sour and silly'*, and may well have been referring to some of his professed followers.

Wincott targeted his attack on monetary policy, continuing week after week until his death in 1969, but it was not until ten years after his death that people with beliefs similar to his own won power. In the meantime there was a drift, encouraged no doubt by the International Monetary Fund, towards a more monetarist approach to problems, and in particular towards the use of the weapon of interest rates. Wincott may have exercised some posthumous influence on this trend. His fame was perpetuated by the creation of the Wincott Foundation with the purpose of sponsoring an annual lecture in his memory under the auspices of the Institute of Economic Affairs. Appropriately, the Harold Wincott Memorial lecture for 1970 was given by Nobel Prizewinner Professor Milton Friedman, a zealot for monetarism, which he put forward as a correction of corrupted Keynesianism (which might be called *post-Keynesianism*). By contrast the following year's lecture was given by an eminent associate of Keynes, Professor James Meade, who later won the Nobel Prize.

Another effective publicist for monetarist views was Enoch Powell, M.P. In the 1950s he had been a Treasury minister in the Macmillan government. He and the Chancellor of the Exchequer, Peter Thorneycroft, along with another Treasury minister, Nigel Birch, had all resigned from the government in January 1958 over the issue of the proper control of government spending and its effect on the money supply, a monetarist viewpoint. Viewed a generation later the whole affair of their resignation looks bloated out of all sensible proportion. The true problem, as it always is in Britain, was an unwillingness to be realistic over the exchange value of sterling. To avoid devaluation some deflation was needed and monetary restraint, partly in the form of credit controls, was being used. By later standards inflation was so trivial it would be regarded as a Chancellor's dream. The money supply position was anything but liberal. In 1951 the total deposits of the London clearing banks had been 49 per cent of GNP. By 1958 the proportion was 35 per cent. The banks' advances to non-government borrowers, which are what really matter in the financing of GNP, and which had been 14.8 per cent of GNP in 1951, were 9.6 per cent in 1957, and 11 per cent in 1958. In 1959 the figure rose to 13.6 per cent of GNP. The 1957 figure was a big decline on the position in 1950, and in such a situation one can conceive that Friedman would have wished to see an expansion of the money supply. It is paradoxical, therefore, that one of his most vociferous allies should have taken the opposite attitude.

Powell was recognised even by his opponents as a man of impressive intellect. He was an outstanding scholar, educated in the intellectual hothouses of King Edward's School, Birmingham, and Trinity College, Cambridge. He also rose to high rank in the army during the 1939-45 War. His ability as an orator put him in the top division of the parliamentary speakers' league of the twentieth century. His voice raised in support of monetarism was a potent influence, even if not immediately effective. It is very sad that he aided the introduction of some of the most damaging economic policies of his century.

Notes on Chapter Eight:-

1. Such distortions in the economy are rarely corrected and in 1950 the Churchill Award was still being paid to armaments workers.

2. I had brought the importance of the capital base to the attention of several leading economists in 1973. They could not plead ignorance.

3. In those days consumer finance was often a very informal affair. Many workers were members of local savings schemes called with typical working class humour *'diddlums'*. The proportion of the population who had access to commercial bank overdraft facilities was tiny. For an insight based on 300 interviews into social conditions in the deflation of the 1920s see *A Land Fit For Heroes* by Christopher Grayling, 1987, Buchan and Enright.

4. Media historians could write a very interesting study of the long series of fashions in thinking, sometimes called *trendy attitudes*, which the press, television and radio have encouraged almost to the point of mass hysteria and monomania. The study would perhaps start with the fraudster, Horatio Bottomley, and his magazine *John Bull*. In the sphere of economics it would cover not only the Gold Standard but the 1930s campaign for reduced government expenditure, the 1940s campaign for social security, the 1950s *'never had it so good'* syndrome, the 1960s

slogans of '*the white hot technological revolution*' and '*the social contract*' coupled with pressure for social engineering by taxation. In the 1970s there was the '*dash for growth*' regardless of the effect on the environment. But one campaign run by the British Broadcasting Corporation is always in fashion, and has the same life span and regularity as *The Archers* programme; it is the daily reporting of the sterling/dollar exchange rate. The announcer's voice is grim if the pound has fallen and bright if it has risen, thus brainwashing the public with the erroneous notion that an overvalued currency is a good thing. The wheel came full circle when the 1990 campaign for adoption of the Exchange Rate Mechanism echoed precisely the campaign for the Gold Standard in the early 1920s.

5.   Professor A. V. Hill, Keynes' brother-in-law talked to me about Keynes' move from radicalism at our one meeting which was in 1974 or 1975. '*Of course Keynes was a radical, but he had also been to Eton, and this led to strata in his character which were well known to his friends.*'

6.   I never met Keynes. He died the year before I arrived in Cambridge. But during the 15 years I lived there (1964 to 1979) I met and talked to so many of his colleagues, friends, and relatives by marriage, I began to feel the aura of the man. I was told that he was a polymath, eager to hold forth on any subject, but not always accurately according to one close source!

Regrettably I never met his brother either. I should warn that anyone who reads the autobiography of Sir Geoffrey Keynes in the hope of getting an intimate picture of Maynard Keynes, will be somewhat disappointed. Reading between the lines I get the impression the brothers were not good friends. The book, *The Gates of Memory,* is well worth reading for Sir Geoffrey, a surgeon, architect of the blood transfusion service, and a distinguished Doctor of Literature, was also a great man.

7.   It was Keynes' practice of demonstrating economic functions by algebraic equations which convinced Professor A. V. Hill, and other great scientists with a mathematical background, that economics was now a science. I pointed out to Hill that in the physical sciences one could deduce arithmetical constants to replace the algebraic symbols in the functions, but that in economics there are no demonstrable constants, and therefore no functions which are valid over time. The symbols in the functions can never be replaced by absolute values. Hill did not reply and after a brief silence changed the subject. Unfortunately I was not then aware of Hayek's similar criticism. Friedman's defensive attitude regarding economists' techniques also came to my notice much later.

CHAPTER NINE

THE INFLATION OF JAMES CALLAGHAN

'All money nowadays seems to be produced with a
natural homing instinct to the Treasury.'
THE DUKE OF EDINBURGH

IN APRIL 1965 the new Chancellor of the Exchequer, James Callaghan introduced corporation tax to Britain. He applied it in its classical form, that is a tax on company profits over and above any income tax charged on dividends paid by the company. Previously companies had been subject to the same income tax system as individuals, plus an additional tax called profits tax. Since a company had already paid income tax on all its income, dividends paid out of that same income were regarded as taxed already. Profits tax was charged at a fairly low rate, 15 per cent at its highest on retained profits, and at a rather high rate, up to 45 per cent, on distributed profits, giving an incentive, it was hoped, to plough back profits. Germany did the opposite, taxing retained profits at the higher rate. Theorists preferred the latter system. Their rationale was that investors were better judges of the correct investment opportunities in the general economy than company directors. The classical corporation tax hit distributed profits even harder than the previous system.

Chancellor Callaghan justified his decision by arguing that corporation tax was a more modern tax, that it would enable companies to be taxed at a lower rate than individuals, and that it would motivate companies to retain a higher proportion of profits for investment in expansion of their businesses.

A few days later France abandoned the classical form of corporation tax, thereby casting much doubt on its modernity. As regards the second argument, corporation tax has never been levied at a lower rate than the standard rate of income tax. In contradiction of the third argument, the proportion of profits retained by companies fell from 44.82 per cent in 1965 to 31.97 per cent in 1969. In real terms the fall in retentions was even greater. Because inflation doubled between 1965 and 1969, much of the profit retained in 1969 and after was truly additional depreciation, charged to comply with the principles of inflation accounting by which depreciation should be calculated on the replacement cost, not the historic cost, of plant and equipment. Although it was logical to believe that corporation tax would encourage retention of profits there were overriding factors at the time which rendered the logic of Callaghan's Treasury officials and academic advisers totally ineffective. These factors were practical ones, not likely to be anticipated by pure theorists. The main one was the need for directors to maintain dividend rates as a way of discouraging take-over bids.

Inflation grows
There was a delay of about 18 months before the new tax became fully effective. Not long after that inflation started to increase.

Year	Inflation rate (per cent)
1966	3.0
1967	2.9
1968	4.73
1969	5.64
1970	6.8
1971	8.6
1972	7.55 [1]

The inflation rate measures what one could call kinetic inflation, on the analogy of kinetic energy. It relates to manifest price changes. But just as there is also potential energy, by analogy there is potential inflation too, that is inflation which has already been caused, but whose appearance in the statistics is prevented either by consumer subsidies, or by an artificially bolstered exchange rate which keeps import prices low. It is quite usual to say that a devaluation causes inflation. Professor Sir Alan Walters, in his contribution to the volume of essays published in 1975 by the Institute of Economic Affairs and called *Crisis 75*, made a most perceptive comment about inflation in connection with his own proposal for a devaluation of sterling at that time:-

> *'Such a devaluation would not **cause** inflation. On the contrary, devaluation is simply a **consequence** of the inflationary expansion of public spending and the money stock which has persisted since 1971. Nevertheless the devaluation will be associated with a considerable acceleration in the rate of inflation as the prices of imported foods and raw materials rise. And it is likely that cause and effect will be confused yet again and the devaluation will be blamed for the further inflation.'*

What Sir Alan believed to be true in 1975 had also been true in 1967, for bolstering of the exchange rate was then taking place. Therefore some of the kinetic inflation of 1968 and 1969 properly relates to the period before the 14 per cent devaluation of the pound in November 1967. Similarly the low inflation of 1992 may prove to be an illusion to be revealed by devaluation, unless falling interest rates bring about a balancing fall in costs.

Although there are always very many complex agents at work in the causation of any inflation, in the specific environment of the British capital market it is justifiable to believe that there was a causal relationship between the upward trend of inflation after 1965 and the introduction of corporation tax. There are reasons why it should be true as will be seen in the following pages.

The encouragement of debt capital

The classical form of corporation tax cheapens debt capital relative to equity capital, because it ensures that a net of tax dividend on equity requires about 1.8 times more earnings to service it than the equivalent net interest payment on a loan. Corporation Tax thus encourages the raising of loan capital in preference to equity. The consequence was that whereas in the period 1959 to 1964 58.7 per cent of new company finance had been equity, in the five year period 1965 to 1970 only 27.1 per cent was raised by equity issues.

The collapse of Rolls-Royce Ltd. in 1971 was attributed partly to its directors' over-reliance on loan capital; significantly five of Rolls-Royce's seven quoted fixed-interest loans had been issued on the stockmarket after the introduction of corporation tax. But for the classical corporation tax system, Rolls-Royce directors must have preferred to raise new equity capital rather than borrow money. For the adventurous new project they had undertaken, the RB 211 engine, which was essential for the company's survival, equity was surely much more appropriate than loan capital.

When an economic slump takes place, many heavily borrowed companies, which would have survived if all their capital was in the form of equity, are forced into liquidation. Therefore cautious economists favoured equity capital, but Chancellor Callaghan seemed unaware of such important implications, or unconcerned by them. Perhaps it would be fairer to suggest that the failure of understanding lay with his principle economic adviser, Professor Nicholas Kaldor. Later events demonstrated just how dangerous it is to rely on borrowed capital.

Unwanted fixed-interest issues

The change to a taxation system which encouraged borrowing was imposed at a time when professional investment managers were becoming increasingly reluctant to invest in fixed-interest stocks. They were well aware of the depreciatory effects on such issues of the mild inflation which had become endemic after 1945. Consequently they no longer regarded fixed-interest or fixed-nominal issues as safe investments. Moreover, rising interest rates had caused the price of gilts and other fixed-interest securities to fall, and investors feared that the falls could be extended by further rises in rates of interest. Ordinary shares had come back into favour from 1953 onwards, and the so-called *cult of the equity* had by 1965 reversed the traditional yield relationship between fixed-interest issues and equities. No sensibly cautious investor wanted large holdings of fixed-interest stocks, while the less wise investors were attracted only by the consequent high yields on such stocks. Before corporation tax the best British companies had been able to capitalise themselves with equity at very low cost, 3 per cent being an acceptable dividend yield on rights issues of ordinary shares. After corporation tax had caused inflation to increase, all the shrewdest investment advisers discouraged investment in gilts, preference shares, debentures, building societies accounts, and mortgages. It was a confident prophecy to make that some day a Trust Corporation would be sued for damages for having invested trust money in gilts. The case of Nestle v. National Westminster Bank, 1984, eventually fulfilled the prophecy. The defendant won the case only because a high proportion of equities had been retained in the trust even in the deflationary period of the nineteen-twenties and early nineteen-thirties. But an expert witness for the plaintiff went so far as to maintain strongly that there should never have been any fixed-interest investment at all throughout the whole life of the trust which had started in 1922.

Until 1961 the trustees of trusts without specific investment powers were almost entirely restricted to fixed-interest securities. The Trustee Investment Act of 1961 ameliorated that restriction which had become more a benefit to borrowing governments than a protection for trust beneficiaries. From 1961 onwards there was a reduced demand by trustees for both fixed-interest investments, such as debentures and preference shares, and fixed-capital investments, such as bank deposits and building society accounts.

The plight of the non-professional investors

Although the professional investor did not want to invest in debt capital, the general public was still happy to do so, as the growth of the building society movement amply confirmed. Though even an undergraduate economist would advise investment in equity assets in an inflationary period, the evidence of the government statistics tends to suggest that inflation slightly increases the public's preference for monetary assets. Inflation certainly does not reduce the public's appetite for building society deposits. Japan, which had experienced this phenomenon as an accompaniment to severe inflation after the war, had in the early 1950s provided avenues by which the people's monetary savings could be channelled into debt capital for industry. The avenues were *Money Trusts* and *Loan Trusts*, run by institutions called *Trust Banks*. The Japanese public happily deposited money in Loan Trusts for fixed terms of two or five years, and from these deposits medium-term loans were provided for industry. They were something like a unit trust of industrial loans. The loans could be readily rolled over at maturity because of the medium-term nature of the deposits financing them. According to an official of a Japanese Trust Bank questioned in 1974, as much as 95 per cent of a Trust Bank's deposits from the general public might be for five years fixed.

A similar system of harnessing savings for the use of industry is also carried out in Japan through the medium of the Post Office. The Japanese Trust Banks and the Japanese Post Office appear to have provided the financial foundation stones for that country's industrial success. British political leaders have remained, it would seem, unaware of either system. They preferred to explain the Japanese miracle as being genetic in origin, or due to culture or religion. They suggested that all major countries have their economic Achilles heel. In France and Germany it was the agricultural sector (even though product per hectare was above Britain's); in Britain it was the manufacturing sector; in Japan it was the distribution sector. Such platitudes had just enough truth in them to make them quite acceptable in Whitehall. The Bank of England however, had it cared to, could have known better. But arrogance blinded its senior officials. One of them was outraged in 1975 by the question, *'Do you at the Bank of England ever go abroad to look at other peoples' central banking and capital systems to see what you can copy and improve upon?'* 'Of course not,' was the furious answer. Then after a pause to regain his lost temper he added, *'Sometimes we make foreign visits to tell them what to do.'* At that time sterling was on the floor, and foreign opinion of the British government and its advisers was down to the pre-cambrian level. The official was taking part in the annual Cambridge Seminar of the Chartered Institute of Bankers, probably as a course leader. The following year the future prime minister John Major, then still a banker, attended the seminar as a course member.

In Britain the provision of long-term fixed-interest capital had been one of the functions of the stockmarket. The big banks had never been willing to provide it. Under the British arrangement, while it lasted, it was stockmarket investors who provided long-term fixed-interest capital for quoted companies. After 1965 the supply of such capital gradually evaporated. The stockmarket had, of course, never been a prolific source of long-term loan capital for private companies, a major defect in the British capital market. Other sources of debenture and loan capital for private companies had also steadily dried up.

Loan Trusts are natural partners for a classical corporation tax system. Could they have been promoted to partner the tax in Britain? In 1974 Barclays Bank studied the possibility of promoting such a form of saving in Britain. Two serious obstacles soon became apparent: amazingly one was that the interest income of *Trust Deposits*, as the British version of loan trusts were to be called, would be subject to corporation tax, preventing a competitive yield being offered to investors. The tax handicap could be avoided, but only by creating a form of unit trust which it was then illegal to market openly. Secondly, there was no hope of competing with the building societies, which not only still had the advantage at that time of favourable tax treatment, but were also allowed to lend for twenty-five years money which was callable by depositors at a few days notice. Such a mis-match was not acceptable to commercial banks in 1974. In such an environment there was no hope of success for far-sighted lending institutions which wished to match the maturity of assets and liabilities. Trust Deposits had to be rejected. Japanese style loan trusts were not viable in Britain: the loser, on a massive scale, was, of course, British industry, especially capital-intensive manufacturers and small businesses. Later Barclays Bank set up a Trust Bank in Japan: it was much easier, and perhaps more profitable.

Interest rates rise

Following the introduction of corporation tax, the laws of supply and demand caused long-term interest rates on loans and debentures to rise. In the early days of Japan's surge of economic growth bank loans at nine per cent were common, but in the late 1960s when Associated Portland Cement Manufacturers, later renamed Blue Circle, issued a debenture with a coupon of nine per cent, there was consternation that a blue-chip British company should have to pay such a high price for a loan. At lunchtime in Christ's College, Cambridge, on the day of the announcement of the issue, a senior fellow who was very knowledgable and interested in financial matters asked for the author's comment. The answer was a forecast that if the pattern of equity yields remained as it then was, the interest rate on industrial loan stocks would rise to 14 per cent. That forecast astonished many of those around the table, though not, if memory is accurate, Professor James Meade, later to be awarded the Nobel Prize for economics. He seemed to take the point with his usual calm. Corporation tax's lack of neutrality no doubt inspired him to oppose it. The forecast was in due course more than fulfilled.

The general rise in interest rates increased the government's own borrowing costs, making necessary an increase in taxation. Unbelievably, one of the taxes raised was corporation tax, a move which had the knock-on effect of increasing the rate of interest which a company would be willing to pay rather than resort to an equity issue. Only when equity yields were very low, such as in 1968, a year of stockmarket boom, was any substantial amount of new equity capital raised. In 1970 industrial and commercial companies raised only £39,000,000 in equity capital, compared with over £1,200,000,000 borrowed from banks. Naturally these borrowings by the business community gave rise to another large increase in the intermediated money supply.

The influence of corporation tax was most effective upon the longer end of the interest yield curve, but the shorter end of the curve was dragged up by the necessity, consequent upon rising inflation, to bolster the exchange rate. In a desperate attempt to avoid devaluation, the Bank of England raised Bank Rate to 6.5 per cent on 8th November 1967, but devaluation came anyway on the 18th. It had to be supported by an increase in Bank Rate to eight per cent on the same day, a level which later would not seem high, but which caused a sensation at the time; it was three per cent higher than the rate imposed in 1925 to help return sterling to the Gold Standard at an excessive valuation. It was one per cent higher than the rate set in 1957 during the financial crisis following the Suez War. Such was the transformation in interest rates triggered by Chancellor Callaghan's corporation tax. There was never a satisfactory intellectual basis for corporation tax; nor had any been put forward publicly.

The 1960s provided no empirical evidence whatsoever to support that most cherished of British economic myths, the belief that raising interest rates to a high level will reduce inflation without adverse effects on the economy.

The notion that high interest rates cure inflation rests on two arguments which have already been set out. The first, it will be recalled, is that high interest rates discourage borrowing and thus hold back the expansion of the supply of credit. The second is that high interest rates cause recession and unemployment, and that these act as a brake on high wage claims which are the root cause of cost inflation. The second process proved to be effective but undesirable. It works especially well when high interest rates cause the currency to be overvalued with the result that British exports of goods and services are inhibited.

High interest rates cause inflation

Let us now look, hopefully with a deeper insight, at the opposite contention, that a high interest rate, far from curing inflation, is truly a principal cause of it. There are a number of reasons why this should be true:-

1.   High interest rates raise the cost of all business borrowing and thereby increase unit costs, causing cost inflation throughout the business sector of the economy.

2.   High interest rates cause recession, which leads to reduced turnover and a consequent rise in unit costs.

3.   Recession induced by high interest charges leads to greater expenditure on unemployment benefits, which can also translate into higher costs through the tax system.

4.   The most compelling reason is even more apparent. High interest rates immediately raise the cost of servicing mortgages. That stimulates wage claims by workers.

The unorthodox British system of financing long-term housing loans with the short-term deposits of savers enables mortgage borrowers to be charged short-term interest rates, which are commonly lower than long-term rates. This once seemed an inspired move as it meant that in the 1940s mortgagors paid only four per cent interest. When the government in pursuance of orthodox monetary theory tried to cure inflation by increasing interest rates, the most marked effect was on the short-term market: interest rates not only rose, but were higher for short-term money than for long! This was a traumatic blow to mortgagors, most of whom are economically active young wage-earners. Hit by high interest rates, which transfer purchasing power from the young to the old, because the level of wealth ownership increases exponentially with age, the young fight back with unrelenting demands for compensating higher pay, and they always win. The circulation-seeking popular press supports them sympathetically. The annual round of wage rises becomes an ingrained habit, and wage-cost inflation becomes endemic.

This was the simple genesis of wage inflation in Britain. A unique feature of the British system of financing house purchase amplified normal inflationary pressures.

Many young mortgagors are intelligent and perceptive enough to see that inflation favours debtors. They are happy to encourage it actively. They are told that inflation will cause unemployment, but they are unconvinced. It is, indeed, the foolish things done in response to inflation which cause unemployment, not inflation itself, which can stimulate economic growth as postwar history has shown. The oft-repeated statement that inflation causes unemployment is irrational. There is no compelling reason why it should. The argument that it makes export industries uncompetitive is true only if the government acts to reverse the natural decline of the exchange rate which inflation generates. Only if the money supply is restricted as part of an anti-inflationary policy will inflation necessarily and directly cause unemployment.

'*Facilis descensus Averni: noctes atque dies patet atri ianua Ditis; sed revocare gradum superasque evadere ad auras, hoc opus, hic labor est.*' Thus wrote Virgil in book Six of *The Aeneid*, and the translation should decorate the walls of Whitehall offices to inform those who are more conversant with classical economics than classical poetry that, '*Easy is the descent to hell; the doors of the dark ruler of the underworld are open day and night; but to retrace one's steps and escape to the upper air, that is an achievement, that the laborious task.*'

It is the government's own actions, not inflation, which causes unemployment. Nor does inflation necessarily cause high interest rates, as is so often alleged without logical justification. Deflation is a much more horrifying experience. Only hyperinflation is worse, declared Keynes, and some brave souls might be tempted to dispute even that qualification.

Experience in other countries

In some other countries mortgagors can still borrow at a fixed rate of interest, not at a variable rate as has long been the norm in Britain. Consequently a rise in interest rates in those countries does not stimulate wage inflation so intensely or so immediately as in Britain. In America, instead of causing inflation, an increase in interest rates paid to depositors bankrupted the Savings and Loan Associations, the U.S. equivalent of building societies, as the Associations' interest payments rose higher than their fixed-interest income. This effect was precipitated by two unlucky events. The first was that the government abolished a statutory limitation (*Regulation Q*) on the rates of interest which could be paid to depositors, but did nothing to enable lenders to charge more interest on existing mortgages. The Savings and Loan Associations were crippled by being bound to the rates of interest which they had contracted to charge when the original mortgage agreement was made, while they had to make higher payments of interest to depositors as the Federal Reserve Bank pushed interest rates up to unheard of levels. Circumstances had changed in a way it was impossible for them to anticipate when they made the loans. They could not help making massive losses as interest income fell below interest payments. The second unfortunate event was a decision by an American court that existing mortgages could be assumed by, that is transferred to, the purchaser of a property which was already mortgaged. The mortgage went with the house, regardless of the credit-worthiness of a buyer. Thus the time that a mortgage with a fixed low rate of interest might continue without revision was not ended by a sale of the mortgaged property.

That these two unfortunate decisions were made showed an appalling lack of understanding by those who regulate a great country's capital system. The court decision revealed a total ignorance of banking by the judges who hold absolute power over American business affairs. With such great authority should come a parallel responsibility for judges to ensure that they fully comprehend the consequences of their judgements, and they should not be bound by foolish legal precedents if the result is to bankrupt the trustees of the nation's savings. The legal system can have profound effects on the progress of an economy and some changes in the law should first be subjected to criticism by competent economists before they reach either the statute book or the body of Common Law. It is a tragedy for Americans that they not only inherited the poorer of the two British legal systems, but have also managed to make it far worse.

In Germany the level of home ownership is little more than half the British level. Not only have housing loans there usually been at fixed rates of interest but also the amount lent to each borrower has been much more prudent. Consequently a rise in interest rates is less of a burden, and therefore has less influence on workers' demands for wage increases. Moreover for decades Germans have not paid interest on their mortgages at anything near British rates. But at the time of writing German interest rates have been pushed up to a level which may cause a repetition in Germany of the credit explosion which affected Britain in the 1970s and after. The critical factor was that in 1991 the profits of German banks rose dramatically because of what is called *the endowment effect* of very high interest rates. The rise in profits was followed up by calls for additional capital which could provide the base for a surge of credit. High interest rates were also pulling in foreign money. Without preventive action a direct repeat of the British experience seemed very likely. The long-term effect of German monetary policy in 1992 should, if continued, be as disastrous to the German economy as the similar British policy was in the 1970s and 1980s.

Low interest rates and low bank profits

In the 1930s the major factor which restrained monetary growth was surely that with low interest rates there was little profit in banking, and consequently the propensity to increase lendings was muted. Just how small the profits of the banks were in the low interest rate era is not known as true banking profits were then secret. Because of secrecy popular imagination was inclined to magnify them enormously, but in the late 1960s, the chief accountant of a clearing bank, an enemy of all secrecy, stated privately that the banks were barely profitable as late as the early 1950s. If banking is not profitable, banks can neither attract new capital nor plough back profits in order to increase their capital bases. If they cannot get new capital they cannot expand their lendings because, as we have already seen, they must keep a reserve of their own shareholders' capital which is directly proportional to the amount of their rising liabilities.

It might be thought odd that banking profits were so low for until 1971 the clearing banks maintained a cartel of interest rates. In theory they should have been able to use the cartel power to raise profits. For reasons which can only be guessed at they sustained the rate of interest at a level which happened to be just high enough (five per cent) to make borrowers prefer to resort to the bond market. The rate seems to have been too high to tempt borrowers, and too low to encourage lenders to try to overcome borrower resistance by effectively marketing credit.

When competition between lenders was established in 1971 the first effect was a rise in interest rates charged, and a rise in banking profits. But by then the bond market had been destroyed by inflation, so that there was no serious competition.

The true limit on the money supply

The capital base of the banks is important. It must be repeated that if banks cannot raise additional capital they cannot expand the intermediated money supply. In such circumstances the only way they can continue to provide the fodder for inflation is to persuade some customers to fund their debts, for that releases part of the capital base of the banks to support the creation of new credit. The analysis of overfunding in Chapter Seven has shown that an increase in non-intermediated credit which substitutes for, and therefore reduces the intermediated credit supply, simply paves the way for the further creation of intermediated credit. The effect is to restore the level of intermediated lending to what it was before the funding (disintermediation) by customers took place.

Whenever empirical evidence is in conflict with received dogma, *Towards True Monetarism* tries to follow where the evidence leads, no matter how many pronouncements asserting the truth of the dogma have been disseminated over the world from the Grove of Academe. In Britain the evidence is that very low interest rates are associated with, and may even cause, low inflation. While they assist and encourage some economic growth they do not necessarily propel it to the optimum possible level.

Not only do the messages from the Groves of Academe need to be rewritten, but the equations they have inspired must not form part of the Treasury's computerised emulation of the British economy. The emulation must take into account the truths we have already put forward. Should it fail to do so, the British government's management of the economy will continue to generate both high inflation and high unemployment.

The suggested rule might not be eternal. In some future era of low interest rates the margin between the interest rate charged on loans and that allowed on deposits might widen without the impediment of the restrictive cartel which was characteristic of the last low interest rate era. Bank profits might therefore remain at a satisfactory level, and a liberal supply of intermediated credit could consequently be maintained despite low interest rates. There might also be a great and rapid increase in new issues of non-intermediated credit.

High interest rates, high bank profits

In the particular environment of the 1960s corporation tax helped cause interest rates to rise and thus made banking much more profitable. Capital-raising exercises by banks then became more frequent. In October 1971 the paper *Competition and Credit Control* heralded the abolition of the interest rate cartel. Interest margins then rose. The resultant high level of bank profits even prompted a Labour Party election poster in 1974 which read '*Bank Robs Man*', though in their book of evidence to *The Wilson Committee on the Future of the Financial Institutions,* which reported in 1980, the clearing banks were rightly able to show that their high profits were partly an illusion of historic cost accounting. Inflation-adjusted accounts showed a very different picture. The adjusted profits may not even have covered the dividends paid.

British clearing banks had been sleeping giants who were at last awakened to their great profit potential, and the government policy of encouraging competition was also effective in stirring them to life. In 1972 a major bank subjected all its staff to intense training in marketing, and backed it up very successfully with the powerful management tool called *Management By Objectives*. This produced agreed targets for all staff to achieve, including very specific sales targets. Bank managers quickly found that proper marketing could make nonsense of economic theories that high interest rates discourage borrowing. People were eager to borrow more than they had previously been allowed to, and only needed the opportunity to do so, even if the percentage rate charged was as high as 31. It is now clear that the limitations on the appetite of the public for credit are first, the borrower's ability to service his loan, and second, the lender's prudence. The latter was relaxed. Few now remember, for instance, the time when building societies refused to lend money on houses built before 1919, or would not take into account for loan limits the earnings of a married woman of child-bearing age. Partly under pressure from do-gooders, such restraints have long been abandoned by lenders who, once their protecting inhibitions had been sloughed off, or flayed off by the whips of the popular press, rushed to find new customers who would soak up the ever-expanding supply of credit.

Any inflation of the price of houses beyond the level of general inflation increases the value of building plots. Even at a rate of interest of 14 per cent or more the willingness of the public to borrow on mortgage, once the credit was available and well-marketed, was sufficient to push the value of houses up so much that in 1989 the value of the plot of a new house rose to perhaps 40 per cent of the total price, and as high as 60 per cent for larger houses. In the 1950s it had been normal for 85 per cent of the price to reflect building cost, and only 15 per cent the cost of the site. It seems right to attribute much of the rise in house prices to credit creation rather than to underlying demand. Admittedly demand was strong for another reason as well. With house prices rising on average three per cent faster than the Retail Prices Index from 1957, houses for occupation had become a very popular investment, largely because they appeared to be an investment that hedges against inflation. Because they were a hedge against inflation their prices rose faster than inflation. Chicken and egg! Which of the two comes first? No-one thought to try to answer the question for thirty-five years. When the house-price bubble burst, and house prices headed sharply downwards to correct the anomaly in values, no-one in government had a sensible remedy to prevent hundreds of thousands of people from suffering bankruptcy and poverty. Of the leading press commentators one, Anatole Kaletsky of *The Times*, was brave enough to suggest that even increased inflation was preferable to such fast increasing homelessness.

The capital base revisited

As we shall see in a later chapter, the final blow to the old monetary theory came in 1988 when it was clearly demonstrated that it was easy to expand credit, and therefore the money supply, once the capital base was available.

After the 1939-45 War the raising of capital in Britain was for a long time controlled by *The Capital Issues Committee*. Did the Committee reject any applications from banks to raise new capital or were none made? Because of the very long period of low interest rates bank shares were not then a profitable investment. One financial journalist (Harold Wincott?) sarcastically dubbed them *'vaguely participating preference shares.'* The raising of new capital for banks by way of a right issues did not recommence until 1961. There was a jump in the aggregate capital adequacy ratio of the banks about that time; it had fallen to a very low level in the 1950s. The rights issues made possible the rebuilding of the banks' portfolios of loans to the private sector.

Bank losses as a method of credit control

The expansion of the money supply after 1965 could have been even more rapid if the banks had not experienced some occasional severe losses by misfortune or government action among the periods of booming profits.

There was the secondary banking crisis of 1973-74. From 1971 to 1984 there was confusion over leasing, a clever contrivance which had its origin in an anomaly in the rules of corporation tax. Leasing would eventually have caused taxation problems for the banks even if Chancellor Nigel Lawson had not made it less profitable by changes in the depreciation rules for corporation tax in 1984. The banks' object in engaging in leasing was to secure the deferral of tax liabilities, but the trick depended on the continuance of inflation to achieve an indefinite deferral of the liabilities. By the time the Chancellor acted to reduce the taxation advantage falling inflation was already threatening to make the huge postponed tax liabilities mature for payment.

Lawson's action followed only three years after the imposition of a windfall tax on bank profits which also savaged the banks' capital bases. The enormous reduction in capital resources which followed these two actions of the government may have helped the marked reduction in inflation which followed them.[2] A little later the banks also ran up huge losses through recycling the deposits received from Latin Americans and other foreigners (possibly including illegal deposits from Eastern Bloc citizens) back to the free-spending governments of the countries from whose citizens the deposits originated. Then came the interest swap crisis. Finally there were the huge losses which resulted from the over-expansion of credit in 1988, 1989, and 1990.

Taxing capital gains

Corporation tax was not the sole taxation blunder of Chancellor James Callaghan. At the same time (April 1965) he brought in a full-blooded capital gains tax. This was a blow for the non-intermediated credit market. It is theoretically quite sound and justifiable to tax capital gains, but one must understand that for the community in the aggregate all capital taxes are really burdens on current income, even though they are computed by reference to capital values.

Taxes on capital stimulate the growth of a virulent cancer of the economy in the form of a strongly growing tax avoidance industry. Fine brains, which might be underemployed in a socialist system because they are unable to carry out important tasks in the expansion of the real economy, are instead attracted into this industry. Those who should be leading the drive towards the target of economic growth are tied up with defensive measures which have only a little relevance to the creation of real wealth.

A more anaemic form of capital gains tax had been applied in 1962. The Conservative government then introduced a short-term capital gains tax levied on realised gains. Its short-term aspect was that it was assessed only on gains made by the sale of an asset within six months of purchase. Anything held longer than that was exempt. The logic behind it was that anyone who took a profit so quickly was a trader in assets, not a true investor. But in addition to the logical reason there was also the moralistic attitude that anyone who took a quick profit was a speculator. Speculation was commonly regarded as an evil. The short-term tax was an intentionally half-hearted attack on the problem of taxing capital gains. The Conservative government had instincts which told it that such a tax was nothing but damaging. They might not have known quite why. Nevertheless they pandered to popular pressure, which was in truth pressure from the many clever but sadly ignorant young people who were common among the writers on such matters in the newspapers.

The wider benefit of speculation

The main effect of the short-term gains tax was indeed to discourage speculation, as was intended. One odd result was a distortion in the market in new share issues. There tended to be a dearth of sellers for six months after a new issue as few investors wanted to incur tax on any profit. This created an artificial one-way market for a while: prices would rise for six months, then fall back. The tax was no more than a bureaucratic money-waster for the compliance cost to the taxpayer was greater than the revenue raised, and the administration cost was also high.

In 1965 Chancellor James Callaghan decided to tax all capital gains which had been realised by the sale of assets. The rate of tax was a flat 30 per cent, regardless of the size of the gain. Its most damaging immediate effect was to destabilise the market for company shares, an effect which increased over a period of years. All markets can be stabilised by the operations of successful speculators. Unsuccessful speculators can damage a market, but they are, like butterflies, a short-lived species. They quickly lose the wherewithal for financing their attempts at speculation. On the other hand speculators who are successful can go on indefinitely, though the more of them there are, the smaller are their profits. Successful speculators are people who buy when prices are low, and sell when they are high. They shore up a falling market, limiting its fall. They take the froth off a rising market, limiting its rise. The sounder their judgement, the freer is the market from erratic short-term movements, and the smaller is their profit. Good speculators can make only small profits in a free market: if they are operating in a market which the government is trying to manipulate, (and the most frequent instance of that is in the foreign exchange market,) speculators make colossal profits, a fact which sound economists know very well.

The destabilising effect of introducing a full capital gains tax in 1965 showed up in the movement of the stockmarket index. In the five years before the introduction of the tax the FT Ordinary

Share Index fluctuated in a band whose maximum was 40 per cent above its minimum. In the five years following its introduction the band of fluctuation was twice as wide. In the subsequent five years it increased a further fourfold, the minimum point being well below that of the previous two periods. That was the effect of removing the moderating speculator from the market. It has since continued to be volatile, but the fact that a large and growing percentage of company shares are held by tax-free funds, like pension funds, may have latterly somewhat improved stability. It has not eliminated instability completely, because there is a tendency for investment fund managers, a brotherhood which enjoys togetherness, to move like a stampeding herd, fast, furious, and unitedly in one direction. Their herd instinct is so well developed they keep in very close and frequent communication with one another, not in order to fix the market deliberately, but just to know what the other man is thinking, and thereby gain psychological support for making their own similar decisions.[3]

Side effects of capital gains tax

The stockmarket instability caused serious problems for those institutions which, because their reserves are invested in stockmarket securities, depend on the stability of stock and share prices. The insurance companies especially faced difficulties. They were also suffering from the effect on share prices of the introduction of the classical corporation tax, which, by reducing the net of tax profits of companies, indirectly lowered the value of shares, whose prices are normally set at a multiple of the net of tax profits per share. The insurance industry was very important to the British economy, partly because it earned very great amounts of foreign exchange. Its welfare, and especially its competitive ability, should have been carefully fostered. It was very silly to weaken its financial reserves at a time when it was beginning to face intense competition from foreign insurers.

In the longer run capital gains tax gave an odd kind of boost to life assurance companies, for, although they had to make reserves for a contingent capital gains tax liability, little of that liability had to be paid immediately. The tax is payable only on realised gains. But when investment values rise, even if it is only as a result of inflation, it is necessary to reserve for the contingent tax liability, however remote. When a with-profits life assurance policy matures, the payment made to the beneficiary of the policy suffers a deduction which reflects at least a part of the tax that might some day have to be paid in respect of known capital gains which have not been realised. Calculating the correct amount to deduct from the maturity value is an impossible exercise because there are three assumptions which have to be made, (i) when will the tax be payable, (ii) at what rate will it be levied, and (iii) what profit will the investment representing the tax earn in the mean-time? Faced with such an impossible calculation how can an assurance company decide what premiums to charge?

The reserves for tax made by the insurance companies remain with them to earn income and further capital appreciation, but they belong to no-one. They do not belong to the Inland Revenue, because the tax is not yet payable. They do not belong to the policyholders; they do not belong to the insurance company's shareholders, though the policyholders and the shareholders can benefit from the income and the capital profits earned by these reserves. Within a very few years of the introduction of the tax old-established assurance companies had reserves for contingent tax which may have been greater than their shareholders' funds. As the old-established companies benefited most, competition was distorted. Industrial companies too had huge contingent capital tax liabilities, almost wholly as a result of inflation. They made no reserves against the liability to tax as in practice it would only be payable in the event of the winding-up of a company. This fact could cause declining companies to continue to trade longer than they should, prolonging their death throes.

Between 1965 and 1982 there was no provision for adjusting for inflation when a capital gain was calculated. One commonly found that capital gains tax was payable even though, because of inflation, the proceeds of sale of an asset had a lower current purchasing power than the original acquisition cost.

Inflation adjustment was introduced in 1982, and in 1985 Chancellor Nigel Lawson corrected some of the remaining mistakes which his predecessors had been persuaded to perpetrate. James Callaghan's version of capital gains tax gave a government a strong financial incentive to encourage inflation. Inflation converted the tax into an arbitrary and harsh wealth tax, extremely erratic in its incidence. Capital gains tax is undoubtedly an extremely effective instrument for diverting attention from the real problems of an economy. It ensures that resources of skill and energy are wasted in dealing with the purely artificial problem of avoiding a tax which had been made, almost deliberately, irrational and destructive. A vast effort had to go into the study of the ways of reducing the impact of capital gains tax. Superficially estate and inheritance taxes may seem to be more destructive of private wealth, but whenever one tried to tackle the problem of preserving a business from the ravages of the other capital taxes, one found that there was a preliminary difficulty, usually quite insurmountable, of avoiding capital gains tax. As that meant that inheritance taxes could not be ameliorated, capital gains tax was doubly destructive in its effect.[4]

Notes on Chapter Nine:-

1. The inflation rates are calculated from the National Income Blue Book 1973, Table 16: *Index of prices of all final goods and services sold on the home market.* The Retail Prices Index figures differ somewhat but are less appropriate in this analysis.

2. Figures for the effects of the 1981 windfall tax on banks' shareholders' funds are given on page 30 of Bernard Wesson's *Bank Capital and Risk.* (Institute of Bankers, 1985, ISBN 0-85297-134-6).

3. Daily observation of an investment research manager revealed that he spent the first hour of every day on the telephone to his opposite numbers. The time he spent on original thought was surprisingly short. To take an individual line on any topic was dangerous. If one was alone in being wrong one was condemned, but to be wrong with the herd was accepted as just bad luck.

4. Comments made here on taxation are based on direct experience of the principles and practice of tax planning.

Many taxes were introduced as political window-dressing, and legal loopholes were provided to avoid wrecking the economy completely. Many businessmen were uneasy about using loopholes; they were less cynical than the politicians. Eventually the judicial comittee of the House of Lords refused to play along with the politicians' devious game, and schemes whose sole purpose was tax avoidance were declared void.

Some would-be tax-avoiders were deceived by fraudulent advisers.

CHAPTER TEN

THE KALDOR AND JENKINS S.E.T.

*'There are two problems in my life. The political ones
are insoluble, and the economic ones are incomprehensible.'*

SIR ALEC DOUGLAS HOME

IN THIS CHAPTER we must make a digression from pure
monetary theory, for the decline of the British economy in the
1960s and after was not due only to a failure to understand
money. Nor was James Callaghan the only Chancellor to damage
the economy by pursuing false theories. His better educated
successor as Chancellor, Roy Jenkins (Lord Jenkins of Hillhead),
did much damage while apparently under the influence of an
economist whom the press made infamous rather than famous.
But another reason for the digression is to show the meretricious
depths to which the study of economics had fallen since death
took Keynes from the scene.

The most notorious of the economic gurus of the incoming
Labour government in 1964 was Professor Nicholas Kaldor, later
made a life peer as Lord Kaldor. He was a fellow of King's Col-
lege, Cambridge, an honoured status once held by Lord Keynes.
Kaldor was very influential and had some ardent supporters.
When he gave his much delayed inaugural lecture as Professor of
Economics on the 2nd November 1966, several hundred people
were assembled in Lady Mitchell Hall in Cambridge to hear him.
His topic was the cause of the slow rate of economic growth in the
United Kingdom. He started the lecture by quoting the rates of
growth for the ten years to 1964 of the leading industrial

countries. They were 2.7 per cent for the U.K., 4.9 per cent for France, 6.0 per cent for Germany, and 9.6 per cent for Japan. He then deduced that the factor which characterised the successful economies was a high rate of growth of manufacturing, known in the jargon of economics as the secondary sector of industry.

His figures showed that in 1963 Britain had 44 per cent of its workforce in secondary industry. That was a bigger proportion than any other country. So why was not Britain already the richest country on Earth? Kaldor did not explain, except to say that Britain had reached 'premature maturity'. He concentrated on what is called The Verdoorn Law. That law asserts that with an increase in the rate of growth of output, both productivity and employment grow at a faster rate. Kaldor deduced that to obtain an increase in manufacturing production and in productivity there must also be an increase in employment. The Japanese annual growth of 13.6 per cent in manufacturing had been accompanied by a 5.8 per cent increase in employment. He deducted one from the other to deduce an increase in productivity of 7.8 per cent. Here we have a beautiful example of a statistical correlation that proves nothing. If there was a correlation between an increase in employment and an increase in productivity, it did not prove that the one was dependent on the other. Kaldor assumed it did. The statistics of the early 1980s must surely show a negative correlation and throw Verdoorn's Law into doubt. Probably it is true only in newly industrialising countries.

Kaldor was happily confident that he had found a significant correlation because his mathematics showed a regression line with a high factor of correlation. Having indulged in mathematical mischief, he went further on that course by giving a pat on the back to countries which departed from the regression line. The United Kingdom's increase in manufacturing production was 3.2, and in employment was 0.4 per cent, giving by his method of calculation an increase in productivity of 2.8 per cent. He regarded this as a better performance than Japan's increase of 5.8 per cent in employment and 7.8 per cent in productivity, because the second figure divided by the first was higher for the United Kingdom than for Japan.

Kaldor's arithmetic was very strange, especially his way of calculating an increase in productivity. Can one really calculate it by deducting the percentage increase in employment from the percentage increase in production? Not accurately! The correct method is to divide the new index of production by the new index of employment, deduct one from the answer and multiply by one hundred. Taking the Japanese figures the new index of manufacturing production is 113.6, and the new index of manufacturing employment is 105.8. The first divided by the second is 1.0737. Knocking off one and multiplying by one hundred gives a percentage of 7.37, not 7.8. That is the percentage increase in productivity. The result for the United Kingdom was 2.78 per cent. The Japanese increase in productivity was 2.64 times that. No reputable economist could possibly twist that result into a success for the United Kingdom to crow about.

Kaldor's elementary arithmetic being faulty what faith should one put in his more advanced mathematics? As his regression analysis included his faulty arithmetic the answer is none. His correlation factor of 0.844 for rate of growth of employment on rate of growth of manufacturing production is inaccurate as well as irrelevant. Three of the countries whose statistics are in the correlation showed little or no growth in employment though they enjoyed economic growth, in one case substantially more than the United Kingdom. Either a law is universal, admitting of no exceptions, or it is not a law at all, but merely a tendency, which might, or might not, be repeated. A carelessly applied regression analysis can highlight an interesting coincidence, while it obscures the obvious truth of the raw data. It happens in other sciences. In the field of biological research some fancy smoothing of the crude data, another dubious technique, hid the existence of several subcategories of white cells in the blood, while a simple bar chart revealed them to a far more careful researcher.

Switching sectors

An increase in employment in manufacturing is achieved in most countries by a compensating reduction in employment in primary industry (agriculture and mining). The United Kingdom already had the lowest proportion of its workforce in primary industry of any country of the industrialised world. It was 6.7 per cent compared with Japan's 30 per cent. The scope for a further switch was therefore much less than in other countries. In order to achieve higher employment in secondary industry, and thereby a faster rate of growth if Kaldor's theory was correct, workers had to be taken from the tertiary sector of the economy, that is from the service industries.

The government decided to take Kaldor seriously and give a push to employment in the secondary sector. The attack on the problem was two pronged. The first prong was already in place, the fifteen year-old policy of facilitating immigration of workers. The second prong was to be a tax called *Selective Employment Tax* (S.E.T.). The tax penalised employers of workers in service industries, and favoured those in manufacturing.

The question we posed earlier of why Britain, with the highest proportion of its workers in secondary industry, was not already the richest country in the world, was never answered by Kaldor. The obvious explanation is that Britain had industrialised first, and its equipment was therefore out of date and labour intensive. Also the interwar stagnation had discouraged investment in productivity. If this was what Kaldor meant by *premature maturity* he would have been right. In fact Kaldor meant by that phrase that real income per head had broadly reached the same level in the different sectors of the economy. That was a totally different thing; he had missed the point completely.

Selective employment tax was imposed in respect of those workers who were not involved in manufacturing. At first there was even a premium paid to employers of labour in manufacturing though it was soon dropped. S.E.T. encouraged the inefficient use of labour in manufacturing. Exemption from the tax was not given unless the proportion of production workers at a plant was above a certain level. That ruled out the modern highly automated plants. An example of such a plant was Ciba-Geigy at Duxford in Cambridgeshire where, of the 800 workers, a mere 36 were engaged in production. One plant there appeared to chunter along producing methanol without any workers at all. In total there were twelve workers on each shift. This was considered too low to qualify for exemption from S.E.T. Chancellor Jenkins was unwittingly sabotaging the profitability of Britain's most modern plants.

While true at an earlier stage of industrial development, the relationship Verdoorn had seen breaks down in the advanced economies, for in the later stages of economic development the proportion of people in secondary industry declines and that in tertiary industry grows. It is, however, a rather different type of tertiary industry. No longer is it girls in domestic service, but those employed in banking and insurance and other high value services. Such services were in the 1960s important growth points of the economy. The government, or its advisers, failed to see that.

Industrialisation releases workers for other tasks. Indeed the first effect of industrialisation in Britain was to release women to look after the home and children. It is said that the proportion of married women who worked fell dramatically, from a level which may have been as high as 85 per cent.

Did Jenkins' policy activate Goodhart's Law, *that any observed statistical regularity will tend to collapse once pressure is placed upon it for control purposes?* It was even worse than that: he was trying to push on a rope. If the increase in employment was a consequence of manufacturing investment, why should one be able to increase investment by increasing employment? That a causal relationship functions in one direction is no proof at all that the causal effect also works in the reverse direction. Some causal relationships are reversible, but none can be assumed to be. The rolling of a ship may make one sick, but being sick will not cause a ship to roll. Truly reversible causal relationships are detected by experiment, and then explained by analysis of the physical mechanism of the process. Nowhere in his lecture did Kaldor try to prove that the relationship he was talking about was a reversible one, nor did he analyse the mechanism which might make it so. The thought that he needed to prove it does not even seem to have entered his mind. It was slipshod reasoning, unworthy of a great university which had recently given the world of science more than a royal flush of Nobel Laureates in other sciences.

In his lecture Kaldor warned about the abuse of statistics:-

'*We must beware of attributing causal significance to a statistical relationship unless it can be shown to be consistent with some general hypothesis which can be supported by other evidence.*'

Is this a sufficiently high standard? One should go further and assert that the relationship should also be a logical one; that means it should be capable of rational explanation, and the link of physical cause and effect should be shown. The policy that Kaldor fathered needed foundations which were completely firm, not dubious. Let us amend his warning and insist that, *'causal signifi-cance should not be attributed to a statistical relationship until the physical reason for the relationship has been elucidated and demon-strated beyond all reasonable doubt.'*

Probably the greatest body of statistical data ever assembled was that which indicated that there was an association between smoking and cancer of the lung (and many other diseases). The statistical evidence was overwhelming, but no medical researcher would be content until the physical link between the two could be detected and proved. Statistical evidence was regarded as no more than a pointer. Real proof is a long and often a continuous process. Many decades of research would be needed to find all the links in a convincing chain of cause and effect.

A secret agenda

On shaky grounds Kaldor had built a policy edifice which the government swallowed, but a secret agenda was also there. It reveals itself in his urging that we should,

> *'concentrate our efforts on a more rational use of manpower in all fields, and limit the absorption of labour into those sectors where the marginal social product is likely to be appreciably below the marginal private product'.*

This obscurantist phrase seems to imply direction of labour, restriction of private choice in expenditure, more state control, and blind acceptance of Kaldor's private set of values.

Businessmen would have supported him if his words had meant that there should be fewer people employed in devising, computing, assessing, collecting, and paying 'reformed' taxes. They would have agreed also to fewer people engaged in teaching or studying erroneous economic theories, and in pushing dubious statistics into dubious computer models of the economy. But neither businessmen nor economists have a right on their own to make effective value judgements as to the social desirability of different economic activities. Such judgements are for democratic decision. The community has the right, if it wishes, to decide whether a tax should or should not, as S.E.T. did, favour the manufacturer of roulette wheels at the expense of the lawyer or the banker.

When Kaldor finished his lecture wild applause greeted him; enthusiastic colleagues rushed down to the podium, competing to be first to congratulate him. They created a scene of revolting and misguided adulation. The following morning *The Times* ran a leading article about the lecture, but the leader writer, in the brief time available to him, had not seen all the gross errors in it.

Roy Jenkins continued selective employment tax throughout his chancellorship of the Exchequer (1967-1970). At the end of it there was not more employment in manufacturing but less. The tax did not achieve its purpose. Manufacturing output went up at a slightly lower rate than GNP between 1965 and 1971, and at 12.8 per cent was much lower than the 16.9 per cent of the period 1960-65. Primary industry's output fell 18.5 per cent, but the output of banking insurance and finance, the sector most savaged by S.E.T., went up 32.5 per cent. Even a damaging tax cannot stifle completely what is a natural trend of the time.[1]

The episode provides more proof that those who are most effective in destroying an economy are very often those who are so determined to secure its well-being that they do not wait for the flaws in their policies to be pointed out. In that Roy Jenkins was a worthy predecessor of Sir Geoffrey Howe.

The press regularly treated Kaldor with outrageous contempt. Among those fellows of Kings who were not economists familiarity bred proverbial contempt for his views. One who claimed a very long acquaintanceship with him, and who had also known Keynes, announced at King's College's High Table, '*It is my considered opinion that if on an economic topic Nicky Kaldor said that so and so was true, then the opposite must be true.*' The considerable faith the government had in him must have been some consolation to Professor Kaldor for the wide-spread hostility to him.

Note on Chapter Ten:-

[1].   The figures are calculated from data in the 1973 National Income Blue Book.

CHAPTER ELEVEN

PETROLEUM VAPOURS

'My boy…always try to rub up against money for if
you rub long enough some of it may rub off on you.'
DAMON RUNYON

T HE DISCOVERY OF major deposits of oil in the North
Sea not only presented a prospective bonanza to the British
people but it also posed an economic threat to the British
economy. Sterling faced a danger that, once it became a petro-
currency, it would be overpriced in the world currency markets.
Far-sighted economists proposed prophylactic action to prevent
this, or to compensate for it. There are ways of securing the
benefits of an overvalued currency without suffering its disadvan-
tages. Much depended on the calibre of the fashionable economic
advisers who were dealing with the situation. In 1964, long before
the oil bonanza, Professor Nicholas Kaldor had made a crude but
promising proposal to protect an economy against the ravages on
its industries of an overvalued currency; he suggested the introduction of a universal value added tax which would be used to
finance a 7.5 per cent wages subsidy. Kaldor was later heard to
claim that if his proposal had been accepted the devaluation of
1967 would have been avoided. It certainly would have been
postponed, at the very least.

Four years after that embarrassing devaluation sterling was
freed from the straitjacket of a fixed exchange rate by a more
market-oriented administration. The scene was set to run Britain's
economy on a more realistic basis, promising an era free from

exchange rate crises and unnecessary abandonment of worthwhile projects. But confusion reigned at the Treasury. The government was tugged this way and that by the conflicting views of rival parties of advisers. One group saw that all successful economies of recent times had grown with the help of an undervalued currency, and the other group saw a highly valued pound as a cure for inflation. At the height of the confusion both policies were followed, and there were exchange controls both to prevent money from leaving the country, and to prevent it coming in!

A freely floating pound could float upwards as well as down. In the mid-1970s far-sighted observers wanted to avoid the possibility of an upward floating pound making Britain in the 1980s the richest nation of unemployed in Europe because of the competitive disadvantage in international trade of having a highly valued *petro-currency*. By 1976 the flow of oil from the North Sea was making the danger of overvaluation an imminent one. In the next three years the flow increased ten-fold. The problem was foreseen but never tackled. Luckily economic mismanagement depressed the pound and postponed the danger for a while, even though the potential danger had been made far greater by the huge rise in the oil price which had been engineered in 1973 by the Organisation of Petroleum Exporting Countries.

When the oil-producers put up the oil price, some countries, including Britain, responded by raising interest rates to prevent or cure the inflation it would cause. The reaction was hardly logical because it was not an irrational inflationary price rise of the kind so common since 1945. So far as consuming nations were concerned the increase in the price of oil was a genuine rise in real costs, a factor external to their economies. No amount of tough anti-inflationary measures was going to prevent prices rising as a consequence. Instead, of course, the rise in interest rates was itself inflationary for the usual reasons which have already been set out. The problem was compounded. The oil price rise even became a smoke screen for the raising of other prices too.

Trade imbalance

There was another reason for the interest rate rise, which by now was presented as the wide-spectrum antibiotic for all economic ills. The increase in the price of oil put many economies into a trade deficit. Government economists hoped that high interest rates would restrain demand and correct the trade balance. It was a vain hope. In principle the only way to correct the imbalance of trade was to increase exports to the oil-producing countries. Events showed that the only way of even starting to eliminate the deficit was to sell arms or capital assets to the oil-producers. Many of the oil-producing countries which were members of OPEC were thinly populated desert countries. For them it was difficult, if not impossible, to use all their new-found purchasing power for the benefit of their peoples by importing goods and services from the oil-consuming countries. The salesmen of the industrialised countries worked hard to turn the tough tribesmen of the deserts of the Middle East into sybaritic consumers of every plaything, whether useful or useless, of the so-called 'advanced civilizations'. Occasionally they were spectacularly successful, but, as always in human affairs, there was also an ascetic reaction. The area was dominated by one of the world's most moralistic religions. Its fundamentalist preachers attacked Western values, and grew in numbers almost as fast as petro-dollars. At least arms sold in vast quantities. Some oil-producers made matters worse by building industrial plants whose production not only made imports less necessary, but also supplied exports, probably subsidised, and thus increased the imbalance of trade yet more.

Compounding a problem

Raising European and American interest rates merely sharpened up the problem, for it meant that the burgeoning oil revenues of the producers were further gilded by the addition of high interest earnings. At their highest British interest rates had the effect of doubling the cash deposits of the oil-producers in only five years, or 16.3 times in twenty years! British policy makers seem to have been wholly unfamiliar with the effect of compound interest. The wisdom of an earlier age, which had led to the passing of 'Thellusson's Act' to discourage the establishment of funds which compounded interest indefinitely, had been forgotten. The legislators of that Act knew that at a low four per cent rate of interest Mr. Thellusson's trust fund would eventually own the whole national debt. No-one cared that Arab oil-sheikhs could do the same thing. In practice the oil-producers had no alternative but to recycle their revenues back to the oil-consuming countries. So why was it thought necessary to give them an unnecessary bonus of high interest? The action taken was not rational: it was lunacy.

An old problem reborn

The scenario was almost a repeat of that during the 1939-45 War when Britain was buying war supplies from all over the world with borrowed money. Then the British government saw no need to gild its suppliers' rewards, and interest rates were kept at an ultra-low level: indeed when adjusted for inflation they were negative. If in the 1970s the oil-consuming industrial nations had been shrewder, they would have responded to the producer cartel by setting up *The Organisation of Petroleum Importing Countries* ('OPIC') with a cartel of its own - a cartel of low interest rates. Commonsense did not prevail; it was not even heard. Instead, the consuming nations competed for the bank deposits of the oil-producers. As a result they experienced more inflation than they need have done. They also thereby took on the dangerous and difficult task of safely lending the OPEC deposits.

If the top industrial nations had not offered such enticing rates of interest on bank deposits, the developing nations might have been successful in getting in on the act and in attracting deposits to their own banks. The next stage would have been to use those hard currency deposits to finance purchases from the industrialised countries. The banks of the industrialised countries would have been saved from making unsound loans themselves. The megalomaniac desire of the bankers of the industrialised nations to become bankers to the world was one that they would eventually have reason to regret. In ringing phrases they preached their philanthropic duty to help recycle the deposits. Loans to Third World governments were given the noble sounding name of *sovereign lending*. The borrowers were called 'LDCs' for *Less Developed Countries*. Privately bank chairmen beamed with delight; it was easy money. The OPEC countries were saved the moral responsibility for their huge accumulation of money, and the blame for the huge debts of the LDCs was heaped not on the ultimate sources of the money, but upon the intermediaries. The blame fell mostly on the bankers of America as so many of the loans made with the oil money were denominated in dollars.

Profitable banking but unprofitable manufacturing

Initially Britain found that acting as international banker was profitable, and the profits helped reduce the balance of payments deficit. Later, when sovereign lending had become *the sovereign debt crisis*, and the time had come to write off the loans which had gone sour, were the write-offs fully reflected in the figure for the trade deficit? One suspects not. In the end the whole recycling exercise in international banking was an expensive disaster.

As Britain's own oil-production grew the trade figures came into balance, but no worthwhile surplus appeared. Instead British producers of visible exports found overseas markets made more difficult because of the frequent overvaluation of the pound. As long ago as December 1974 Professor Alan Walters suggested the pound ought to fall to $1.60. Despite having a poorer record of inflation than the dollar, the pound averaged $2.33 in 1980. Although it declined to $1.09 in February 1985, it was way up to $2.00 in May 1988, and again in October 1990. Against European currencies it was continously overvalued until September 1992.

Tremendous increases in productivity were achieved in British industry in the 1980s through trade union reform, better quality investment, one hundred per cent initial allowances on plant and machinery, and more intelligent marketing, but no country can forever remedy the effects of an overvalued currency by superior efficiency. They are essentially one-off improvements which, if reflected in their turn by a further increase in the value of the currency, achieve no permanent benefit. High efficiency is made more difficult to maintain in Britain by the pleasanter alternatives to hard work which are always on offer in Britain's beautiful land, where bountiful nature has provided so many more seductive ways of passing the time. Moreover, whatever improvement in efficiency is achieved in one country can be repeated in time in any other country. There can be no permanent advantage from cost-cutting and improved productivity.

At the root of the survival of the British economy are the twin factors of exchange rate policy and taxation policy. The first should encourage exports. The second should ensure that the cost of the welfare state is born not only by British manufactures but by imported wares as well; it should therefore be financed by value added tax, and not by direct taxes on domestic industry.

A banking crisis

Around the time the first wells in the North Sea began to produce large quantities of oil, the supply from the Middle East was reduced by a revolution in Iran, inspired by religious fundamentalists. This made Britain's growing oil-production even more valuable. The Iranian revolutionaries were anti-American. They indulged their extreme hostility by taking hostage the staff of the American embassy in Teheran, the capital of Iran. The Americans reacted by blocking Iran's very large cash deposits in American banks. The American hostages were eventually released following an agreement to release Iran's dollar deposits, which were estimated at $7billion, and to allow them to be removed completely from America.

Readers who fully understand the principles and mechanics of bank bookkeeping will immediately say, *'But that is impossible. Those dollar deposits have already been lent in America and used to finance all kinds of real things. You cannot remove wealth from a country except in kind, not money. But how do you remove to Iran a vineyard in California, a house on the coast of Cape Cod, or any of the myriad other things which have been financed by those loans? If the dollar deposits are removed, the loans in dollars which match them in the banks' balance sheets have to remain.'*

The Iranians were not interested in removing real wealth from America. They merely wanted the money: it was a matter of national and religious pride.

What was to be done? The answer was obvious and simple. The removal of the money had to *appear* to take place. There was no other alternative. The deposits would have to be transferred from the American banks to a bank abroad which would then agree to lend them back again to the banks from which they had come. Of course no private bank could digest $7billion. That it would not have the capital base to support such an increase in its deposits was only one reason. Nor would there be much profit to be derived from recycling deposits back to where they had come from. A central bank had to be found which had the power and the discretion to act quickly, and in contravention of all banking prudence. Which should it be? The British have quite as big an inferiority complex towards the Americans as the Americans have towards the British. Therefore the British banking hierarchy welcomed the chance to prove its superiority to the Americans. It was the moment for the Governor of the Bank of England to play hero, or was it the sucker?

The Bank's finest hour

It was the Bank of England's greatest hour. The Old Lady of Threadneedle Street showed her alleged skill. There was a great danger to be faced, the possibility that the Iranians would want the money converted out of dollars and into sterling. If that happened, who would carry the exchange risk of the reconversion back into dollars when the money was lent back to the American banks which needed it? The American banks? Not if they could help it. The Bank of England? One assumes the question was considered, but one cannot guarantee that it was. There is no certainty that the American government was made to guarantee the Bank of England against loss. Fortunately for Britain the Iranians surprisingly allowed the money to remain in dollars; the lucky Chancellor of the Exchequer was saved the embarrassment of more billions of pounds sloshing around the world, and playing havoc with his monetary targets.

How did the American Banks pay the money over? Did they send drafts drawn on themselves? Such a remittance does not change the debtor/creditor relationship: willy-nilly the Bank of England would be a creditor of the paying bank. Did they draw cheques on the Federal Reserve Bank ('the Fed')? If so, how was the payment to be covered? By a creation of money by the Fed? Or by the Fed taking over some of the paying banks' investments? Was the payment perhaps made in the form of an assignment of securities? That does not seem to have been the case. The Bank of England received the remittances and opened an escrow account for the Iranians, not an ordinary deposit. The reason for this was that the investment of the money was to be left to the Iranians. The escrow was a sort of trust account. It is not clear whether that meant that the Bank of England took no responsibility for the safety of the investment of the money. One trusts not, for if he is on risk for $7billion no sane banker hands over the decision on its investment to the customer!

The Iranians appear to have asked that the money, (after the repayment of a loan of some hundreds of millions of dollars from a consortium of banks,) be placed in the short-term money market. That was realistic of them. The money thus returned to the banks it had left, something which every practical banker knew would have to happen, whether it returned directly or indirectly. It would have been no different if the money had been deposited in the Moscow Narodny Bank. It would still have gone back to America. All was well. The Iranians had made it look as though they now had their money in London. The international money markets remained stable, and all was sedate and beautifully British. The Old Lady had done it again! But how was she, or her servants, rewarded? There is silence on that question. One trusts that it was something more substantial than a few good lunches for the Bank's Governor and senior staff.

The world's money

There was one big change, however: the world's money supply had gone up by nearly $7billion. The balance sheets of the American banks remained the same, except for the one that had received a repayment. Even that bank probably had to lend the returned money on to the other banks who had parted with Iranian balances. That would balance the books. If so, the American money supply was no different after the withdrawal from what it had been before. The Bank of England's balance sheet total had gone up dramatically. A huge rise in the world's money supply had happened in a split second. It was not, however, a matter for any immediate concern. It was merely a book entry, but one which could not have taken place if the Bank of England had worried about its capital adequacy ratio. If the figures for the banking department of the Bank of England are as given in the Financial Statistics, it does not have any significant capital! However the statistics do not show the Iranian deposits either, perhaps because they were treated as a trust. To parody Mark Twain's words, '*There are lies, damned lies, and the Bank of England's balance sheet.*'

Was the Bank of England on risk for an additional $7billion against which it had no reserves at all? If so, the credit of the British nation itself had been pledged. Unless the Iranians generously exonerated the Bank of England from all risk one must hope that the banks with whom the money was placed did not include Bank of Credit and Commerce International.

Money beyond control

Another interesting thing about that $7billion in London was that it was a dollar balance over which the United States Federal Reserve Bank had no control or power of supervision of any kind. It could demand no reserve deposit from the Bank of England. The most it could do was twist the arm of the Governor of the Bank. The incident showed how it was possible to create money over which the country in whose currency it was denominated could exercise no supervision. It was not the only bundle of dollars to be created outside the Fed's jurisdiction. That did not mean that dollar holdings in non-U.S. banks were completely unsupervised. But supervision was the task of the central banks of the countries in whose banks the dollars were deposited. In many small countries where the deposits were located for tax reasons that might not mean very much. There was, too, a large dollar bond market supplying non-intermediated credit, and that was largely unsupervised because it was located in tax havens.[1]

The affair of the Iranian dollar balances is a good example of monetary principles in action. Did the econometricians, the economic forecasters, the money supply watchers, do anything to their computer models to take account of the biggest ever aberration in the sequence of British monetary statistics, or do they normally ignore the Bank of England's banking business? Did they notice anything at all? Did they understand what was happening? Luckily they did not need to on this occasion. It was a non-event! It could, however, easily have been a financial disaster.

One exciting suggestion has been put forward for ameliorating the difficult problem of foreign deposits in banks. Mr. Gunnar Tomasson has proposed that all non-resident holdings of money be denominated in Special Drawing Rights (SDRs).[2] Of course the concomitant borrowings to match the deposits would also have to be denominated in SDRs, as there are unlikely to be banks which would be prepared to shoulder the exchange risk which would arise from owing money denominated in SDRs while their assets are in national currencies. The implementation of the idea requires the solution of many associated technical difficulties, but the benefit of this suggestion is that it would free all national currencies from the influence of so-called *hot money*, which sloshes about the world like bilge water in a foundering ship.

Notes on Chapter Eleven:-

1. In the early 1970s I was my company's London liaison point with the whole gamut of off-shore tax havens so I knew much of what was going on. It was very big business and profitable for Britain.

The commonly used explanation of the market for Euro-dollars, Euro-marks, Euro-whatevers, seems to me to contain more fantasy than fact. I am not even sure that I understand it. It is usually ascribed to the interest equalisation tax imposed in the United States, coupled with the U.S. trade deficit, or was it the trade surplus? One can concede that the equalisation tax may have been a precipitating factor, but why should not the true impulse have been the desire of Europe's bankers to conduct business in the world's leading currency? What need is there to bring in the factor of the U.S. trade surplus/deficit? Bankers can create credit in any currency which takes their fancy, and having been created in the intermediated credit market the credit leaks through, in the time-honoured way, into the disinter-mediated market.

2. Christopher Meakin has informed me from his personal experience that denominating deposits in SDRs has been tried, but the suspicion that it would be difficult to get people to take loans denominated in SDRs proved to be correct. The way around the problem was the very complex one of arranging that the bank's loans should together reflect a basket of currencies, as nearly as possible identical with the basket which determines the SDR itself. See Table 10.4 in B. Kettel's *Monetary Economics* for details of the basket in 1985.

CHAPTER TWELVE

THE MONEY VOLCANO ERUPTS

'Felix qui potuit rerum cognoscare causas.'
('Happy is he who has been able to learn the causes of things.')
VIRGIL

IN THE SPRING OF 1988 the Bank of England lowered minimum lending rate to 7.5 per cent. The huge monetary explosion which followed is blamed by monetarists upon this reduction. There was the best of reasons for lowering interest rates. It was the need to lower the exchange value of the pound which was then far too high, pulled up by the combination of high interest rates and sterling's status as a petro-currency.

The argument that the lowering of interest rates alone led to the credit explosion does not bear close examination: average interest rates were little different in 1988 from the rates in earlier years. According to the Central Statistical Office average base rates and the percentage rises in M4 for five successive years were as follows:-

Year	1986	1987	1988	1989	1990
Average base rates (%)	10.90	9.74	10.09	13.85	14.77
Rise in M4 (%)	15.88	16.35	17.60	18.42	12.07

The lowest level for base rates was in the second quarter of 1988 when the average was 8.15 per cent. The increase in M4 in that quarter was at a rate about 10 per cent greater than in the previous two quarters. However in the third quarter the increase in the rate of expansion of deposits was 50 per cent, even though the average of base rates for that quarter at 11.08 per cent was 3 per cent higher than in the preceding quarter. One suspects, of course, that the sharp rise in the second half of the year was in part a consequence of the exploitation of the £920,000,000 which Barclays Bank had added to its capital base by way of a rights issue in April.

Lift off for M3

When added to other increased capital resources this fresh capital enabled Barclays to expand its balance sheet by almost £17billion (19 per cent) by the end of the year, to be responsible for 33 per cent of the increase in M3, to expand its UK lending by 32 per cent, and to increase its mortgage lending by 51 per cent. The following year, despite even higher interest rates, its balance sheet was expanded by a further £24billion. This was done while high interest rates, the Treasury's favourite homeopathic remedy, were supposed to be discouraging borrowing and therefore controlling inflation. Surely they were promoting its growth? Although the rates of interest at the time of the rights issue were lower than for some years, they were higher than in other countries. Even at its lowest, minimum lending rate (MLR) was nearly five times the level of Bank Rate during the 1939-45 War.

Barclays Bank's performance in increasing lending was in no way exceptional; it was virtually matched both by the other clearing banks and by the big building societies. It was, however, exceeded by foreign banks operating in Britain by a factor of at least three.

These happenings exposed fully the fundamental error in monetary theory. In the 15 years between 1948 and 1963, when the lowest Bank Rate was two per cent, and the highest 7 per cent the deposits of the clearing banks rose 34.5 per cent; in the late 1980s, when the lowest MLR was 7.5 per cent and the highest 14 per cent, Barclays Bank needed just over two years to increase its deposits by the same percentage. Could this have been achieved without high interest rates? Could it have been achieved without the ending of the interest rate cartel? The first of these questions must receive a negative answer, but the answer to the second is less certain.

The Chancellor is disarmed

The Chancellor of the Exchequer had already abandoned the weapon for controlling the growth of credit. In March 1988 Mr. Nigel Lawson announced that he was going to throw away an effective but idle instrument of control, the Control of Borrowing Order. Such an order, which could control both share issues and borrowing, had the statutory authority of the Borrowing (Control and Guarantees) Act 1946, which was a relic, no doubt, of the Keynes' armoury of control procedures. A Statutory Instrument, SI 1958 No. 1208, later supplemented the Act. One oddity of the Statutory Instrument was that it exempted building societies from such orders. This no doubt reflected official opinion about the unimportance of building societies in 1958 as a force in the increase of the intermediated money supply. It was a long time before the authorities realised the error of that opinion.

Control of Borrowing Orders could have controlled credit creation directly, but possibly an even better course would have been to use their power also to prevent issues of shares or other capital raising exercises by the banks. By such simple means the authorities could have kept under control the capital bases of the banks, and of all other licensed deposit takers and moneylenders. Once again the essential truth set out earlier is crucial: if lending institutions cannot increase their capital bases, they *cannot* increase their lendings, because total lendings may not be greater than a prescribed multiple of the capital base.

To be totally effective the limitation of the banks' power to raise capital must be accompanied by some restriction, whenever necessary, of the non-intermediated credit market. The 1946 Act had sensibly envisaged the use of such restrictions. The credit market, intermediated and non-intermediated, is one market and must be supervised as a totality; looking at bits of it is useless. For instance, the long standing debates between academic economists about the relative importance of M0 and M3 as economic indicators is without rational foundation, and the tendency to dismiss the modern bond market as irrelevant to the control of the money supply is wholly unscientific. The attitude of 1946 was much wiser and it was a strange development to abandon such wisdom. True, the 1946 controls were probably overused by busybodying and ignorant bureaucrats of that time, who still thought they were running a siege economy, but the principle was sound and its total abandonment was disastrous.

By coincidence the £920million rights issue by Barclays Bank took place thirteen days after the Chancellor's announcement of the ending of control of borrowing legislation. After he resigned from the office of Chancellor of the Exchequer in 1990 he became a director of Barclays Bank. Obviously he bore the Barclays' directors no ill will for having played a major part in wrecking his financial strategy. Perhaps he was so blinded by the monetarist dogma to which he adhered that he had not understood the significance of the bank's actions.

Competition and uncontrolled credit

What also helped precipitate the vast expansion in the money supply which took place in 1988 to 1990 was competition between banks for increased market share. It was alleged in the press that Barclays Bank intended to regain the status of being Britain's biggest bank. That report alone would surely have been enough to goad the other banks into increasing their efforts to expand their business too. The result was that the British banks and building societies initially expanded their balance sheets at roughly the same rate, and Barclays won only a trivial advantage. A dangerous race had begun, a race to see who could reach Nemesis first. All the competitors finished the course.

They were also fighting intense competition from foreign banks. The chairman of Barclays Bank complained about the low margins which Japanese banks were prepared to take, and foreign banks were successful in winning much of the lending business generated by the Channel Tunnel project. The increase in credit creation by foreign banks was at a rate at least three times greater than the rate of increase of the United Kingdom banks' lendings.

Take-overs and buy-outs

Two other factors which played a large part were, firstly, a craze imported from America, the leveraged company buy-out, and, secondly, a spate of large cash take-overs of companies. Several teams of financial experts were formed whose sole purpose was to seek out or stimulate opportunities to lend money to companies for take-over purposes, or to provoke management teams to buy from holding companies the subsidiaries which they ran. The big accountancy practices and the merchant banks were active in forming such teams.

The pressure generated was intense. It was stimulated by the need for managements to show performance in order to protect themselves from being the victims of take-overs. Many managements also had share options which could become very valuable once profitable growth was achieved. The only thing lacking was the special taxation factor which in America made loan capital so much more attractive than equity. The United States had a tax upon company profits which was a classical corporation tax system. As has already been explained, that system encourages the use of loan capital in preference to equity capital. In Britain the classical corporation tax system had long been amended to reduce the incentive to capitalise with loan capital, though it had not been entirely eliminated. Besides 'gearing-up,' (as 'leverage' was termed in Britain,) was the best way of making the equity capital, and hence directors' share options, more valuable - given a rising tide - but worthless given an ebb tide!

The teams went into action with great success. Table 8.8 of the C.S.O.'s Financial Statistics for the period gives the details. In 1988 the cash used for acquisition of independent companies totalled £11,569million. In 1989 it was higher at £17,052million. Acquisitions of subsidiaries cost £4,421million in cash in 1988 and £5,307million in 1989. Despite very high interest rates 1990 saw an expenditure of £6,175million on acquisitions, raising the three year total to £44,524million. Much of this money must have been borrowed from the banks, especially foreign banks. Money lent to finance the purchase of an existing capital asset is certain to be newly created money. It cannot be money saved from the proceeds of current economic activity (that is, from income), for that has to be used to finance new production of real wealth if the economy is not to run down. True savings, being an addition to capital, cannot finance the purchase of *existing* capital assets unless there is a compensating dissaving by the vendor of those assets. In that case the saving is truly financing the vendor's profligacy, not real capital investment.

The loans made for the purchases of companies were a major constituent in the huge expansion of the credit supply which took place in those three years. The bulk of it may have come from foreign banks which were then subject to a less stringent requirement regarding capital adequacy ratios than the British banks. British banks were observing a capital adequacy ratio of around eight per cent; Professor David Llewellyn has observed that the equity to assets ratio of Dai-Ichi Kangyo Bank, the Japanese bank that is the largest in the world, was in 1988 2.4 per cent compared with a ratio of 6.1 per cent for National Westminster Bank.[1] A bank capitalised that much lower is able to charge a rate of interest perhaps half a percentage point lower than that charged by the bank with a larger capital adequacy ratio, and yet will still achieve the same return on shareholder's funds.

Asset price inflation

Where the acquisitions were of quoted companies the prices paid for the shares were much greater than the value previously placed upon them by the market. The purchases therefore caused inflation of asset values. Most of the increase in lending took place after base rates had begun to rise again from the low level of May 1988, indeed after they had reached 9.5 per cent. Lending for take-overs and buy-outs tapered off briefly when base rates reached 13 per cent, but surged to its highest level in the third quarter of 1989, when base rates averaged 14 per cent. It still continued at a high rate even when base rates were 15 per cent. It was therefore quite wrong to suggest that it was the *fall* in interest rates in the Spring of 1988 which caused the credit explosion.

Why corporate borrowers were ready to pay well over asset value for shares, and also to pay very high rates of interest to borrow the money to do so, seems to be a question for psychologists, or even for psychiatrists, rather than for economists. It made no immediate business sense at all.

The personal sector is a net seller of equity

It has long been the practice of the personal sector of the British economy to be a net seller of company securities, but the amount of the sales hugely increased in 1988 and 1989 to a two year total of £28,586million. Sales of UK company securities totalled £30,631 million, the difference between the two figures being balanced by net purchases of overseas securities. Some of this cash no doubt came from selling privatisation issues, that is issues for cash made by the government of shares in former state industries, but a very large sum must have come from the cash used in take-overs. In 1990 sales of company securities by the personal sector were £8,694million. Though still a very high figure, it was lower than in 1987.

But the inflation of asset prices did not stop with share prices. Once created, the money used for the purchases of shares could circulate, and the route of circulation of a considerable portion of it is easy to guess, for another habit of the personal sector is to use stock exchange profits to buy bigger and more expensive houses, partly as an anti-inflationary hedge. Finally, a third habit of the personal sector, and especially its older members, is to put any surplus cash into building societies deposits. Personal sector deposits in building societies and banks increased dramatically, and 1988 saw a huge surge in house prices as a result. The increased level was maintained throughout the following year.

The credit Krakatoa erupts

Asset price inflation also stimulates the public's willingness to borrow money for consumer goods, and the money was available to borrow. The whole scenario is unusually clear for an event in economics, and it reveals a vivid example of a *multiplier* in action. Of course the money the banks had lent to finance acquisitions had to find its way to the liabilities side of their balance sheets, but its route thither must have gone through many banks, creating deposits and lendings along its way. It left a trail of asset price inflation and a huge increase in the credit supply. We have earlier explained the mechanism by which one act of credit creation can cause an increase in the money supply that is many times the amount of the lending which started the process.

The total for the three years 1988-90 was £171,700million, an increase on December 1987 of 56.5 per cent. The theories upon which the government's interest rate policy had been founded do not begin to explain this empirical evidence. The evidence supports the view that to contain the growth of credit at the right time, direct controls are needed; interest rates alone are not sufficient and, indeed, the evidence proves that a rise in interest rates in the short term aggravates the problem of control.

Of course the banks had to raise lots of new capital to provide the base for the enormous increase in their lendings. So too did the building societies, but for them the task was made easier by the fact that high interest rates increased the speed of increase of their reserves. Building societies do not have their profits drained away by the need to pay dividends: if they are lending profitably they must accumulate the profit and all the interest earned by their reserves. The reserves increase exponentially through compounded interest. The exponential rate of growth of reserves is amplified by a high interest rate. Hitherto monetary theorists do not seem to have taken sufficient note of the fact that reserves earn interest. We saw in the last chapter how dramatically a high rate of compound interest increases a sum of money.

Indeed the building societies were also allowed to join the banks in the raising of subordinated loan capital in order to enhance their capital bases. Later they added permanent interest bearing shares (PIBS) to their methods of increasing their capital bases. Although one could not see a purpose for these increased capital resources, other than a further attempt to push up house prices, there was no indication that the supervising authority objected to the building societies' capital raising exercises. They were just as complacent about the effect of compounding interest on building society reserves as they were about its effect on money owed to oil-producers. The government appeared to be completely oblivious of the way in which it was steadily wrecking its own efforts to reduce inflationary pressures.

Neutral taxation: its effect

The next step is to modify the basic theory of the creation of credit by banks. The principal feature of the process is that the granting and drawing down of a loan must create an equivalent deposit somewhere else in the banking system, and that deposit can find its way to the liabilities side of the balance sheet of the lending bank. Unfortunately for British commercial banks, until the mid 1980s there existed a different tax treatment for the interest paid on bank deposits from interest paid by building societies. The effect was to raise the rate of income tax on interest allowed on bank deposits by a fifth above that payable on building society interest. Only deposits by private individuals were affected.

The result was that deposits at clearing banks were not competitive in the market for the private individual's savings. Any cash accumulating in the ownership of individuals was likely to find its way into a building society account, not into a bank account.

A loan made by a bank would still find its way back to it through the intricacies of the monetary system to become a bank deposit, but it might be at second, third, or even tenth-hand, not direct. By the time it got back to the bank much of the profit margin would have been creamed off. Naturally the tendency of private deposits to flow preferentially to building societies, whose lending avenues were restricted, had the effect of pushing up house prices. This must have been one of the factors which caused house prices to rise faster than the index of retail prices.

The financial market was highly distorted, and it was not until the taxation anomaly was abolished by Chancellor Nigel Lawson that the banks could become true savings institutions. The banks then used their new competitiveness to expand. Part of their expansion was to move into the house mortgage market and their lending for house purchase increased sharply.

It was a paradoxical result. The taxation anomaly had led to an increase in house prices: yet its abolition increased house prices even further! The Chancellor of the Exchequer had made a classic error. It was now possible for banks to compete in the building societies' traditional area of lending, but not the reverse. The building societies could not lend heavily in the non-mortgage market. By ill-chance the change came at a time when the banks were enthused with the safety of lending to private individuals. They had on average been a good credit risk. The banks forgot that this good record had been a function of the severe restriction there had often been on borrowing by private sector consumers during most of the postwar era. The ordinary man and woman had been given few opportunities for a borrowing spree. That was all about to change.

Distortion in the capital market

The British capital market was very distorted. One effect was that the needs of small industrial enterprises were poorly served. A major sector of the savings industry ignored them. But a gigantic lending juggernaut had been created to oversupply the house mortgage market. The building societies were not allowed the chance to provide for industry the resources which equivalent savings institutions in foreign countries were able to give to their industry, either directly or indirectly.

The expansion of lending in the United Kingdom had taken place without due regard for prudence. As a result the banks were announcing in 1991 large provisions for losses. In early 1990 two of the big clearing banks paid dividends out of capital reserves because profits were insufficient to cover them. Shareholders' funds were thereby reduced and with them the capital base for lending. When the shareholders approved the payment of a dividend to themselves they should have also been required to choose which of their banks' borrowers were to be forced to repay a total sum twenty times the amount of the dividends! The payment of dividends out of capital was repeated the following year. Between December 1988 and December 1991 the shareholders' funds of the big four commercial banks fell by £1,735,000,000. Theoretically that reduced their aggregate lending capacity by at least £21,000,000,000, and potentially by up to twice as much.

One way to resolve such a shortage of bank funds is to force creditworthy customers to raise equity capital by rights issues, effectively a reversal of what happened in 1988. In principle this should free the banks' capital for use as support for loans to small business customers who have no source of capital other than the banks. The actual outcome was that the lendings of the banks were cut back to such an extent that their capital adequacy ratios rose well above 8 per cent, indeed in one case to 10.3 per cent.

Vandalising industry

The switch of £44,524million from equity capital to loan capital in the three years 1988 to 1990 was a staggeringly large change in the form of the capitalisation of British industry. It should have stimulated some heart-searching at the Department of Trade and Industry (DTI). The Bank of England too should have taken worried note of what was happening and dreaded the likely consequences of an increase in interest rates in such a radically changed environment. Is there any evidence that anyone in the DTI, in the Bank of England, or in the Treasury was alive to the dangers of this trend? Did *anyone* in those sophisticated institutions warn the

Chancellor that in the circumstances a rise in interest rates would both vandalise British industry and bring untold suffering to those who had borrowed very excessively on mortgage in 1988 and subsequently? Or was the Chancellor so totally obsessed with an erroneous monetary theory that he ignored advice, if given, and continued to pursue a deflationary policy without giving proper thought to its terrible consequences for a host of overborrowed citizens? Hundreds of thousands of mortgagors were dispossessed of their houses. Inflation would have saved them from that cruel experience. No wonder Keynes called those responsible for such an economic policy inhumane!

Some mortgage borrowers were hit two ways: their mortgage payments went up because of higher rates of interest, and they also found themselves unemployed because higher interest rates had put their overborrowed employers out of business. A sad example of this problem was a lady who appeared in January 1991 on a Granada Television programme called *Up Front*. She had taken out a large mortgage in 1988. She had been employed by a large department store group. This had been the subject of a management buy-out from its former owners, a large public company. The new owners could not service their loans, and a receiver was appointed who made staff redundant. The Granada programme also revealed examples of the extreme imprudence of some mortgage lending, even by leading banks.

Were foreign banks to blame?

The total intermediated money supply, M4, rose by 57 per cent, but the lendings of the banks increased by 100 per cent. The accounts of the big British clearing banks do not reflect so great an increase. Although Barclays Bank had promised in 1988 a period of rapid growth, it achieved only a 53 per cent increase in its assets in the three years. One deduces therefore that foreign banks increased their lendings in the United Kingdom at a far greater rate than 100 per cent. They were reported to be responsible for much of the funding of the construction of the Channel Tunnel, and to be active in lending for company acquisitions and management buy-outs.

What constituted the capital base for their loans in Britain? Was it represented by sterling assets or by their overseas assets?

Japanese banks had much lower capital adequacy ratios than British banks yet do not appear to have been restricted in their lending in Britain by the supervising authority.

It was during that period that the Basel Capital Accord on capital adequacy ratios was agreed internationally, though its full implementation was postponed until 1993. The convention adversely affected the Japanese banks. There were reports in the financial press that they had found it necessary to restrict their lendings, and indeed, that they were moving out of the British market. That would have been good strategy as it was important for them to use all their lending power to support asset values at home, otherwise they could precipitate disaster for themselves. Even so the reduction in their lendings in Japan is said to have caused land values in Tokyo to fall dramatically. If that is true it is strong vindication of the theory that it is the capital base of the banks which is the critical factor in determining the amount of credit which can be created, the level of the intermediated money supply and, indirectly, asset values.

If press reports are reliable, the Japanese banks had discovered, quite accidentally one suspects, an easy way of expanding their capital bases. With their capital base they bought equity assets, such as company shares. Loans to portfolio investors and to companies would both have had the effect of causing equity assets to increase in price. As a banks' holdings of shares rose in value, so did the value of its capital base, and also therefore, subject to government permission, its maximum lending capacity.

The Distribution of Wealth Law

The greater part of the personal wealth of the nation is held by those over the age of fifty; the bulk of the borrowing, especially for house purchase, is done by those under fifty. The *haves* therefore belong to the older generation, many of them retired, and the *have-nots* are the workers and their young families. An increase in interest rates effects a transfer of income from the have-nots to the haves, from the young to the old, from the workers to the retired, from those best able to cause inflation by high wage claims to those who cannot. The switch of gross income in 1990 from the young to the old could have amounted to as much as £15billion. What greater incentive could there be to cause wage inflation, and therefore, because of the government's intransigent pursuit of its disinflationary and recessionary policies, to cause unemployment? The government said it was aiming to avoid unemployment by checking inflation. Truly it was causing both. Inflation is not, on its own, either an inevitable or a major cause of unemployment. Indeed experience suggests that it is much more likely to increase employment. As we have already stated, it is what is sometimes foolishly done both by governments and by ordinary people *in response* to inflation which increases unemployment!

The desire of young married people for wage rises was further aggravated by a factor which was not part of the monetarist philosophy, but of the government's attitude towards the welfare state. To demonstrate this point one must compare the relative financial positions of a young family man with a non-working wife and three young children in 1963, and his successor a generation later in 1990 with the same job, same family, same house, and same proportion of its value on mortgage. Although the salary for the job had increased 25 per cent more than the index of retail prices, the successor in 1990 would have had £4,000 (in 1990 money) less to spend than his 1963 predecessor. In practice this meant that he would not have been able to afford such a good house or the third child. This is a very significant change, but seemingly it is not understood by many of the experts who hold the limelight on the fiscal studies scene.

Some of this difference was due to higher interest rates, plus the inflation of house prices at a rate higher than general inflation. But part was due to the reduction in family allowances, the ending of tax allowances for children, and the abolition of the lower rate bands of income tax. These last three factors strengthen the motivation to seek pay rises, which go to all workers, not merely the family men. The government did not seem to understand that generous family allowances, by subsidising the family wage-earner, make it possible to keep general wage rates down, thereby assisting international competitiveness. The government's policy on tax and national insurance benefits was therefore highly inflationary. The French scene is different. Although French social security charges on employers are very high, the burden may be balanced by the fact that generous benefits and tax reliefs for the family may help keep general wage rates down.

The so-called trade cycle

Much academic effort has gone into the discussion of the origin of the trade cycle, but surely the cause is a simple one: it reflects booms and dearths in the demand for credit.[2] The booms are periods when too many people simultaneously decide to borrow in anticipation of future income. The recessions are when too many people simultaneously attempt to reduce their accumulation of debt. If all these decisions were nicely phased over time there might be no trade cycle. In the absence of a steady, phased replacement process, a credit explosion, such as that in 1988, must be followed by a period of consolidation when people try to pay off their debts. Having consumed in advance of receipt of their income they have to cease consuming while the income to repay debts comes in. But the cessation of consumption and the consequent reduction in economic activity reduces peoples' aggregate income and, therefore, their aggregate ability to repay. The banks become worried at their losses and reduce lendings, thereby further aggravating the problem. A downward spiral takes place. It is a very simple scenario. One wonders why so much academic ink has been wasted on the subject. One look at the unemployment figures for the nineteenth century reveals the constant oscillation.

The problem is made worse still if the lending has been effective in inflating asset values. One recalls that the American stockmarket crash of 1929 followed a period of rising share prices which had been stimulated by dealings 'on margin', that is, on credit. When the inevitable reaction came many banks were in trouble and a grievous recession followed. The banking failures reduced the money supply. The credit available to American stockmarket investors more than halved. Stockmarket values, and indeed all asset values, collapsed as an inevitable result.

Bankers at bay

In the expansionary boom period of the late 1980s the British banks reversed their traditional attitude and made much more credit available to the small business sector of the economy. Perhaps they were led to do this because the foreign banks had competed so successfully with them in the large corporate market for credit. The recession induced by the government's interest rate policy caused much of the lending to small businesses to go sour.

The chairman of one large bank announced that his bank was losing a million pounds a day of its loans to small businesses, and that it was therefore going to reduce its lending to the small business sector.

Injurious taxation

Small businesses in Britain have tended to be undercapitalised. This is a natural tendency, and is probably universal among small businesses. In Britain it is exaggerated by adverse taxation policies of very long standing. At the root of the problem is the socialistic impulse to try to redistribute wealth. Tax policies designed for this purpose achieve a far more sinister effect: they prevent the accumulation of capital in businesses, or they divert any accumulation of capital away from the business.

An example of diversion of capital is the tax allowances given to pension funds. In the 1970s the tax on an entrepreneur's profits could be as high as 83 per cent, though on a current cost accounting basis the tax charge might be nearer 100 per cent. In the 1980s the maximum rate of tax was reduced to 40 per cent. It was possible to avoid tax altogether in respect of the amount of profit permitted to be put into a pension fund. But profit accumulated in a pension fund is not available to the entrepreneur to capitalise his business. A special tax privilege was therefore introduced for the benefit of directors of private companies, though curiously not for the unincorporated trader. The privilege was that the directors of a company could start their own pension fund into which profits could be syphoned, and the directors could then control the investment of the fund. They were allowed to invest up to about half of the money back into their own business. Often the money was used to buy premises which were let to the company, or to make loans to the company. This privilege was a help to businessmen, but only to a limited extent: the money was not available to provide an equity base for the company's borrowings. Indeed any loans to the company from the pension fund would probably result in a pro-rata decrease in the credit limit allowed by the company's bankers, for the equity base of a business should logically set the limit for total borrowings from all sources. The maximum ratio of loans to equity should be constant whatever the source of the credit.

The expenditure tax

A tax régime better designed to help businesses grow would have been that proposed by the Nobel Prizewinner, Professor James Meade, in his report on direct taxation for the Institute of Fiscal Studies. It was called an *Expenditure Tax*. Seven years later in 1985 the Confederation of British Industry adopted Professor Meade's proposal but gave it little publicity. Probably it was realised that there were aspects of the scheme which would not have been comprehensible to most of the electorate, and may not even have been comprehended by the Confederation's general membership. Under an expenditure tax there is no tax at all on any form of savings, so there is no special tax privilege for a pension fund. Money for pensions can be saved in the business!

The small business at the mercy of the banks

The bankers' decision to cut back lending to small businesses was an attack on the foundations of the economy. The smaller businesses have become dependent on bank loans for, on average, 31 per cent of their capital needs. Moreover most of this borrowing is at short-term interest rates. One of the effects of continued inflation has been to make the traditional forms of long-term fixed interest capital no longer available to smaller businesses, which are therefore very vulnerable to increases in interest rates. It was most unfortunate for them, therefore, that high interest rates had become the favourite tool of government in pursuance of its vain attempt to control the money supply.

High interest rates have another effect: they discourage people from paying their bills on the due date. Many small businesses are suppliers of goods and services to large companies whose finance directors became ruthless in delaying payment. In 1991 a bill that was contracted to be paid at thirty days was on average paid after eighty-one days. As a result of this practice a large proportion of bank lending to small companies indirectly finances large companies. If 15 per cent of all the capital of small companies was absorbed in this way, and if bank borrowing is the marginal capital source of small businesses, it means that in the aggregate one half of all bank credit to small companies is indirectly financing the capital requirements of larger companies on an interest free basis. The true proportion could be higher.

Was the chairman of the bank referred to earlier aware of this fact? Was he happy to bankrupt many of the suppliers of his larger customers, or would he prefer to try to persuade his larger customers to pay their bills on time? Would he lend them the money to do so? To refuse would be an effective way of killing off British business from its most sensitive small roots upwards.

At the local branch level bank staff have been well aware of this problem and have marvelled at the lack of action by their superiors, and at the failure of parliamentary lobbying promoted by business organisations such as the Forum of Private Business and the Federation of Small Businesses. Bank staff know the problems of their small business customers because they face them regularly across the counter; bank directors on the other hand face only the finance directors of multi-nationals across the claret glasses in the lunch rooms of Lombard Street.

To Civil Service mandarins small businessmen are a nuisance; to some Labour Party members of Parliament they are vermin fit only for elimination by destructive taxation. The minds of Conservative members of Parliament have been fuddled by incorrect monetary theories. What chance has the small businessman of getting fundamental reforms of the financial system which might aid him and also make the banker's life less stressed?

Notes on Chapter Twelve:-

1. See Professor Llewellyn's article in the January 1992 issue of *Banking World*, the journal of the Chartered Institute of Bankers.

2. I have not seen the full report of the Macmillan Committee of 1928 (of which Lord Keynes was a member), but I understand that it contained a recommendation that the term *trade cycle* be replaced by *credit cycle*.

CHAPTER THIRTEEN

THE GENERAL THEORY OF SAVING

'Saving is a very fine thing, especially
when your parents have done it for you.'

WINSTON CHURCHILL (*attributed*)

IN CHAPTER SIXTEEN of his book *The General Theory of Employment Interest and Money* Lord Keynes analysed the nature and effects of saving. He pointed out that when a man saves he is postponing consumption, possibly, but not necessarily, with a view to consuming later. The consequence of this, Keynes suggested, is that saving reduces the immediate demand for goods and services. The first conclusion the reader is led to draw from his analysis is that saving must cause unemployment.

He also suggested, however, that if the saving were for the purpose of some future consumption, the entrepreneur might think it worthwhile to invest capital immediately in order to be ready to supply the future demand when it appears. This would counter the tendency for unemployment to rise as a result of an increased propensity to save. But he seems to expect that the normal knock-on effect of the reduction in the demand for goods for immediate consumption would be to reduce also, not increase, the demand for capital equipment such as machine tools.

Keynes' remarks must have had great influence on political economists and politicians. Some have favoured the second of the alternative results of saving, and have used his analysis as a reason to inhibit saving during a recession. Others have chosen the more optimistic version, and have encouraged saving on the principle that it will artificially stimulate investment, and therefore the expansion of the economy. An extreme example of the latter policy would be the adoption of an expenditure tax. Such a tax would have the effect of making all savings an allowable deduction from income for tax purposes.

If one looks at the bookkeeping related to the saving process in close detail one finds that Keynes' comments are defective. His analysis needs much correction and refinement.

A better analysis of saving

The most elementary form of saving takes place when an income earner retains part of his income in the form of currency, tucking banknotes in a deed box at the bank, in a jar at home, or even in the legendary old sock.

If a person collects and keeps banknotes as a store of wealth, the government must increase the number of banknotes in use. Still commonly used for most day to day purchases, banknotes provide the medium of exchange for a large proportion of the ordinary citizen's expenditure. It is, however, a somewhat diminishing proportion because of the great increase in the popularity of cheques, debit cards, and credit cards. If people also use banknotes as a store of value, that is as a medium for saving as well as a medium of exchange, then a greater supply of banknotes must be required. The quantity of banknotes needed in an economy is determined by the normal market forces of supply and demand, and although governments pretend to limit the value in issue, in truth they have no choice but to supply the quantity which the economy needs. Failure to do so would either cause banknotes to stand at a premium to other forms of money, or, much more likely, would cause the populace to invent a substitute currency for use as a medium of exchange.

When saving increases the demand for banknotes, the government meets it by having more printed. It could, if it wished, introduce the notes into circulation by paying for its own purchases with them. That would make the printing of banknotes a means, additional to taxation, by which a government acquires purchasing power for its own needs. By making purchases with newly printed banknotes the government mops up the purchasing power temporarily relinquished by the hoarder of banknotes.

The Bank of England and the Note Issue

In Britain the government does not introduce new banknotes into circulation by directly using them to pay for its own purchases. That is seen, quite rightly, as the tempting and sure route to hyperinflation, the real life business of printing money.

The issue of banknotes is handled by the Issue Department of the Bank of England. When a bank wants to buy banknotes from the Issue Department, but does not have sufficient cash on its account at the Bank of England to cover their purchase, it can acquire them with *category one money* obtained by selling (usually indirectly) commercial bills of exchange, (which are short-term loan instruments), or short-dated government stocks to the Bank of England. The securities which the Bank of England acquires from the bank which sold them are retained as asset backing for the note issue. The Issue Department of the Bank of England shows in its balance sheet the issued banknotes as a liability, and its holdings of government stocks or bills of exchange as assets.

The result of the British system of issuing banknotes is that the Bank of England gets an interest free loan. As the government owns the Bank of England it is the true beneficiary of the cheap loan as any profit made by the Bank of England belongs to the government. Indeed there appears to be an agreement between the Treasury and the Bank of England for the interest on the assets held by the Issue Department to go straight to the Treasury. It is not treated as the income of the Bank of England at all.

Banknotes are normally expected to be a fast circulating part of the money supply and are therefore referred to by some monetary theorists as *high power money.* Yet if they have been tucked away in our saver's old sock they cannot circulate at all! To some extent therefore the intensity of the future demand for goods and services will depend on the frequency of circulation of the assets which back the increased note issue. Some of the assets which the Issue Department of the Bank of England holds to balance the liability of the note issue are bills of exchange, and they turn over comparatively quickly, though not as quickly as the faster moving part of the banknote issue.

When the Bank of England purchases financial assets from the bank which needs banknotes to supply to its customers (who may well include our saver and/or his employer), these financial assets represent existing liabilities, not new ones. Is Keynes right after all? Has a normally fast circulating component of the money supply (banknotes) been rendered immobile by being tucked away in the saver's old sock, and is it now balanced by a more static, *low power*, investment (gilts or bills)? Surely not, because our saver's demand for banknotes for the purpose of hoarding is *additional* to the regular demand. It is replacing a potential bank deposit which would have been equally static as it would represent permanent saving with no frequency of circulation. Thus the fast circulating component of the money supply, true *high power money*, is not reduced by the saver's decision to stock up with banknotes.

The capital adequacy ratio may rise

There is another important compensating factor. When a bank supplies banknotes to a customer who has a credit balance at the bank, and obtains those banknotes by selling to the Bank of England an asset, be it a government stock or a commercial bill of exchange, the bank's balance sheet total, both of assets and liabilities, is diminished. The customer's balance has been reduced and the bank's investments have been equally reduced. The reduction in investments must improve the bank's capital adequacy ratio, with the result that the bank has the capacity to increase its lendings and borrowings: it can create money (credit) in order to restore its balance sheet totals, and its capital adequacy ratio, to the previous figure. Effectively the total intermediated money supply is increased as the Bank of England has taken over part of the bank's lendings. Therefore the effect on demand in the national economy of some citizen saving banknotes will depend almost wholly on whether the banks are able to restore their levels of lending in order to exploit fully the potential of their capital bases. We have already remarked on how strong is their incentive to do that.

Lord Keynes' idea could on occasions be right, but there is no compelling necessity for it to be so always. In the 1980s it was certainly not true, as all banks regularly made very full use of their capital bases. When capital ratios rose above the normal minimum in 1991-1992, the fall in bank lending reflected, at least in part, an increase in the proportion of credit provided through the non-intermediated market, that is the stockmarket.

Demand for credit overrides all

The strength of the demand for credit is what determines whether the credit supply is increased. An increased propensity to save may affect its strength, but there is no necessity for it to do so. An increased propensity to save by one section of the community may be matched by an increased propensity to consume by another section of the community. The latter may be prepared to borrow in order to indulge its wish to consume. In practice it is the older citizens who are, in the aggregate, the net savers, and the young who are the net borrowers. In the real world, therefore, the two propensities happily exist side by side, and balance one another. Moreover, when the propensity to save is strong, the banks must step up the sales pressure upon potential borrowers. Luckily for the banks the propensity to borrow appears to be readily stimulated by marketing pressure from the lending institutions. By definition savings and borrowings have to be equal. The creation of credit tends to slow down only when the populace is already imprudently overborrowed. That is the lesson from the 1980s.

One possibility is that the government could take advantage of the opportunity created by the banks' need to lower their capital ratios and itself borrow more from them. Because the government owns the Bank of England any government debt held by the Bank is interest free. So, when the Bank has bought up government debt (government stock or Treasury bills) to provide the asset backing for an increased banknote issue, additional funds to the same value could then be borrowed by the government at no additional net cost in interest, because it is getting back all the interest it pays on the gilts owned by the Issue Department of the Bank of England. The government could then use the additional borrowing to finance a reduction in taxation, and thereby leave a greater quantity of spending power in the hands of the public.

What happens if taxes are reduced, but taxpayers, instead of spending the money, increase their savings by an amount equal to the tax reduction? Further research will be required, possibly into a very extended sequence of transactions, to find out where the consumption power released by savers is balanced by increased expenditure by some other person or persons, or by some company, corporation, institution, or government department. Analysis of all the possibilities is very complicated, but one truth is clear: one way or another the public's saving will be balanced by dissaving in some other sector of the economy. The combined effect of the laws of accountancy and of arithmetic ensure that. This absolute truth can never be repeated too often. *One man's saving is another man's debt.* They *must* always be in balance. If any debtor cannot repay a loan, and it has to be written off, some lender loses an identical amount. The balance is thus preserved.

Saving by increased deposits

Let us revert to our hypothetical saver and assume that instead of saving banknotes in an old sock he decides to increase his deposit at a bank. This begs the question of how the saver acquired the money he is saving. His income will consist of money which he has received from someone else, perhaps from his employer. If the employer has reduced his own credit balance at the bank in order to pay wages to his employee, the deposit by the employee neatly replaces the amount withdrawn by the employer. That is very convenient for the bank as it means that the liabilities side of the bank's balance sheet still matches its assets side. Our saver has merely replaced another saver. Nothing has happened to reduce either aggregate demand or the total money supply.

But the money paid to the employee could be new money, created, in the manner already described, when it was lent to the employer. Here again the saver is merely providing the necessary deposit to match the loan which the bank has made to his employer. With that loan the bank has expanded the intermediated credit supply, and has thereby increased both the asset and liabilities sides of its balance sheet. If the intermediated money supply is to remain at the increased level, there has to be someone who is willing to hold a deposit which balances the loan which has been taken up. In such circumstances the saver, far from reducing the availability of credit, is playing an essential role in the process of increasing it!

If our saver increases the level of deposits in the banking system by his saving, that additional deposit has to be lent by the bank. As we have already seen, all bank deposits have to be matched either by a holding of currency notes (which is a free loan to the government or the Bank of England), or by some other form of lending. An obvious truth that follows from this analysis is that the effect which an act of saving has on the progress of the economy is determined by the subsequent action of the borrower of that saving - and there must be one - not by the person doing the saving.

The loan which the bank makes with our depositor's money may be lent to finance the purchase of a vehicle, thus inflating the demand for vehicles rather than the demand for other goods and services. Alternatively it may be lent to help some improvident person out of a temporary shortage of cash required for the purchase of the immediate necessities of life. In this case, as in the previous one, the saving is financing expenditure on consumer goods and services, and therefore the act of saving has done nothing to reduce demand.

Thus Keynes' analysis is quite wrong. It grossly overstates the likelihood that saving will cause a reduction in demand. This could happen if the saving served to reduce a borrowing, and thereby reduced the amount of money circulating. It could also happen if the saving caused a part of the money supply which has a high frequency of circulation to be replaced by money which has a lower frequency of circulation. It must be well nigh impossible for any economic forecaster to predict which of these eventualities will happen in any given situation.

Capital formation

The savings might finance loans for the creation of productive resources. It is in this scenario that saving provides the where-withal for the eventual expansion of the economy; and it is this scenario which the economist may wish would take place. There is a regrettable tendency among some economists to assume that a high rate of saving will be coupled with a high rate of creation of productive capital assets. In reality no necessary connection exists between an act of saving and *real capital formation*, as the creation of physical capital assets is called. Whether savings are used to finance real capital formation or only consumer expenditure will depend on market forces in the overall capital market.

Throughout Keynes' earlier book, *The Treatise on Money,* he appears to be under the impression that savings always finance investment. Presumably he means by investment what the Central Statistical Office much more sensibly calls fixed capital formation.

Moreover he also appears to believe that savings have to precede investment. It is this mistake which makes a very large part of his *Treatise on Money* wrong and misleading. An act of true investment *precedes* an act of true saving in the same way that borrowing must *precede* an increase in money deposits. An attempt to save which is not matched by an act of real capital formation must end up financing consumer expenditure; that is a logical necessity.

Keynes got himself deeply confused over the definition of saving. On no other aspect of economics does he seem to have failed so lamentably in his analysis. Seven years later, in Chapter Six of the *General Theory of Employment Interest and Money*, he has another go at clarification and writes,

'*So far as I know, everyone is agreed that saving means the excess of income over expenditure on consumption.*'

But everyone does not agree. Saving is the failure to exercise a right to consume to the limit of one's income. That right can be lent to others who may use it to purchase consumption goods. Keynes' definition of saving is the aggregate expenditure of the whole community on non-consumption goods - whatever they may be. He sets out his proof on page 63 in three equations:-

Income = value of output = consumption + investment.
Saving   = income - consumption.
Therefore saving = investment.

Keynes has neatly and idiosyncratically fudged the discussion by defining saving in terms of investment. He has tried to avoid examining what the ordinary man sees as savings by looking only at the net aggregate saving of the whole community. At the individual level the definition does not work at all. He was aware there was some problem for he returns to the issue in Chapter Seven. On page 75 he defined net investment as the net addition to all kinds of capital equipment. Then he had a cup of coffee, had a bright idea, and wrote the next sentence in which he expands the term '*capital equipment*' to include '*working capital or liquid capital*'. Yes, savings can also finance work-in-progress and stocks of consumption goods. How true indeed!

The *Treatise's* other errors

The Treatise on Money contains two other serious mistakes. The first is the ridiculous '*Widow's Cruse*' simile, postulating an eternal and inexhaustible supply of profit. The second is Keynes' definition of *profit*, and all the long reasoning derived from it. He seems to cherish the illusion that one man's profit is always some other man's loss. This is not true; profit is the entrepreneur's reward for his work and skill, or the return on his capital. It is perfectly possible for *all* entrepreneurs to make a profit at the same time. Perhaps Keynes' mistake is due to his personal preoccupation with financial speculation, through which he became very rich. In stockmarket and currency speculation, in both of which he was active and successful, one man's profits may well reflect another man's losses. But gambling and productive industry are two totally different things.

The useful parts of *The Treatise on Money* are some technical discussions which have their parallel in *Towards True Monetarism*. An example is the discussion of the definition of the effective money supply. There is also a perceptive discussion of the problem of constructing indices of prices. That problem has not gone away. Some sixty years later people quote the latest Retail Prices Index as if it were a divine truth, not a digest of messy averages. It is only one of a number of deflators. Earlier economists preferred to use the level of wholesale prices, not retail, as the base by which to measure inflation, as it was simpler to ascertain, basic commodities being few in number and very much easier to price.

The financing of real capital formation

In Britain it was most unusual in the postwar era for the savings of its ordinary citizens to help finance the creation of new productive resources because for several decades British industry was, in the aggregate, more than self-financing. In the year 1987, for instance, industrial and commercial companies spent £28,411 million on fixed capital formation in Britain, yet their undistributed earnings amounted to £46,415 million. There was no need in 1987 for the personal sector of the economy to save in order to provide the finance for any of private industry's capital formation. In the aggregate industry itself was well able to finance it. That is nothing to be proud of as it reflects a low level of industrial capital formation. This position has changed dramatically since, but only because so many capital hungry utilities have been transferred to the private sector from the government sector of the economy.

In 1990, despite the privatisation of capital hungry industries, the whole of the company sector of the economy, which includes financial companies as well as industrial and commercial companies, was still in the aggregate self-financing. Aggregate retained earnings plus depreciation were roughly equal to aggregate real capital formation. The position may have been even better than the official statistics suggest, as the official figures for real capital formation include the cost of land. That should be excluded, as it is not true capital formation but is merely the transfer of the ownership of an existing capital asset. True real capital formation needs to be measured by the amount of human effort which has gone into creating totally new assets. The lending of money for the purchase of an existing capital asset does not have to be matched by an act of true saving, that is by the postponement of a right to consume which has been earned by a worker's contribution to the current production of goods and services. When land is bought with money borrowed from a bank, the bank deposit balancing the bank lending is that of the vendor of the land, who has merely exchanged one asset for another, a real asset for a financial asset.

We repeat, there is no automatic association between a high level of individual saving and a high level of capital formation in production capacity. Saving can just as easily finance consumer credit as finance capital expenditure on production facilities. In an economy such as the United Kingdom's, which has regularly been internationally uncompetitive because of an overvalued currency, saving is much more likely to finance the consumer rather than the producer of goods and services.

To put it simply, we may rewrite Keynes' definition to state that savings is always equal to borrowing: saving is not equal to investment, if by investment one means the creation of new real capital assets (real capital formation).

Primary and secondary capital markets

Our notional saver may not deposit his savings in a bank: he may use them to purchase a financial asset such as a life policy, an investment in stocks and shares, or a unit trust (mutual fund), or a host of other investment instruments. In such cases the money may find its way into either the primary or secondary capital market; the saver does not know which. If it is the primary capital market, it could finance the purchase of durable things which will become the real capital of future generations. But that will not necessarily be so, as the primary capital market can finance stock in trade, debtors, or consumer borrowing as readily as it can finance factories or machinery. If the saving finds its way into the secondary capital market, it may be buying an asset belonging to someone who is dissaving, and who proposes to turn his financial asset into the wherewithal to purchase part of the current production of goods and services of the economy. In either case the saver finances demand which will completely replace his own deferred demand, the value of which is measured by his saving.

The principles restated

Let us restate the principles yet again. In a developed economy all positive saving, that is saving which takes place not merely for the repayment of existing debt, will be matched by an equivalent dissaving. One man's postponement of the right to consume, which he has earned by his work, will normally be replaced by someone else's active anticipation of his expected future right to consume. The routine process of matching each act of saving with an act of borrowing, whether it is to finance consumption or to finance real capital formation, will be achieved through the financial system's capital markets.

All wealth is debt: one man's wealth is someone else's liability. Saving cannot exist without dissaving; thrift cannot exist without profligacy. All moralists please take note!

Although Keynes' analysis is wholly misconceived, we could no doubt construct a scenario of events which do run an economy down. If an economy can expand, it can also contract. But it is most unlikely that the horrifying picture of a declining economy which Keynes paints in the third section of Chapter 16 of *The General Theory of Employment, Interest and Money* would result solely from the propensity to save without assistance from another factor. An increased propensity to repay debts is that other factor. So the problem activity is what may be called *negative saving*, the reduction of debt.

Investment, and the meaning of capital

Investment is therefore a much misused word. The misuse has led to the very mistaken or very misleading statement that *'savings equals investment'*. One can only avoid misunderstanding by the laborious process of redefining the word every time one uses it. Keynes should have been less general in his statement and content just to say, *'A certain kind of investment is equal to a certain kind of saving'*. The kind of investment is that which results in the creation of new structures which produce real wealth faster than did previous structures, and the kind of saving is that which finances such structures.

The word *investment* can in popular parlance include portfolio investment as well as referring to real investment. Portfolio investment is the purchase of existing productive assets, whereas real investment is the creation of new productive assets. To avoid confusing the two we have used the alternative expression *real capital formation* for the latter. Unfortunately not all real capital assets are productive: they are merely fixed, permanent. Thus we can go on refining our terms and perhaps arrive at *fixed real productive capital formation*.

Aristotelian classification always prompts further questions, and so does our refined term. Is a new road, which is obviously something real and fixed, a productive asset? *'Yes,'* one could say, *'if it assists the economy to be more productive.'* Is a school a productive asset? *'Yes, because it provides a service.'* Is a dwelling productive? *'No, because it is an object of production, one of the goods we desire.'* However it is capital, is it not, for it is real and fixed?

Then what is capital? We tend to feel that a house is capital but a washing machine is not. We therefore invent a new term, and the washing machine is consequently classified as a *durable consumer product*, as if that distinguishes it from true capital assets. Truly all it does is distinguish it from non-durable consumer products. Is not a house truly a durable consumer product too?

What is Income?

Let us approach from another direction. The opposite of capital can be income. Is not the aggregate income of a community the totality of all its production of goods and services? Surely it is; in that we agree with Keynes. But that totality includes *all* of the current production of capital goods. Gradually we discover that the popular meaning of *capital* has no logical foundation. It is pure nonsense. It has a vague instinctive meaning, incapable of precise definition. Let us therefore drop the popular use, try to be more scientific, and, like Lord Keynes, apply terms to definitions, not definitions to terms. Now the thought process becomes quite easy. Income is the current production of all goods and services, and capital must therefore be the surviving results of *past* production. If it exists, it is real capital. If it is being produced, it is income. Because creation can be a speedy process, the transformation from being part of income to being an item of capital can also be quick. So to measure income we take a fixed period and count up the value of all production in that period. The production of one day would be the ideal time period, but a year is more convenient. We have thus defined as income the gross domestic product for a year, exactly the definition used in the official statistics.

Some goods remain capital for only a brief period in time, as production and final consumption may be very close together, and the consumption may leave no residue. Food is consumed and thereby destroyed, but if we think of the purchase of a washing machine as consumption we must admit that it is consumption which certainly does not *consume* in the sense of *destroy*.

An individual's own production of goods and services has a value, and he is entitled to consume other goods and services to the same value. He may choose not to exercise all his proper entitlement. The difference between his entitlement and his actual consumption is his saving, and he will want his saving to be represented by some store of value, something of continuing value. As has already been demonstrated, for production and consumption to be in balance, some other person must borrow in order to finance the acquisition of the exact value of current production whose consumption the saver has deferred by his act of saving. That other person becomes a debtor for the value of his borrowing: the debt becomes the saver's store of wealth.

A vital purpose, indeed the basic purpose, of the financial system is to match the underconsumption of a saver to the overconsumption of a borrower. This statement should finally make it clear that savings can finance the production of *any* goods and services, whether of lasting nature or not.

Through positive investment the community tries to make a proportion of the current production of food, lighting, heating, clothing, lodging, etcetera, available to other workers who are producing no immediately consumable goods or services. Instead they are fully engaged in producing new capital structures, which may eventually enhance the production of goods and services. In return for their abstinence savers are rewarded by getting some of the new wealth generated by those new assets.

Promotion of productive investment

We have already mentioned that Keynes' old associate, Professor James Meade, wanted to make the encouragement of saving the prime object of the taxation system, and that in 1985 his views were adopted by the Confederation of British Industry.

A taxation policy to promote saving is not the real need: we need a policy to promote productive real capital formation. If the community decides to produce capital assets, the saving to finance them automatically takes place. It has to, because there arises a deficiency of goods to consume upon which to spend the money incomes earned. At any particular moment in time some persons or institutions must have on their bank accounts the money which was borrowed and paid to the workers who built the new productive asset. These bank balances may get passed from hand to hand, chasing an insufficient supply of consumer goods. Some inflation may ensue. However a successful project of productive real capital formation will result in the supply of goods at a lower price than before. So deflation could then result.

If the continued creation of real capital assets does cause some inflation, it is worth tolerating as the price of the expansion of the economy. However the inflationary effect of capital projects is in any event only marked if there is a dearth of resources, either of workers, skills or materials, so that demand exceeds supply. But if there is no deficiency the inflationary effect will be slight, being limited to the difference between the workers' wages and what they would receive in unemployment benefit. If that difference increases demand, unemployment will be further reduced.

The increased demand may even lower unit costs with yet more benefit to the economy. Retail prices may therefore go down, not up. Oddly enough that is not entirely a blessing,

because the truly dangerous side effect of real investment is deflation, rather than inflation. The inflationary eventuality which one
will prefer to prevent is the growth of an over-liberal credit supply
which *cannot* be applied to real investment, and which therefore
merely pushes up the price of existing assets. Failure to prevent
that was the tragic error of the late 1980s. The violent credit explosion of that era was primed, as already shown in Chapter
Twelve, by high interest rates. If interest rates had been low, there
would have been a much greater likelihood of the credit increase
being absorbed by productive real investment. A lower exchange
rate would have also helped that result. The exchange rate would
have been lower if interest rates had been lower, a double benefit.

Capital taxation

When a government taxes its people, what it is trying to obtain is
the power to use some of the current production of goods and
services for its own purposes. For the most part any existing
goods, that is the community's capital assets, are of no use to it. It
follows that the taxation of capital, except in kind, is impossible. A
government wanting its taxes paid in cash can tax only income.
What are called capital taxes are truly income taxes computed by
reference to capital values. If a taxpayer has insufficient income to
pay a tax on his capital he must sell an asset to someone who is
saving. Then it is the *saver's* income which finances the tax. Those
economists who have advocated increased capital taxation, and
they are legion, have not clearly understood what they are about.
Some proposals, such as those emanating from the Trades Union
Congress, have envisaged tax revenues exceeding the net savings
of the personal sector of the economy. Not only is that a logical
impossibility, but it also has the effect, when attempted, of deflating capital values. Thomas Cromwell and John Russell discovered
that in the sixteenth century when they carried out the dissolution
of the monasteries. Russell, of course, turned the phenomenon to
the very long term advantage of his descendants, the Dukes of
Bedford, by buying up Abbey lands on the cheap!

In 1974 J.S.Flemming and Professor I.M.D.Little published a
pamphlet called *Why We Need a Wealth Tax*. The pamphlet avoids
any discussion of the effect of such a capital tax on security values.
Nor does it mention the natural limit which the aggregate net

saving of the community places on capital taxation, a limit which their tax proposals came very near to breaching. There was room in the pamphlet to do so, but the authors preferred to use it for emotive pictures of people hunting, of an art auction, and of the Stock Exchange. Little was Oxford University Professor of the Economics of Undeveloped Countries. His tax proposals could have helped add Britain to that category. Flemming later became economic adviser to the Bank of England. He was in due course made a Director of the Bank while Lord Lawson, not an obvious friend of capital taxation, was Chancellor of the Exchequer. His seeming inadvertence in allowing the choice evoked a protest. The reply was that Flemming had a fine academic record. Such a record may be the proper reward for being receptive of the views of one's teachers. If those views are wrong, the academic honours system perpetuates errors.

Foreign investment

Foreign investment can take several forms, only some of which necessitate savings in the home country. Often it simply means borrowing money in a foreign country and using it to create new productive assets in that country. Sometimes it can mean the purchase of existing foreign assets with capital raised in the home country. In such cases the transfer of money abroad will of necessity be matched by a movement of bank funds in the reverse direction. Sometimes the purchase can be made with capital raised abroad so that no transfer of funds abroad is required.

But sometimes foreign investment is the production at home of goods and services for use in the creation of productive assets abroad. That production may be financed either by savings, or by newly created credit. It is inevitable that this last form of investment causes an export of goods and services. Keynes knew that, of course, but he preferred investment to be made at home. This was because he, and others, believed that there is no multiplier effect when investment is made abroad. That opinion must be wrong. Because the money invested in the production of the goods and services for export is spent in the country doing the exporting there *must* be a multiplier effect: the money will circulate *only* in the home country. Moreover, as there has been an export of goods and services there must be a deficiency of the same in the home country relative to the total income of workers. The wages of the producers of the exports will therefore drive up demand for goods and services in exactly the same way as any other investment, unless it is balanced - coincidentally - by true saving (a postponement of a right to consume). Foreign investment of this kind is creating a demand for goods and services at home, but is not supplying it. If the finance for the investment is new credit, not savings, home demand will be enhanced.

Conversely a true disinvestment of assets abroad results in a real inward transfer of goods and services, which is financed by the proceeds of sale of foreign assets. It must cause an increase in imports. That too is axiomatic.

In 1985 the Trades Union Congress and the Labour Party Conference both advocated government action to force a return of the investments made abroad by British investment funds. No government action was taken, but by coincidence a substantial disinvestment from foreign assets took place at the end of 1987. It was accompanied, as one might expect, by an increase in imports and the appearance of a trade deficit. As the distribution of goods is about as expensive as their production, one of the paradoxical effects of a trade deficit, whether financed by a sale of foreign investments or by borrowing from abroad, is to increase the number of people employed in distributive trades in the importing country. Even though it may also tend to precipitate some reduction in employment in home manufacturing industries, whose competitive position is eroded by the effect of the disinvestment or borrowing on the exchange rate, an overall fall in unemployment must inevitably accompany the appearance of a trade deficit. In the three years after 1987 such a fall duly took place. The British government, failing to distinguish fact from fancy, deemed it *a recovery*. Presumably the work of distributing the increased quantity of imports was counted in the statistics as part of Gross Domestic Product, and the economy was deemed to have grown.

CHAPTER FOURTEEN

IRVING FISHER'S EQUATION

'Parturient montes, nascetur ridiculus mus.'
('The mountains will give birth;
a funny little mouse will be born.')

HORACE

'I do not believe in mathematics.'

ALBERT EINSTEIN

MONETARY THEORY boasts a fundamental equation. It is MV=PT, and its derivation is credited to Professor Irving Fisher. It states that the money supply (M) multiplied by the velocity of circulation (V) is equal to the number of transactions involving money payments (T) times the average price of each transaction (P).

The purpose of the expression 'PT' is to give the total value of all transactions during a period. The period usually chosen is a year. Ideally one would like to know the figure for each day.

The word *velocity* means speed. It is not the appropriate term for the equation. What is truly meant is the *frequency* with which money changes hands during the chosen period. If the frequency is high, one could rightly say that the money must be moving faster, but as the equation stands MV is meaningless, if not ridiculous. Only when *velocity* is replaced by *frequency* is the expression capable of calculation.

We will be pedantic and rewrite the equation as M*f*=PT, '*f*' indicating frequency, exactly as in the science of electronics.

How does one discover the average frequency with which money changes hands? It must be axiomatic that it is the total of all transactions in a certain time period divided by the total of money in use during the same period. That seems to be the only way of discovering the value of 'f'; there is no independent means of calculating its value. Unfortunately the amount of money in use is not constant for a day, let alone a year, and so a calculation of 'f' that is based on a time scale of a year gives a result which cannot be more than vaguely accurate if the active money supply is increasing or decreasing sharply. For purposes of comparing periods the figures thus derived can be misleading.

Note that we have introduced a new expression, for *the total of money in use* is not necessarily the same as *the money supply*, however one chooses to define it. There is plenty of money on bank accounts which is not used from one year's end to the next for any transaction: it remains static and is financing a permanent investment, not a transaction. No-one has yet found a way of estimating with any precision the proportion of the total money supply which is being used for transactions at any particular point in time. Moreover there are, by contrast, transactions which do not involve money on bank accounts because they are accounted for by bookkeeping entries.

PT or GNP?

Economists long ago introduced what they seemed to think was another form of the equation for, as they had no practical way of ascertaining the number and value of all transactions, they made a mental jump and assumed that PT must be the same as the total of all goods and services produced in the community during a year. For PT they therefore substituted gross national product (GNP). Table 11.5 of the 1992 Financial Statistics published by the Central Statistical Office gives frequency (velocity) of circulation ratios for M0 and M4, calculated in just such a way. The ratios show a big variation, so that over a seven-year period the highest ratio for M4 is 50 per cent above the lowest.

These published ratios are interesting but they have nothing to do with $Mf=PT$. Money transactions do not relate solely to goods and services; PT must surely include *all* transactions for which money payments take place. A vast number of movements of money relate to transactions in financial assets which are in no way part of Gross National Product. Stock Exchange transactions reached a total value of over £1.7trillion in 1987, or 5.78 times the money supply as measured by M4, whereas the ratio of Gross

National Product to M4 was only 1.48:1. Obviously a part of the money supply is tactically more important in the economy as the basis of the liquidity of the securities market than it is in financing the supply of goods and services. It helps make many non-intermediated debts and many other varieties of financial assets readily marketable. They thereby become more significant for economic activity, and, indeed, in the problem of the control of inflation.

Should one then restrict PT only to transactions which involve the sale of goods and services? If one does, how much of M does one ignore because it is not actively financing our new PT? It does not matter how one answers the first question because no-one knows for certain how much of M is used only for financial transactions. A slight indication is provided by the total of cheque clearings in the town clearing. Much of the town clearing is concerned with activity in financial markets, for it relates only to the cheque clearings between branches of banks located in the square mile of the City of London, the branches whose business tends to monopolise the transfer of money around the financial markets. However there is no reason to suppose that the figure would be consistent from year to year, or even from day to day. Money used today for a purely financial transaction could tomorrow be used to finance the purchase of a Rolls-Royce motor car.

PT is greater than GNP

A second objection to the replacement of PT by GNP is that the sale of goods and services does not take place only at the point of final consumption. An item can be the subject of many sales during its progress to the consumer, and each transaction includes the value of every previous transaction, plus the value added since the last transaction. Every industry would have to be fully integrated vertically for PT to equal GNP. PT *has* to be vastly greater than GNP, and it *must* be PT, not GNP, which dictates what monetary resources a community needs.

Moreover the need for money will be affected by changes in the industrial structure. If a vertically integrated business is dismembered into its smaller components (as was Bowater), those transactions which were once intercompany transfers involving internal book entries become external sales and purchases which require the use of the money supply. The frequency of circulation will probably increase following such a change, but the quantity of money may need to be higher too. A merger which brought about more vertical integration might have the opposite effect.

GNP a function of M?

It is undeniable that at any one moment in time a certain supply of money, and of credit, is required to sustain a particular level of economic activity. The precise requirement will differ greatly both from country to country and from one time to another. The exact level of money requirement for a given level of production will be dependent on the interrelation of a host of factors. Some will be environmental or customary, some will be legal, some will depend on the structure of the capital market. All the relevant factors are liable to change at one time or another. Predicting the changes or their effects is difficult, if not impossible, though economists have not been discouraged thereby from trying to make forecasts.

Monetary theorists, such as Professor Milton Friedman and Anna J. Schwarz, having observed that a certain level of economic activity requires a certain level of money supply, went on to claim that if one controlled the money supply one would also control the level of economic activity. But economic man reacts against government controls, and the consequence is that they produce dynamic reactions which are neither intended nor anticipated. Cynical observers are inclined to conclude that the public's reaction will wreck *any* control system. This phenomenon led Professor Charles Goodhart to propose a new law of economics,

> *'that any observed statistical regularity will tend to collapse once pressure is placed upon it for control purposes.'*

Goodhart's Law, as it is called, may seem to some economists to be just a joke, but it is undoubtedly true. The public is not a set of programmed robots, mindless and unreacting, to be manipulated by arrogant economists. For every action by a government which is attempting to control the economy there is bound to be a reaction by members of the public, a reaction beyond the expectation of the planner. The reaction does not even have the simple virtue of being *equal and opposite* as in Newton's famous Third Law of Motion! Unfortunately Professor Goodhart's cynical but wholly accurate observation has not, it would appear, demoralised enthusiastic monetarists, nor has it dissuaded many interventionist politicians from fruitless actions.

The constant velocity syndrome

Before monetarists could suggest seriously that monetary controls would be effective they had to prove that they could accurately calculate the money supply requirement for a given level of economic activity. Studies were made of the relationship of GNP and other key variables to the money supply in both America and Britain over a long period of time. The chosen measure of the money supply in Britain was £M3, which is very roughly the sterling deposits of the clearing banks. The claim of the experts (notably Professor Milton Friedman and Professor Sir Alan Walters) was that these studies showed a remarkably stable relationship between GNP and the money supply except in unusual circumstances such as war. Can the frequency of circulation of M3 money really be a constant? If so, why?

As a wrong application of the control of the money supply can devastate an economy, there must be no doubt about the answers to the two questions in the last paragraph before any monetarist is allowed to try to exercise control. Unfortunately, the gravest of doubts must remain. Even if there were no doubts about past relationships of the money supply to economic activity, would not Goodhart's Law apply in the event of the *statistical regularity* being made use of *for control purposes*?

Irregularities

Those who have carried out the studies admit that they have had to ignore periods of great irregularity such as war, and that raises the question of why war should cause an irregularity in a constant. They have also had to assume that the relationship is a lagged one. Rather tricky statistical techniques have had to be used. Are they reliable techniques, or are they being used to make the wanted result appear? The great '*Why*' question, the root question which any physical scientist will ask, does not seem to have been answered at all. That question is, '*Why should the money supply and the Gross National Product and other "key variables" have a precise and constant functional relationship?*' What mechanism of cause and effect makes the stable functional relationship exist? Why does it cease to be stable in a war?

The detection of lagged relationships is a statistical minefield. By lagging a response one can prove that black equals white. Lag the response to the sun's rise by twelve hours and the rising of the sun is the cause of night! Such statistical tricks can provide many marvellous opportunities to charlatans and quacks.

Causes of instability

One can readily think of many reasons why there can be no stable functional relationship. Some we have already mentioned, but we must now list a few more of the phenomena which we would expect to accompany, of necessity, a stable relationship between the money supply and the gross national product. They are:-

1. The structure of the capital market must be constant. There must be no variation at all in the ratio of the total quantity of intermediated capital to the total of non-intermediated capital. The ratio of capital to GNP must also remain forever constant, or, alternatively, a change in the latter must be compensated for by a change in the former.

2. There must be no change in the level of the requirement for consumer finance. It must be a constant ratio of GNP.

3. There must be no change in the overall effect of vertical integration in industry, or in the overall effect of mergers. Therefore any move to vertical integration by one business must be balanced by a disintegration of equal effect in another industry.

4. The proportions of people paid weekly, two weekly, monthly, or for any other period must remain constant. Any switch from weekly payment to monthly payment would tend to require a greater money supply as the frequency of circulation is likely to be reduced by more than three-quarters.

5. The amount of housing finance required must maintain a constant ratio to GNP.

6. The introduction of new methods of payment, such as credit and debit cards, must have no effect on the overall demand for currency ('M0'), or on the overall level of outstanding debt.

7. The increase in the level of saving through pension schemes which has taken place over decades must be exactly balanced by compensating falls in other forms of saving in order to have no effect on the money supply.

8. There must be no big swing towards endowment mortgages from subscription mortgages as the former require a larger money supply. (In practice the use of endowment mortgages went from one per cent or so to 80 per cent in the course of 40 years, most of the swing taking place in a decade.)

9. There must be no variation in the proportion of the banks' assets invested in government bonds and bills. (Over a period of forty years the proportion has in fact gone from 67 per cent to 0.5 per cent.)

One could surely add substantially to this list of things which would have to remain constant as ratios to GNP or, alternatively, whose changes must be negated by an equal and opposite change in some other influence on the quantity of money required. But is it necessary to go further? Is it not axiomatic that none of those things which are required to remain constant ever do so? Because they are not immutable it is impossible to arrive at an econometric formula which will determine what change in the money supply is needed for a given alteration in GNP. The Friedman-Schwarz edifice of theory collapses under the impact of reality.

For monetary strategy to work with any precision a constant relationship between the Gross National Product and the money supply is essential. If there is no constant relationship how can one determine the desirable level of the money supply? Only by inspired and experienced guesswork.

Some eminent monetarists have long conceded that there is no constant relationship. Professor Sir Alan Walters, writing in 1969 in the Institute of Economic Affairs publication, *Money in Boom and Slump*, puts the position as follows overleaf:-

'We cannot predict at all accurately the effects of an increase in the quantity of money on prices and incomes.

'On the other hand, it has been argued by Professor Milton Friedman of the University of Chicago, and by a rapidly growing school of monetary economists in the United States that the velocity of circulation, although not a constant, does behave in a systematic and predictable way. Broadly speaking they argue that, as the quantity of money is increased, the velocity of circulation also increases. Thus, money incomes increase even more than the increase in the quantity of money. Similarly, when the quantity of money is decreased, so the velocity follows it down. (This implies inter alia that the monetary leverage is large, i.e. a small change in money has a large effect.)'

Professor Sir Alan Walters was sensitive to the criticism that the velocity of circulation is not a constant. In a footnote on page 28 of the book he writes:-

'It is remarkable that the "constant velocity" strawman is the one most frequently attacked by the anti-money school. Sometimes they attribute these views to monetary economists: demonstrating that the monetarists are wrong is then like taking candy from a baby. An example is Mr. Jay's allegation that Professor Friedman is trying to prove that the velocity is constant ("The Times" 29th May 1968.) Professor Friedman has always insisted that only a rigid orthodox quantity theorist would pretend that the velocity is constant; rather one seeks systematic variation and enduring regularities.'

So there is no constant, but there is a regularity! Even if there were, would it survive the intervention of government economists? Or would there just be a Mad Hatter's Tea Party?

When 'M*f*' does not equal 'PT'

At the beginning of this chapter we defined 'T' as being the total of transactions which involve money payments. That distinction is made in order to exclude non-money, or book entries, of which there are myriads being made every day by way of entries in books of account, and these make no use of the intermediated money supply. If the distinction is not made then M*f* does not equal PT. The standard textbook on monetary economics by B. Kettel does not make this distinction.

How to hide money

It is also possible for accounting practices to hide a great part of the true money supply. Multi-national companies, and other big holding companies, commonly have departments which they call their 'treasuries', and these act as bankers to their self-accounting subsidiary companies. The use of a treasury diminishes the apparent money supply as the bank accounts of the group are netted down to one bank balance in the name of the parent company.

Some subsidiaries may be borrowers, while some carry large credit balances. The parent company lowers its financing costs a little by using the credit balances to fund the debtor companies. That could also be done by intercompany loans, but it is much more effective for the holding company to act as banker for the subsidiaries so that all daily variations in debit and credit balances are automatically netted out immediately. Possibly the largest treasury operation is that of the British Petroleum Company (BP). If that operation is as large as rumour avers, one would expect the Bank of England to insist that BP's treasury be recognised as a bank, that the individual balances of subsidiary companies be reported, and thus included in the official statistics.

There was once a proposal that the Law Society should act as banker for all solicitors in order to get a cheaper banking service. The aggregate of the balances under the control of solicitors must be enormous. If the debit and credit balances were netted out so that only the net figure was reflected on an account at a recognised bank, the implications for the money supply figures would be very significant. But a more serious practical problem would then be that a slice of the banking system's free capital reserves would become redundant, making it available to support the creation of more credit. If the Law Society had gone ahead with its proposal (it is presumed that it did not), it should have been treated as a regular bank and required to hold reserves equal to eight per cent of the gross credit balances as reflected in the books of each individual solicitor's practice.

A philosophers' stone for economists?

Given the many probable defects in the money supply figures must we conclude that econometricians have been pursuing a philosophers' stone that cannot exist? Their confident assertion of a predictable regularity in the frequency of circulation of money must be rejected for want of proof so long as the money supply cannot be defined and measured. The definition used by Professor Friedman in those of his papers which were published by the Institute of Economic Affairs under the title *Monetarist Economics* was the one known as *M3*. But publication of M3 has ceased. Presumably the official statisticians decided that it was no longer valid as a useful measure of the money supply. As British research into the regularity of the frequency of circulation used a measure of the money supply no longer considered valid, the tempting conclusion is that the result of the research into the relation of M3 to GNP is not valid either.

On page 177 we claimed that PT, and not GNP, determines the level of M. A constant functional relationship solely between M and GNP is impossible because PT, which determines M, has no constant relationship with GNP. Any function relating M to GNP must therefore include in its parameters the variations in the relationship of PT to GNP. Estimating the variations looks likely to be beyond the predictive power of any economist.

At the commencement of this book it was asserted that true monetary theory must accord with empirical facts. In the latest argument we have sought to prove that some facts discovered by painstaking research are invalid because they are inconsistent with basic theoretical considerations. By relying on theory, not facts, have we betrayed our principles? Would it not have been better to have proved that the facts discovered by the research were wrong? Much as we feel that our theoretical arguments are overwhelming, we accept that they do constitute only a hypothesis, not proof. However as no factual research is possible without a proper definition of one of the key variables in the function which we are discussing, what more can we do?

The significance of M0

In the late 1980s, after every other indicator of the money supply had proved misleading, the government acted on advice that it should regard M0 as the most significant monetary indicator. M0 is banknotes and coin. One can see that as it is mainly used for retail purchases, it could be a better indicator of overall economic activity than M3, a greater proportion of which is perhaps used for transactions before the point of final sale to the consumer.

However the figure for currency in circulation arouses both one's curiosity, and some suspicion. Why is the figure so large? Sterling banknotes in circulation in April 1991 amounted to £15.4billion. That was £275 for every man, woman and child in Britain, or more than £660 per household. As the pockets of the populace do not obviously bulge, the large figure can only be explained on the basis that a large proportion of the currency in issue is tucked away out of sight, being held primarily as a store of value and not as a medium of exchange.

Why should this be so? The popular assumption is that it reflects the frequent use of currency in the black economy and by criminals, the two sectors of the population which prefer the anonymity of currency. So for M0 to be a useful economic indicator one needs to assume that the level of activity in the black economy, and in the criminal world, is a constant proportion of all economic activity. Rising crime statistics rule out that assumption. According to the little memo of interesting statistics which the C.S.O. has been distributing to celebrate its fiftieth anniversary, crime has increased ten times in fifty years. Is that trend reflected in the Treasury's computer model of the economy?

In fact we do know exactly where about one third of M0 is; it belongs to the banks, and is kept in their tills and strongrooms.

Blind belief

There can be little if any doubt that the level of the money supply, in that it reflects the level of the intermediated credit supply, is of great concern to governments. Professor David Laidler, who is one of the leading philosophers of monetarism, is quite correct when he writes in the introduction to his collection of essays called *Monetary Perspectives* (Philip Allan, 1982),

> *'Above all, the essays which follow are motivated by the belief that the behaviour of the quantity of money is very important (though not all-important) for the behaviour, not*

just of real income and employment, but also and in particular of the general price level.'

His very next sentence, however, moves from the realm of belief based on truth to that of blind belief. He says:-

This belief in turn is related to another belief, which, I insist, is the sine qua non of monetarism: namely, that there exists a stable aggregate demand function for money.'

If one translates the word *money* into *intermediated credit*, as we have advocated, a destructive question immediately suggests itself. How can the intermediated credit supply be stable when it is liable to be converted into non-intermediated credit at any time, and in any quantity? If the ultimate determinant of the intermediated credit supply is the capital base of the banks, it is the *supply* of money which is more likely to be stable, so long as the banks' capital base is stable, and not the *aggregate demand function for money*. Otherwise the banks would have to raise new capital every time the demand for money rose, whether it was profitable to do so or not. Or is a stable demand function for money equivalent to an *unaltering* demand for money? As the demand for credit and its supply are interactive, there can be no simple answer.

The effect of the level of income

Professor Laidler's *stable aggregate demand function for money*, though connected with the theory of a constant velocity for money, is more subtle than the often criticised and oversimplistic form of that belief, for his function takes into account factors other than the GNP and the money supply. One additional factor is the individual's level of income. There must surely be some relationship between aggregate individual incomes and GNP, though the relationship could be variable because of the irregular supply of, or demand for, credit. The granting of credit increases demand above the level determined solely by income. An increase in the level of personal sector debt relative to personal sector income increases spending, and thereby GNP. At first sight this appears to increase the ratio of GNP to income. But as it also raises aggregate income, because money lent becomes income in the hands of the person supplying the goods and services on which it is spent, there is a tendency for the ratio of GNP to income to be restored. This must encourage Professor Laidler.

Although much research and ingenuity has been devoted to finding an equation which emulates the demand function for money, it must remain very doubtful whether any emulation can produce accurate calculations. It is right to be very agnostic as to whether the function can be stable, for, as we have already suggested, there are many factors affecting the demand for money which must change erratically and with considerable but irregular frequency. All these factors would have to be emulated. There is, in addition, far too much doubt about the reliability of the estimation of the constants in the function for it to be used for the management of the economy as if it were a truly scientific tool. Finally, it is not *the aggregate demand function for* **money** which is of first importance but *the aggregate demand function for* **credit**. The demand function for money *must* be subservient to the demand function for credit, for it is the latter which initiates the creation of money. By looking for a demand function for money one is on the wrong side of the looking glass, as well as on the wrong side of the balance sheet.

Models

In determined pursuit of the philosophers' stone econometricians have constructed mathematical models, which are designed to emulate the functioning of the economy. They should indeed be called *emulations*, and not *models*, a term which sometimes confuses students. Emulations are dubious intellectual exercises but they fascinate many economists. If there were no faults or assumptions in them, they would work in the same way, and with the same accuracy, as an electronic circuit. Put in only one assumption and the emulation ceases to be reliable. All emulations must contain many parameters which are assumptions, and many constants which are unreliable and not constant at all.

One would certainly not want to travel to the moon if the spacecraft's computer were filled with equations and data of the quality with which applied economists have to be content. Yet the lives and well-being of countless millions are affected by the decisions influenced by such calculations, not just a couple of spacewalkers who know they are risking their lives. Put into such perspective the complacency of econometricians is horrifying.

Professor Alan Peacock[1] in the Seventh Wincott Memorial Lecture (Institute of Economic Affairs Occasional Paper 50, Page 15) put the criticism as follows:-

> '...the illusion that mathematical skill is a protection against the penetration of ethical bias and a complete substitute for imaginative insight into the workings of the economic system is widespread.'

In such circumstances the inspired guess of an experienced observer of the economy is likely to be more accurate than the computerised emulation. The human brain, when working in its *super-logic* mode (unconscious reasoning, a process sometimes called *intuition)*, and when well programmed by long and close experience, can sometimes compute the likely result of a huge mass of varied and variable inputs far better than any computer which has been programmed with conscious logic. Unfortunately, the processes of unconscious logic are, to use computer terminology, transparent. That means they cannot be observed while they are proceeding, and therefore one cannot test the programming of the individual's mind for correctness, nor decide whether his intuitive reasoning is reliable. On the other hand the level of unreliability of the most sophisticated economic model is fairly obvious.

The real problem for monetarists

At the risk of repetition we again emphasise the importance of the underlying problem in monetary theory, the definition of the money supply. Money is declared to have three purposes. It is a store of value; it is a medium of exchange; and it is a measure of value. But money is not the only store of value, for any debt is a store of value. Other stores of value can in certain money markets be used as a medium of exchange. As a measure of value, money is variable and inconsistent, but it is the best measure, indeed the only universal measure, which can be devised.

Money (or debt) is very easily created and its creation brings prosperity. To reduce the quantity of money (or debt) does the opposite. Much money has been created by the granting of loans which one cannot realistically expect to be repaid. Such debt overhangs the world economy like a sword of Damocles. When the public is overborrowed is it not better slowly to erode away its excess debt by gentle inflation? That is preferable to the prospect of banks going into liquidation. Is it not possible that inflation, though wholly condemned by moralists as well as by politicians and economists, has on many occasions saved mankind from more terrible sufferings? In the days when currencies were based on precious metals, and therefore less easy to depreciate, debt led to revolution. The condemnation of usury by several religions must surely stem from this phenomenon.

A flawed concept

Before we leave Fisher's famous equation we should contemplate the possibility that it is based on a conceptual flaw. Fisher was a great mathematician but his approach to money is just as simplistic as that of the man in the street whose attitude is, '*I have money in my pocket, and some more in the bank, and I shall spend it.*' Fisher has totalled all the money in all the pockets and in all the bank accounts, and considered what that total means for spending potential. He has ignored the fact that there are accounts in debit at the bank totalling slightly more than the deposits, and the *negative money*, to coin an expression, on those accounts can circulate. In fact there is a strong possibility that one-quarter of all money payments are made from accounts with debit balances upon them to other accounts which are in debit.

A bank manager watching the transactions going through his customers' accounts sees four classes of payments:-

1. From an account in credit to an account in credit.
2. From an account in credit to an account in debit.
3. From an account in debit to an account in debit.
4. From an account in debit to an account in credit .

Classes one and three have no effect on the total money supply. Class four increases the money supply by the amount of the payment. Class two reduces the money supply, but how much it does so will depend on whether the payment pushes the receiving account out of the red. For the money supply to remain constant all the payments in classes two and four must have no net effect. A bookmaker who accepted a bet at odds of infinity to one on that ever happening could sleep very soundly.

Fisher's equation assumes that all payments are class one, yet they may be only a quarter of all transactions. Half of Britain's smaller businesses are in debt to their bankers, and payments taking place among them will mostly be from or to overdrawn accounts only. Such payments must represent a considerable proportion of interbusiness transactions.

How does one reflect the power of *negative money* in an equation? Should one add the assets and liabilities of the banks together to arrive at the true money supply? How does one take into account the constant change in M because of class two and class four transactions? The equation has a variable in it which needs to be invariable if it is to be of any practical use.

Fisher's equation has very little use; it is a classroom curiosity whose variations may have some obscure meaning which patient work may ascertain, but only long after it has ceased to matter. By then the current meaning of the frequency of circulation will be different. The equation is an academic's plaything, like Rubik's Cube. The determination of the correct level of the money supply can never be a matter of mechanical computation suitable for a computer emulation; it will remain an affair of inspired guesswork resulting from constant careful observation of what is happening in real time in the financial world. The question to be asked is, *'What tricks are the financiers up to today?'*, rather than *'What is the level of the money supply?'* It was the lack of real time observation which caused the supervising authority of the banking system to fail to check the eruption of the great volcano of credit in 1988.

Note on Chapter Fourteen:-

1. The whole paragraph from which this quotation is taken, and the one which follows it, are a savage attack on the remoteness of young researchers from reality, even though Peacock prefaces his remarks with the words, *'I do not wish to promote knocking copy for those who would jeer at the developments.....'*

CHAPTER FIFTEEN

HIGH INTEREST RATE PROBLEMS

'Debt is the worst poverty.'
THOMAS FULLER, M.D.

1. ALLOWING FOR INFLATION

MONETARIST LITERATURE contains many references to the importance of inflationary expectations and to the effect of changes in such expectations. In any emulation of the economy the demand functions for money and/or credit should therefore incorporate subsidiary functions which will enable the emulation to predict the effect of changing expectations.

But what rate of inflation is to be applied? There are many different indices of inflation, all unsatisfactory in some respect. Keynes described many of the problems of constructing inflation indices in his *Treatise on Money*. Those problems have never been resolved, but we have learned to live with them, which is another way of saying that we have ignored them.

Whose inflationary expectations are to be taken into account? That too must vary with circumstances. Moreover the general public's understanding of inflation, even after a lifetime's continuous experience of it, must still be quite defective or no money would be invested in building societies, or in any investment with a fixed redemption value. Even professional accountants do not want to know about inflation. When accountants were pressed in the 1970s to introduce a form of inflation accounting, the leaders of the professional institutes and associations found that there was strong opposition from a large proportion of their members.

Every individual in the population has a different expectation of inflation (or none at all). An example of the inability to understand inflation is the great philosopher, mathematician, and Nobel Prize winner, Bertrand Russell. Russell was one of the mainstays of the radio programme, *The Brains Trust*, which was so popular during the 1939-45 War. He owned a fine modern house with large grounds and a fine view. When he sold the house it was against his principles to make a profit, so his price was what he had paid for it. In the time between purchase and sale there was considerable inflation, especially of house prices, so in real terms the great Russell was making a loss. If any man ever came close to knowing everything about everything, it was Bertrand Russell, but even he could not distinguish a real profit from a nominal one.[1]

An average of extremely divergent expectations is a meaningless and useless statistic. Consequently there is *no* satisfactory way to emulate the effect of inflationary expectations.

Current cost accounting

Allowing for inflation is a very technical subject, and economists who have no accountancy experience can go badly awry in their understanding of it. This was regrettably illustrated by a paper published by the Bank of England in the May 1988 issue of its Quarterly. This paper argued that the real rate of interest (that is after deducting inflation from the nominal rate of interest) was lower in Britain than the real rates experienced by Britain's trading rivals. It therefore urged industrialists not to hesitate to go ahead with schemes of investment, and not to be inhibited by high nominal interest rates. It also argued that as interest was deductible against profits for the purpose of assessing corporation tax, it was the *net of tax* real rate of interest which should be taken into account. It was suggested that the net of tax real rate of interest at that time was negative!

There were three faults in the paper. One was a matter of fact about the rates of interest experienced abroad. Confidential information from the treasurer of a major multi-national company revealed that the rates of interest his company was paying in the countries mentioned was lower than those stated in the paper. The author of the paper said that special care had been taken to get the rates right. Nevertheless something must have gone wrong.

The second fault was the author's lack of knowledge of the detailed procedure for inflation accounting. The third error was his assumption that all money borrowed for business expansion is spent on assets whose prices rise with inflation.

Money borrowed to provide capital for a business may well finance debtors and work-in-progress. Indeed something like half of all borrowing by small businesses may finance debtors. In the terminology of inflation accounting debtors give rise to *a holding loss*. Borrowings, on the other hand, give rise to *a holding gain*. In less technical language this means that one profits from inflation in respect of borrowings, and loses from inflation in respect of lendings. If money is borrowed to finance debtors, a holding gain is cancelled out by a holding loss. Therefore one may not deduct the rate of inflation from the rate of interest on the loan. The real rate of interest is absolutely identical with the nominal rate of interest paid on any money borrowed to finance debtors.

The same may or may not be true of borrowing to finance stock or work-in-progress. Which way it goes will depend on whether the industrialist is able to charge selling prices which reflect the increased cost of future purchases of stock and of future work-in-progress. Very often public opinion prevents him from doing so. As any increases in selling prices will be wholly profit for tax purposes, in practice he not only needs to raise his prices by the amount of inflation, but by the inflation rate *grossed up at his marginal rate of tax*. Only that way can he obtain from his sales all the cash he will need in order to restock to the same level and to continue to finance the same physical level of production.

If borrowings are invested in plant and machinery, there may be a holding gain from inflation, but additional depreciation will need to be charged in order to depreciate at replacement cost.

The author of the Bank of England paper was also mistaken in suggesting that the true rate of interest is the net rate less the allowance for corporation tax. He was wrong in two ways. The first was his failure to appreciate that for any industrialist all taxes are effectively a cost of production. That is perhaps best proved by pointing out that without a tax burden a producer could cut his prices. It does not matter a bureaucrat's paper clip to him whether he pays corporation tax on his profits, or the receiver of his gross interest payments is liable for tax on them. The money goes to the

Revenue either way. The second fault is that corporation tax may not be an issue if the loan finances new capital equipment. Capital allowances of at least 25 per cent a year (40 per cent in first year from 1992) would probably eliminate any tax charge in the first couple of years, and by the time there is a tax charge, cash flow may have substantially reduced the loan. For that reason too the nominal rate of interest reflects the full cost of the borrowing.

If an industrialist had increased his borrowing in pursuance of the advice of the writer in the Bank of England Quarterly, what would have subsequently happened? The answer is that within a year the company would have been paying nearly twice as much interest, and the expected profit would have turned into a very substantial loss. It is very likely that their inflationary expectations played a far smaller part in the minds of company directors in 1988 than their expectations regarding interest rates. Those whose expectations about interest rates had been optimistic in 1988 went on to see their companies go into receivership.

How does one feed into a computer emulation of the British economy the expectation of worried company directors that the government might fool about with interest rates? How does one emulate the operation of *Goodhart's Law*?

Equity or loans: the decision

An entrepreneur chooses to use loan capital instead of equity capital not because of tax relief, but either because the tax rate is lower, or because he hopes to make a profit with the borrowed money which is greater than the interest he will pay. As at April 1991 the tax rate on profits was 33 per cent. On interest it was 25 per cent. Whether such a difference could produce an advantage would depend upon rates of return on the differing forms of capital. Inflation comes into the calculation, but in a very complex way, not in the oversimplified manner suggested by the Bank of England's researcher.

The Bank of England's paper seriously underestimated the effect of high interest rates because it made a blanket adjustment for inflation and tax which was rarely appropriate in real life cases. Not for the first time the validity of an economist's theorising had been crippled through his lack of knowledge of the principles and practice of accountancy, and of the detail of the tax laws.

There are two worrying aspects of the matter. One is that this paper might have been sanctioned by John S. Flemming, then Chief Economic Adviser to the Bank of England, and later a director of the Bank, for he had written a book on inflation, as well as the pamphlet advocating a wealth tax which was criticised in an earlier chapter. The second was that the paper was recommended and circulated by Walter Eltis, chief economist and later director of the National Economic Development Office. When that was closed he moved to the Department of Trade.

Perhaps the Civil Service College could try harder to correct and improve the technical expertise in accounting and taxation of economic advisers to the British government.

Exchange rates

In the period 1988 to 1990 MLR doubled. Interest rate increases of this order are devastating. A country must never put itself in a position in which it has no option other than to raise interest rates to very high levels. One circumstance which places a country in such a position is when membership of a fixed exchange rate system makes it necessary to raise interest rates in order to maintain the agreed exchange rate for the currency. Three times in the twentieth century Britain has opted to go into fixed exchange rate systems; on all three occasions it did so at a rate of exchange which was above the sustainable valuation of the pound sterling. On all three occasions the move was totally defeated, at very great cost, by market forces. It is impossible to put a value on the trail of irreparable and unnecessary damage which followed these three decisions; cumulatively the destructive effect on the British economy has been enormous.

A non-performing loan

There is another interesting technical difficulty with the argument that only real interest rates matter to a borrower. While a company may legitimately take into account the benefit from the effect of inflation on all its debts when ascertaining its true profitability, it still has to consider its cash flow. In appropriate circumstances inflation may turn a trading loss, as determined by historic cost accounting, into a profit when it is determined by current cost accounting, but the cash flow will still be negative. To benefit fully from inflation a company needs to borrow to pay the interest on its earlier borrowings. At the end of a year of 10 per cent inflation the finance director of a company which has borrowed heavily may say to the bank manager, *'Look, my dear chap, if you add most of the interest to the principal, the total may look more than it was a year ago, but if you adjust for inflation you will find that the amount outstanding after the addition of interest is much the same in real terms as it was last year, and your security has risen in value by the same proportion.'*

To that the bank manager may sadly reply, *'That is very nice in theory, but, as you have paid me nothing in interest, your loan is techni-cally non-performing. I must provide for it in my accounts as a bad or doubtful debt. If I omit to do so, the bank's auditors will report it to the Bank of England and qualify their audit report on our accounts. So sorry, old boy, but you are being a bit too clever-clever!'*

The study paper in the Bank of England Quarterly was there-fore suggesting something which the Bank in its other role as supervisor of the banking industry ought to have some difficulty in countenancing. In practice the point never seems to have arisen in Britain, but only because everyone must have conspired to turn a Nelsonian blind eye to it. That could indeed be a very sensible practical solution, but it is a solution which needs to be adopted consciously, if it is to be a continuing policy. The likelihood is, however, that if some companies get into serious financial difficul-ties, the practice of ignoring technical non-performance of loans will be condemned. Everyone is wise after the ship has capsized.

A crucial calculation

Here is a strikingly important calculation which seems to be consistently avoided:-

The lowest Bank Rate in the period 1920 to 1971 was two per cent; MLR in 1990 reached 15 per cent, a difference of 13 per cent. At the end of 1990 M4 was £473billion. Total intermediated lendings would have been somewhat higher than that figure, but it will quite suffice for our purpose to calculate 13 per cent of £473billion: it is £62billion. This is the approximate figure by which interest charges on intermediated loans, (and therefore costs,) were higher in 1990 than they would have been if MLR had been two per cent. It was the equivalent of 12.8 per cent of

GDP at factor cost. Put another way, high interest rates inflated GDP by 14.7 per cent. We cannot calculate what addition to costs was caused by higher interest rates on non-intermediated loans.

The amount of the additional sum need not be ascertained; it suffices to look at the figure of 14.7 per cent of G.D.P. and say to the government, '*This is the minimum additional cost which was borne as a result of your interest rate policy. Such an additional cost* **must** *have been inflationary. High interest rates* **must** *be a major cause of the inflation of prices. You could achieve a* **true** *reduction in costs by lowering interest rates. Indeed you might even have the grievous misfortune to precipitate a deflationary spiral!*'

Passing the debt parcel

One effect of the raising of interest rates in the unsuccessful fight against inflation was that some finance directors sought to stall the payment of debts to their companies' suppliers. By doing so they successfully passed the debt parcel on to their suppliers, and much of it ultimately ended up with the smaller companies which supplied the big ones. The banks and the media complained about the high rate of failure of small companies. One would like to know how often was the insolvency of a smaller business the result of having to pay high interest rates on money borrowed to finance debts due from a bigger company?[2]

Monetarist economists appear to be unaware of the fact that in the business world a vast amount of debt relates to trading debtors and creditors. Indeed the amount is so great that it would seriously call into question the monetary economists' obsessive concern with only the intermediated money supply even if there were no other compelling reasons for doing so.

A random example illustrates the importance of trade credit. The company's name is withheld for fear of wrongly appearing to imply that it was one of those companies guilty of exploiting its creditors. It is a large multi-national company, and its accounts showed that as at the 31st December 1990 the overdrafts and loan capital of the company amounted to £90.6million, of which £77.8million was lent by banks. But other creditors who were entitled to payment within one year totalled £210.2million. They included trade creditors of £93.9million, and over £50million in taxation; debtors totalled £195.2million.

2. THIRD AND FIRST WORLD DEBT.

In much of the twentieth century the worldwide fashion of state ownership of industry has increased for many governments the problem of getting the tax revenue which they need. For reasons which need not be discussed here state owned industries tend to run at a loss, and socialism seems to lead to expensive subsidies and other social expenditures which are high, and not always rational. Taxation is also used for social engineering in a crude and short-sighted way. As a consequence taxes have to be high, and marginal rates of tax are even higher.

Once the marginal tax rate reaches a certain level, dodging tax becomes a way of life. Few countries seem to have a tax collection system as effective as that in Britain. Britain's success in enforcing very high tax rates may be a dangerous virtue which helps damage the British economy. Even British governments, however, have had deficits which have encouraged inflation. In other countries which do not have such an effective tax gathering system a short-fall in tax revenue has led to the practice of printing banknotes with which to pay for the expenditure. Hyperinflation is caused in this way. Inevitably, those who live in a country which is experiencing high inflation try to deposit their money in a foreign bank, and in a foreign currency. Strict exchange controls only slightly lessen such a tendency. The result is that those countries which have achieved low inflation rates have seen big inflows of deposits from abroad, and the high interest rate policies pursued by First World countries have increased the attraction enormously.

A bonanza for bankers?

The bankers of the industrialised world see this tendency as a wonderful business opportunity. Nor do they limit themselves to deposits in their own currencies. They are prepared to denominate deposits in any good currency they can succeed in lending. Often the result is an element in the money supply which is completely beyond the control of the country in whose currency the foreign based deposits are denominated. Indeed the procedure may make nonsense of attempts to control the domestic money supply. Certainly British regulators concern themselves only with the *sterling* deposits of British banks, the so-called *Sterling M3* (£M3), owned by British residents. The United States government probably has no control over the creation of *Euro-dollar deposits*, nor over the creation of dollar denominated bonds in the non-intermediated credit markets of the world.

Governments should have been more worried at what their countries' bankers were doing. International banking can produce big profits, but it carries with it enormous risks. Those risks are not necessarily confined to the shareholders of the banks; they can threaten the living standards of the whole population.

Transferring wealth around the world

Real wealth is goods and services, not money, and the only way to transfer real wealth from country to country is by a transfer of goods and services. A transfer of money which is unaccompanied by a transfer of real wealth is a two way affair: whatever money is transferred in one direction has to be fully matched by a transfer of money in the other direction. Any difference in the relative demand for the two currencies being exchanged influences the exchange rate between them. If a deposit is made abroad by a citizen of a country which has no trading surplus, there has to be an equal and opposite lending of money back to his country if the books are to balance, which, of course, they must.

For example, when the citizens of the Argentine started to deposit in foreign banks the foreign currency which they had acquired, it was necessary at times when the Argentine had no trade surplus with the outside world for the money accumulated abroad by Argentine citizens to be lent back to the Argentine, normally to its government. Loans to a foreign government were termed *sovereign lending*,[3] which was thought to be safer than lending to Argentine citizens. Time was to tell that the safety of the loans was not so great as was hoped. Many had to be classified as non-performing, and some were written off against reserves.

This experience was paralleled in many countries, even in those in the communist block. Some foreign depositors were not just ordinary citizens but criminals, including corrupt rulers. It is thought that sometimes the money secreted abroad had been received earlier as foreign aid. In one case it was suggested that the president of the country had sufficient money invested abroad to be able to pay off the whole of his country's foreign borrowings.

In another it was said that a drug baron had sufficient dollars in foreign banks to do the same thing.

It is possible that this flight of deposits to foreign banks might not have been so great had First World interest rates been lower. In a free market it is possible that the risks of keeping money in a Third World currency might have been compensated for by a higher rate of interest. If currencies such as the dollar had earned extremely low interest, perhaps Argentinians might have preferred local deposits. With the dollar giving rates of 17 per cent at the height of the high interest rate era there was no likelihood of repatriation of foreign-owned dollar deposits. Another effect of the deposits in America was to enable, if not to cause, the United States to run up a huge trade deficit. This happened with great rapidity once the American banks ceased to lend the deposits back to their country of origin, and instead lent the money in America itself. As the banks became less and less willing to lend to Third World countries, those countries had to become net exporters of real wealth, wealth their populations could ill afford to give up.

'*To him that hath shall be given, and from him that hath not shall be taken away even that which he hath*' is one biblical quotation which might also be a significant law of economics.

The risks of Third World lending

The danger was that the money lent abroad would prove to be irrecoverable, but the deposits from abroad would still remain as liabilities of the banks. A clever supervising authority would have insisted that British banks should accept deposits from abroad only into a subsidiary company, and that all loans abroad should be made only from the same subsidiary company. In the event of the loans going bad the subsidiary company could be allowed to go bust without any recourse to the parent company. (Of course the subsidiary should have been properly capitalised initially with the normal reserves of free capital.) Thus the losers would have been the foreign depositors. There would have been no danger of the parent bank's domestic banking operations being dragged into insolvency because of the failure of foreign debtors.

Table 10.5 of the Financial Statistics for 1991 reveals the extent of the danger: as at 30th June 1991 the external foreign currency liabilities of all United Kingdom banks reached a peak of

£553billion. No doubt this huge figure was magnified by the inclusion of the liabilities of foreign banks which operate in Britain, but which are not truly *United Kingdom Banks*. Only six months later the figure had declined to £497billion, giving an indication, perhaps, that some repatriation of Third World money was taking place.

Two British banks did originally run much of their foreign business through partly owned subsidiaries. Lloyds Bank had a large subsidiary operating mainly in South America which was called *The Bank of London and South America*. Barclays used *Barclays Bank International*, a successor to the bank once known as *Barclays Bank Dominion Colonial and Overseas*. Lloyds and Barclays later took full control over these subsidiaries, and then did a quite amazing thing: they both sought the approval of Parliament to merge the parent bank with the subsidiary which dealt with foreign business. When the wisdom of assuming the liabilities of their subsidiaries was questioned, both banks said that there was no point in maintaining the limited liability of the subsidiaries as the Bank of England would never allow a British bank to use the privilege of limited liability to avoid responsibility for its subsidiaries' debts. That the Bank of England should have such a policy raises doubts about its competence to supervise safely the banking system of a modern economy. The attitude was quixotic and honourable in the romantic tradition of the best British public school fiction. It was potentially quite ruinous.

Blind and suicidal approval

Both decisions were approved by the Banks' shareholders. Did they really understand what they were doing? They obviously did not, nor did the Members of Parliament who approved the private parliamentary bills which Lloyds and Barclays duly promoted to sanction the changes. When the Barclays Bank Bill was debated, attention was concentrated on that bank's connections with South Africa, and nothing was said of the possible liability which might fall on the British people. It seems to be normal for those who are concerned - quite rightly - about Third World debt, to ignore the possible repercussions of writing off those debts on the ordinary British working man. Every written-off debt quantifies the value of some part of the working man's production of goods and services which will remain unrequited. The beneficiaries of his efforts will be those who, often in defiance of the laws of their own countries, have deposited money in British banks. Too many of those who campaign on behalf of the debtor countries of the Third World are unconsciously contemptuous of the interests of British workers. They tend to be middle-class intellectuals, more able to afford loss than the working man, and less than half-aware of the consequences of what they are advocating. The proper policy would be that any charitable write-off of the debts of Third World debtor nations must be accompanied by an equivalent write-off of the bank liabilities to citizens of that country. There has to be a sensible limit to international charity!

Many citizens of Third World countries believe that the billions of dollars lent to their governments are the property of Americans. As America is the biggest debtor of all this is totally untrue. What those countries owe must often be money which is indirectly owned by its own citizens. Although it is true that much foreign lending is financed by deposits from oil-surplus countries, such as those around the Persian Gulf, or from trade-surplus countries, such as Japan and Taiwan, the public - and those who have campaigned on behalf of the debtors - have insufficiently understood the extent to which deposits originating from the debtor countries finance the loans made to them.

The truth became apparent when the Argentine government at last started to make a serious effort to collect taxes. In order to make the payments its taxpayers had to draw down their foreign currency deposits. The amount of cash repatriated was sufficient to drive up the exchange rate of the Argentine currency to an unheard of level, indeed to a level which made Argentine exports dangerously less competitive.

If developed countries have found it hard to be competitive with newly industrialising countries, they can blame it partly on the upward pressure on their own exchange rates of an inward flow of money from abroad. In addition it is possible that British citizens can blame the inflated price of houses on an inflow of deposits from foreigners. The recipient banks had little alternative but to feed the deposits into the mortgage market as there was insufficient demand in Britain for credit for other uses, especially while the government was running a budget surplus, and when

British manufacturing and commercial industries were, in the aggregate, self-financing.

An illusion of curing unemployment

When the debts owed by Third World governments had to be treated as *bad or doubtful,* the provisions which the British banks made were great enough to wipe out all the benefit of Britain's earnings from invisible exports. Unfortunately the reaction to the problem was not to refuse further foreign deposits, but to lend them in Britain. That raised asset prices, and the trade balance became adverse. There was an illusion of a boom. The imported goods and services which were financed by the inflow of deposits had to be distributed, and that used labour. There was a big fall in unemployment because people got jobs in the service industries distributing imports. But employment in Britain's native manufacturing sector continued to fall. The overall fall in unemployment was a dangerous illusion.

The United States had experienced the same effect earlier, and for longer, but began to see the danger. By the second month of 1991 President George Bush was calling for an international agreement to reduce interest rates. He was derided for this by British economists, but he was wholly right.

Correcting asset price inflation

A wrong move is difficult to correct. The actions which led to the huge rise in asset prices in 1988 and after would, if put into reverse, lead to even more damaging falls in values and could bankrupt many. In the past that same problem has been dealt with by allowing inflation to eat away the liabilities without further inflating asset values. The period from 1980 to 1983 was a good example of a period when asset values, house prices in the main, fell in real terms though constant in nominal terms, while there was high wage inflation. Thus the house price inflation of 1978-79 was not followed by a huge number of repossessions of mortgaged houses. There were vastly more repossessions after the 1988-90 house price boom because in 1991 inflation fell. Without inflation coming to the rescue, a recession meant agony for hundreds of thousands of borrowers who had succumbed to the selling efforts of the lending institutions.

The government's determination to beat inflation meant that house prices had to deflate. The dangers of a big deflation were well known. As long ago as 18th September 1821 the economist, David Ricardo, writing to John Wheatley, said that one *'should never advise a government to restore a currency which was depreciated 30 per cent to par.'*

In terms of house prices in South East England that is exactly the deflation which took place.

Yet it was obvious what was going to happen. In the 1970s loans for property development were the craze of lenders. That form of lending went sour in 1974, so the banks switched to sovereign lending with great enthusiasm. When that too went wrong the backroom profit-planners in the banks wrote papers reminding their directors of the impeccable record of the British working man as a borrower. So the main marketing emphasis was switched to him. It was forgotten that the working man's fine record had been assisted by the fact that in the past he had been prevented from borrowing as much as he wanted. The collective optimism of lenders in 1988 was remarkable. *'Those whom God wishes to destroy He first makes mad,'* wrote the Athenian playwright Euripides in the fifth century B.C.

In more modern times the television personality of the 1950s, Gilbert Harding, answered a question on hire purchase with these remarks:-

> *'I would like to quote what a judge said not long ago - that all his experience both as a Counsel and Judge had been spent in sorting out the difficulties of people who, upon the recommendation of people they did not know, signed documents they had not read, to buy goods they did not need, with money they had not got.'*

Marketing credit

Credit must be marketed, just like any other service or product. To get more people to borrow requires a sales force. Instead of creating their own sales force the lenders make use of the sales force of the retailers. They do this by paying commission to any retailer who arranges a loan. So a car salesman, for instance, not only achieves a profit for his business by selling a car, he also achieves a profit for it by arranging a loan for the purchaser of a car. Gradually, as a result of increasing competition, the commission became not just a lucky bonus, but an essential part of the car retailer's profitability. Without the receipt of commission the sale of the car could be unprofitable.

People who have tried to pay cash for a car have had sales directors pleading with them to take out a loan, and even telling lies to persuade them. '*You could earn more interest by putting your money in a building society*', said a sales director to a cash buyer. He had probably been given a target of the number of loans he must secure for every ten sales of vehicles. Targets very soon dispose of honesty. There is a still better ploy for ensuring that a loan is taken out. The car can be priced at a level which includes both loan interest and commission for arranging the loan. The purchaser can then be offered a loan *at a zero interest rate*.

Such a ploy is, of course, designed to increase sales as well as secure commission. Few buyers can resist a freebee, even though a moment's thought must tell them that credit has to be paid for, one way or another. The cash buyer must not be given the option of a lower price, for that would reveal the truth.

Sales techniques can cross the barely detectable line which separates honest dealing from the confidence trick. Human greed is a weakness which can so easily be exploited. '*You cannot play the confidence trick on an honest man*', says the fraudster's proverb.

By such methods the monetary economists' theory of the effect of interest rates on the demand for credit was rubbished. Even without such devious sales techniques credit was sold in vast quantities once a real effort to sell it was made. In 1990 when the rate of interest on building society loans was as near the highest level ever as makes no matter, the value of mortgage loans granted by building societies and the Abbey National bank to the personal sector reached the highest level ever known.[4] That the total of all loans to the personal sector for house purchase was less than in 1988 was due only to the sharp reduction of bank loans for that purpose, a step which may have been due to a policy decision of the banks, and not to an inability to market loans. The building societies seem to have had no problem. The subsequent fall in loans was probably a reaction to the overselling in the earlier period. The level of activity from 1987 to 1990 was too high to be sustainable, especially when Britain's entry into the Exchange Rate Mechanism of the European Monetary System with sterling overvalued turned a recession into a severe and prolonged slump.

Notes on Chapter Fifteen:

1.   I wqs involved in a later sale of the house - at the full market value!

In 1947 I attended a few of Russell's lectures on *An Introduction to General Philosophy*, that is the whole field of human knowledge. He attracted a large audience and was the finest lecturer I have ever heard. I was saddened to discover that he was the archetypal socialist intellectual who rejected the profit motive but lived in some luxury.

2.   The problem of slow payment of debts owed to small businesses has been highlighted constantly by the Forum of Private Business. The Forum's dynamic director, Stanley Mendham, has had every aspect of the matter researched in great detail, and has lobbied unceasingly to get some legislative action. He has passed on to me the results of all this research. I am deeply grateful to Mr. Mendham and his researchers.

3.   A salutary lesson for senior bankers would be some ancient banking history, for there is a 600-year old precedent for the dangers of sovereign lending. In the second half of the fourteenth century two of the great banking houses of Firenze (Florence), the Bardi and the Peruzzi, were bankrupted as a result of the default of King Edward III on the loans they had made to him. Financing Edward's campaigns in France was folly for another reason: they disrupted the supply route by which English wool, the best there was, reached the woolworkers of Tuscany. The marginal income of both England and Tuscany was reduced by the disruption of the trade. Tuscan traders had also sold weapons to the combatants, another folly.

In 1395 another banking house, the Mannini, lent money to King Richard II to finance his marriage to the daughter of the King of France. They too lost their wealth, causing their rivals to say, '....*no man ever allied himself with great lords, without losing his feathers in the end.*' (See *The Merchant of Prato* by Iris Origo, Penguin Books, 1963)

4.   Source is table 4.3 of the C.S.O. Blue Book, 1992 edition, supplemented by Abbey National 1990 accounts. The Abbey National changed from being a building society to a bank in the middle of 1989. This changed its place in the statistics, but not in the mortgage market.

CHAPTER SIXTEEN

PLANNING OR THE MARKET

'This very remarkable man
Commends a most practical plan:
You can do what you want
If you don't think you can't,
So don't think you can't if you can.'

CHARLES INGE

BESIDES BEING MONETARIST the 1979 government
was strongly committed to market economics. There was an
interaction between the two policies: indeed the government
would have seen them as being just two facets of one policy. Both
were attributes of Professor Milton Friedman's teaching. It is
appropriate, therefore, that we should discuss the merits of the
market economy and its rival, the planned economy.

There is a deep ideological division in the acrimonious politics
of economics between those who support a planned economy, and
those who believe in a market economy. There are also those who
support a compromise between the two, the mixed economy. The
fully planned economy implies that the allocation and use of all
economic resources must be controlled by the state's planners:
nothing is left to private enterprise and private choice. In the
market economy market forces are left to operate and react with
one another without government intervention; each individual is
left to make his own economic decisions. The expectation is that
as a result the optimum allocation of resources will come about of
itself, and far more efficiently than could be achieved by the
decisions of any government planner, however knowledgeable,
experienced, and prescient.

Faced with these two very strong philosophies, each claiming to have absolute truth, those who doubt them both, and maintain that an economy must be a mixture of the two, are regarded as weak compromisers and fudgers, which indeed some are.

Yet it is truly inevitable that all economies will be mixed, first, because in a planned economy it is quite impossible to suppress all private enterprise and individual initiative, and second, because in a market economy the sticky-fingered government bureaucracy cannot resist the temptation to exercise its power to interfere in the economy, even if it were not under constant pressure from members of the public to do so.

1. THE MARKET ECONOMY

The philosophy behind the market economy is a strong one, as it is rooted deeply in economic theory going back at least to Adam Smith, the author of *The Wealth of Nations (1776)*. It is based on economists' assumptions about the behaviour of economic man. The belief is that man's natural greed will always lead him to attempt to provide what the consumer wants, because, in doing so, he will profit. It is further believed that in order to maximise his profit he will do whatever is necessary to lower his production costs. To this end the cheapest resources will always be used. With a host of *economic men* reacting quickly, efficiently, and uninhibitedly to each other's actions and decisions the economy is strongly propelled to ever greater efficiency, and growth. Any attempt to interfere with this mechanism must damage it. Planning will fail because of the complexity of the plans required, and because of the lack of incentive to achieve efficiency. There is also the lack of any accurate mechanism to ascertain the true needs and wants of the populace, with the consequence that the planner's own bias dominates decisions. The market economy is therefore based on the belief that if market forces are allowed to operate without artificial hindrance or restraint, the best compromise solution to all economic problems will arise spontaneously and naturally.

The market economy can be confused with the unplanned economy, which some might assume to be the natural economic system. In fact it differs considerably from it. There are strong natural and corrupting forces within the unplanned economy which will prevent it growing into a true market economy. These forces may easily predominate, and prevent the beneficent market forces working properly. Therefore there has to be some state interference in order to enable market forces to work benignly. Even the market economy has to be planned to the extent that action must be taken to prevent the growth of restrictive practices, such as cartels, monopolies and associations. The true market economy is a tough environment, and the weaker citizens find peace preferable to profit. They are, as Adam Smith warned, quite naturally motivated to seek the safety of monopolies, or of markets neatly regulated and allocated by an association. They fear the effect of competition on themselves and refuse to embrace it. The fear is so strong that despite the legislation against restrictive practices all sorts of dodges still survive to keep rivals out of a market.

One common ploy is *the loyalty bonus*, which is a discount allowed to a retailer by a manufacturer if the retailer agrees to stock only that manufacturer's product. To prevent this sort of thing occurring, and to make the market economy work at maximum efficiency, requires constant vigilance and interference by the state, even though the popular cry of the zealous but imperceptive supporter of the market economy is, '*No state interference!*'

The market has no foresight

In ideal conditions the market economy might be able to bring about the perfect allocation of resources which is appropriate for a particular moment in time. But the market economy has little or no foresight. It will tend to do what is advantageous for today, even though that same action could bring disaster tomorrow. The market economy is unable to plan what is best for the future because its natural drive is towards what is best for today. It cannot sufficiently consider the future, especially the more distant future beyond the lives of the current population of the Earth. The market economy, therefore, has no fourth dimension, that is no dimension in time. If there exists a finite resource which is very easily won, the market economy will ensure that that resource is used wastefully right up to the moment of its exhaustion, regardless of the resultant damage to mankind. It will also tend to be blind to growing pollution.

Although the arrangements arrived at by the market economy should be a natural compromise dictated by the interaction of the forces generated by the whole variety of human needs, not merely the economic ones, the forces seeking quiet, comfort, clean air, healthy environment, and generally pleasant social conditions, seem to be submerged by purely economic forces to an extent which may not reflect the true balance of the needs and wants of society. Perhaps this is because those who are most strongly motivated by the acquisitive instinct are the driving force which determines the direction of an economy. One cannot be sure that the influence of the economic pressure from a small group is overamplified in the decision-making process. Judgements on this point are inevitably subjective, and one has to bear in mind the possibility, even though one may be appalled by it, that what happens may reflect the general democratic wish. Certainly, in a poor society the economic pressures are much more likely to predominate, unless it is a very unusual society which is poor only because it is not motivated by greed.

In both the unplanned economy and the market economy the disparity of wealth is likely to grow. If the disparity is great, there may be slow economic growth, and a low average wealth. This may arise from the tendency of the rich to spend their large incomes on menial domestic services, causing the expansion of the tertiary sector of the economy at the expense of the secondary. The greatest economic growth takes place when there is a strong demand for manufactures, the products of the secondary sector of the economy. Such demand is highest when buying power is evenly spread. On the other hand, if there is no disparity of wealth at all, a condition desired by theoretical socialists, but which cannot occur in a market economy, there may be poor economic growth because the requisite motivation for effort is lacking.

Five propositions about the market economy

1. The market economy cannot be a totally unplanned or an uncontrolled economy.

2. The market economy will prejudice the distant future in favour of the present and the near future. It will waste some resources, even non-renewable ones.

3. State interference with the market economy will reduce its immediate efficiency.

4. Egalitarianism will prevent it operating at anywhere near full efficiency, but excessive disparity of wealth will also damage it.

5. The market economy is capable of providing the highest rates of economic growth.[1]

2. THE PLANNED ECONOMY

The advocates of the planned economy insist that it is the only way to ensure there is no waste, that the basic needs of the people are supplied, and that the enhancement of the spiritual and mental well-being of the populace is not sacrificed to its material well-being. The basic philosophical justification is, however, that what is planned must logically, and therefore necessarily, be better than what is unplanned. Although the planned economy is always contrasted with the market economy, it was the evils of the unplanned economy which first motivated the advocates of the planned economy. It is very common for them to confuse the unplanned economy with the market economy.

To succeed, a planned economy needs people who are capable of doing the planning. They must have unerring benevolence, total omniscience, and perfect prescience, and must be absolutely incorruptible. These qualities necessitate vast experience, and must be coupled with complete objectivity in ascertaining the wishes of society. The planners need a total understanding of economics, a quality which has never existed. It is also doubtful whether a person having the other qualities exists, or would rise to a position of authority if he did exist. However, there is no lack of people who are fully convinced of their possession of all these qualities. They are to be found in quantity at every gathering of politicians, and they proliferate in universities.

The likelihood of an economically able political leader getting power is fairly small. Those who propose to use political power to plan the economy usually make known which of the people's economic needs it is their intention to target for satisfaction. Unfortunately the voters do not have the technical knowledge to

enable them to know which are the best policies for the achievement of their needs, so they put their trust in politicians with the
simple answers, or in those who promise the most. Moreover,
even on the rare occasions when they make their choice with
something approaching correctness, they, as individuals, will continue to pursue their own well-being, and thus will give impetus to
the market economy. Their instinctive behaviour will hinder
the operation of the planned economy.

The planned economy is notorious for causing shortages,
which in turn create large windfall profits for traders, for the
enterprising trader who attempts to defeat the planners in order to
provide what the public really needs will find his profits amplified.
It is for this reason that in a planned economy there is always a
prosperous black market. Revelations in eastern Europe after the
fall of the communist rulers tend to confirm the suspicion that
corruption and planning are inseparable. India, too has been a
victim of the overoptimistic attachment of its leaders at the time
of independence to the planned economy. With a market economy
the great talent of its businessmen would surely have made it an
industrial power of the first rank within twenty years of achieving
independence.

A British national plan

Parliamentary enthusiasm for planning was at its height in Britain
in 1965. In that year the Labour Government produced its
National Plan, running to about 700 pages. It is not really one
plan but an aggregation of dozens of plans stitched together. Each
group of planners no doubt worked in ignorance of what the
others were doing.

An economic plan has certain basic requirements. The first
would to some appear to be unrelated to economics: it is the legal
structure. Nineteenth century economic growth was given an
enormous forward thrust when the lawyers invented the joint
stock company. The economic importance of that development
cannot be exaggerated. There was no mention of legal matters in
the 1965 National Plan. One desirable change in the law, a new
form of incorporation for small businesses, was still awaited in
1993 despite the appearance of a government discussion paper on
the subject in the 1970s, and much subsequent lobbying.

A second important requirement is the taxation system. The National Plan had one sentence about fiscal policy but no actual proposals. Five months before the publication of the Plan the government had introduced the classical form of corporation tax with damaging effect. There had been no prior discussion of it.

A third requirement is a good primary capital market. Britain has long had a very good secondary capital market for certain investments, but a primary capital market, such as the French and Japanese industrialists enjoyed, hardly existed in Britain in 1965. The National Plan did not mention primary capital markets.

Nor was there a mention of exchange rate policy. As the economies which experienced spectacular success in the postwar era all enjoyed the benefit of undervalued currencies it was a remarkable omission. Instead a policy of overvaluation for sterling was continued until devaluation was eventually forced by market pressures on an unwilling government on 18th November 1967. The Prime Minister blamed *The Gnomes of Zürich* for speculating against the pound, but he could with justice have blamed those nearer at hand, including members of the investment committees of the Cambridge Colleges, some of whom were friends and associates of his economic advisers!

Finally, there was no mention of interest rate policy, probably because there was none. It was impossible to take seriously any planning document without one.

Six propositions about the fully planned economy

1. A planned economy ought to be an improvement upon a totally unplanned economy, but only because the unplanned economy will have in it those defects which prevent it from functioning as a true market economy.

2. Despite what it ought to be, the fully planned economy in practice is rarely a substantial improvement on anything.

3. To plan an economy totally is not within human capability.

4. The politicians who find themselves in charge of a planned economy are likely to be less than fully competent at planning.

5. Career politicians will hand over the real work of planning to civil servants who will be subject to few of the influences which motivate human beings to perform well, and will have no worth-

while incentive to improve the economy. In addition they may well become corrupt, though Britain seems to have been generally spared that trauma.

6.   A fully planned economy will never expand the economy of a modern industrialised country as fast as a market oriented, but mixed economy.

Perhaps the fundamental reason for the failure of economic planning was best summed up by a sentence in an anthology of quotations. It was taken from a book by Edward Noyes Westcott. A character in the book says:-

> *'I guess the"s about as much human nature in some folks as the' is in others, if not more.'*

The advocates of planning seem to share two characteristics to excess: they have too much faith in their own ability to plan, and too little understanding of the essential natures of their fellow human beings or, indeed, of their own.

3. THE MIXED ECONOMY

It must be obvious that the economy has to be mixed; nothing else is possible. But market forces must be allowed to have their way wherever they can achieve a benefit. Planning has a place, but its most important purpose is to eliminate any hindrances to the proper functioning of the market economy where that has an established record of success. Its main objective should be to add that fourth dimension, which the market economy lacks, in order to prevent wastage of non-renewable resources and eliminate pollution in circumstances where such important objectives necessitate that people should forego some immediate profit.

Governments must ensure that they do not develop the kind of mixed economy which possesses few of the virtues of either of its components.

The mixed economy will always be the battleground of two ideologies, the planners versus the market economists. To build a mixed economy requires knowledge, skill, understanding, and level-headed commonsense, all of the highest order. But what happens in practice is that doctrinaire ideologues pursue utopian dreams while they are mentally divorced from the realities of the community around them. Of course there will be peacemakers between the two battling groups of ideologues, but the would-be peacemakers will tend to be those who always flee from any controversy, and are convinced that the answer to any dispute lies in compromise and fudge.

The post-1979 Conservative Government was right to try to make the economy much more market oriented, but it was too doctrinaire about it, and it failed to exercise the standard of supervision which was necessary to avoid pitfalls.

There are certain areas of economic activity where close state supervision is necessary. Banks, for instance, cannot be allowed to expand the money supply at their whim. An unregulated banking system leads to disaster.[2] It is also desirable to have minimum standards of prudence in lending agreed nationally. Those misguided do-gooders who are always around to plead for relaxation of standards should be firmly resisted.

Success in marketing

The realm of financial services provides an instructive example of the fact that market forces do not always tend to ensure the success of the institution which provides the best deal to the consumer.[3] Rather, it is the institution paying the highest commission to intermediaries which thrives. Before letting market forces rip, one must ascertain whether their natural direction is towards support for the objectives of better choice and service for the consumer. In Mrs. Thatcher's government the ideological advocates of market forces made the unwarranted assumption that by oiling the engines of the economy market forces *invariably* act for the public good. Every ideology has some weaknesses to which its advocates tend to blind themselves. Although the basic assumptions of the philosophy of the market economy are much sounder than those of socialism, which ignore the facts of human nature, every economic doctrine is no more than a rule of thumb which may fail on occasions. Blind adherence to doctrine is a proven route to the wrecking of the economy. For this reason earlier Conservative governments seemed to pride themselves on being pragmatic, but after 1979 the Conservative Party became subject to doctrinal intransigence. A good radical programme of reform was thereby damaged.

Market economists will find unwelcome the suggestion that the system for creating credit should be controlled by the state. It is a suggestion which is made with the greatest reluctance, as there is the utmost likelihood that the control will be badly exercised. Unfortunately it is now crystal clear that one cannot allow credit institutions to compete freely in the creation of credit, or in the creation of money, if people insist on referring to the other side of the balance sheet. Sadly one must accept that although the greatest possible freedom should remain, the final decision as to the rate of expansion of each bank must, when there is risk to the economy, be a state decision, not a result of free competition.

This does not imply that one might as well go to the logical extreme and have only one bank, a state bank. There must be many competing banks. Let them be rivals on quality of service. The potential borrower should continue to be able to hawk a lending proposition around until he finds a sympathetic or understanding ear. It would be totally wrong for one person alone to have both the first and the final say as to whether a proposition succeeds or fails. Nothing written in this book should be taken as an argument in favour of detailed state planning. Let us accept the humane philosophy of socialism which advocates social justice, but not the methods which have been used to try to enforce it, and which have usually attenuated the freedom of the individual and slowed the process of wealth creation.

Notes on Chapter Sixteen:-

1.   The market economy does not always obey the economists' rules for the behaviour of economic man. For instance when food prices fall small farmers tend to increase their output, which is not the response which the market economist wants and expects.

2.   The collapse of the Bank of Credit and Commerce International in July 1991 revealed the need for the proper regulation of banks even in the most market-minded of economies. Depositors who have shown a market-minded interest in high interest rates scream for the regulators' blood when their own judgement of the market proves to be faulty. They seek compensation through the Law Courts.

What caused the regulatory system to fail? Was it a British attitude of don't care towards anything foreign, especially as B.C.C.I was non-European? Was it because the bank attracted mainly immigrants as customers and they did not matter? Or, conversely, was it a fear of the race relations implications if a tough line was taken? Or was it just part of a general ignorance and inertia?

3.   Financial services, such as pensions and insurance, involve the customer in taking an action whose full results may be delayed forty years. He can only take his decision on the basis of an act of faith. His sole comfort is that the authority of the government will be used to ensure that he has a fair deal. Without that authority standards soon fall.

Two decades have elapsed since I took part in a conference on investor protection at the Institute of Advanced Legal Studies of London University, which was attended by representatives from five continents. Since then much legislation has been passed, yet the losses of investors have grown, not diminished. Everywhere one sees practices being invented and exploited which should be banned the moment they appear. When it is so obvious that the government, acting under the influence of unrealistic theorists of market economics, does not care to set up an effective mechanism to enforce legislation, the fraudsters soon become bold.

The legislation can look tough: the Companies Acts' embargoes on share price support operations are specific and absolute, but breaches of those provisions in the 1980s were condoned because no guilty intent could be proved. The Acts were drafted to make these offences absolute ones, with no mention of guilty intent, because the draftsmen knew that such proof is impossible to obtain.

What good has deregulation done for the Unit Trust investor? I used to be an enthusiast for unit trusts and helped launch some of them. But since the ending of controls on fee levels the management charges have doubled or trebled. For this reason I no longer recommend them or use them myself.

But the main protection for the fraudster is the Law of Libel. When Professor Paul Higgins wrote a book about censorship many years ago, I complained to him that he had inadvertently omitted mention of the most effective form of censorship ever invented - the Law of Libel.

CHAPTER SEVENTEEN

CREDIT

'I think that money is on the way out.'
ANITA LOOS

A N UNDERLYING aim of *Towards True Monetarism* has been
to establish the importance of the capital base of the banks.
This powerful regulator was ignored by all economists until about
1990. Before the Basel Capital Accord was mooted, those who
advocated the virtue of regulating the capital base of the banks got
nowhere. The advent of the Accord should at last have helped
focus attention where it is needed. It highlights an economic
mechanism which must be far more effective than the succession
of irrational, ineffective and counterproductive techniques used by
governments in the past to limit the money supply.

In Chapter Five this book suggested in passing that reserve
assets might also be used to control the growth of intermediated
credit provided the control was applied to all lending institutions.
Some economists may wish to see this suggestion put to the test,
but there is little enthusiasm here, given the new era opened by
the Basel Accord. That has put in place the groundwork for a
controlling mechanism able to operate not just nationally but
internationally. The operations of foreign banks in, for example,
the UK would not be easy to control without international
cooperation. The BCCI affair demonstrated the technical difficulties as well as the risks involved. Until there was such an
international agreement, foreign banks which helped expand

Britain's domestic credit supply would need control in more localised form. The rules could insist they maintained a separately defined capital base, made up of assets which are located within British jurisdiction.

But there is another purpose for this book of even deeper importance. In moving towards *True Monetarism*, it argues that it is variations in the total credit supply - not just in one small component, the money supply - which govern the progress of an economy. More specifically, fluctuations in the aggregate credit supply cause the trade cycle. The credit aggregate to watch includes both intermediated and disintermediated credit supplies. Studies confined to bits of the intermediated credit supply, which have been the bread and butter pursuit of academic economists at least since Keynes published his *Treatise on Money*, if not before, are minor irrelevances by comparison.

Monetary theory has been devoted to the study, analysis and classification of the money supply rather than its larger counterpart, the supply of credit. Writers on economics have been obsessed with the people who have currency in their pockets or in their strong boxes, who have deposits of cash in banks or in building societies. They have been far less interested in those people who own bonds, debentures or other forms of securitised loans. They have quite ignored the borrower, without whom the monetary system could not exist. The time has surely come to switch emphasis from the money supply back to the credit supply in its entirety.

Credit was invented long before money. The odds are that it was invented in and for the agricultural industry. The belief that this is so rests on two peculiar and important features of the agricultural industry to which economists give too little thought. These features illustrate some vital basic principles.

Farming is different

The two unusual features of farming are first, that its production cycle for most temperate crops takes a year, and second, that the farmer has little control over the level of his production. The farmer's crops at harvest time can vary in amount from year to year by a considerable factor. As no community wishes to starve, agriculture must aim for a surplus, just in case there is a crop failure. The result is that countries which are big in farming almost always have surpluses, of which they try to rid themselves by dumping them on the world market, often at prices below the cost of production. Britain took advantage of this global surplus-and-dumping phenomenon from 1846 until 1939. By repealing the Corn Laws it had abandoned its own farming industry in order that factory workers could live well and cheaply off foreign surplus production. Only the harsh experience of two world wars changed that attitude to one nearer the policy adopted by the new German Reich in 1875 of seeking self-sufficiency in food. Paradoxically the British ill-treatment of their farmers made those who survived superefficient, in marked contrast to their protected counterparts in continental Europe. When at last entry into the Common Market gave efficient British farmers prices which encouraged investment and higher inputs of fertilizers, Britain, once perhaps the greatest importer of grain, advanced to become the sixth biggest exporter in the world.

Credit has its origins in agriculture

At some point in pre-history human beings started to divide up the workload and specialise. The farmer found himself with a problem: many of the things he needed from other members of the community were produced day by day, but his harvest came in just a few days each year. The solution was obvious; he was given goods in return for a promise to supply food at harvest time. Credit had been invented.

The next stage was to find some way to make the promises assignable. Farmer John had promised basket-maker William two bushels of wheat in return for an immediate supply of baskets in which to collect the wheat. To make the baskets William wanted a supply of willow wands from Thomas, the forester. The answer was to assign one of the promised bushels of wheat to Thomas.

Some undeniable evidence of the promises was needed. Something nice and solid would make a good token with which to provide evidence of a bargain. It might be a shard, a cowrie shell, a piece of bronze, a piece of iron. So long as they could not be duplicated at will, it was an easy next step to treat the chosen tokens as having value in themselves. Thus money was born. Money's importance rested, and still rests, on the fact that it evidences a debt, though its development into a measure of value increased its usefulness.

Once money was invented the farmer's problems started. The obligation he might undertake was no longer to provide a bushel of wheat, but instead to deliver a quantity of the metal, or other solid item, which his community had adopted as its currency. If, however, he had an abundant harvest he might find that his crop was next to worthless, and he could no longer exchange it for all the tokens he had contracted to provide. No longer could he simply pay off his barter debts and retain a larger share of his harvest for himself. Deflation of food prices, the farmer's biggest enemy, could ruin him.

Deflation the rule

Deflation is the natural order of things in a society which improves its production techniques, and it is a disaster for all debtors. History is full of instances of farmers getting into debt, and being unable to repay bankers because of a fall in prices. It is a recurrent theme even in ancient history, and must be the origin of the anathemas of religious leaders against the lending of money. Debt often reduced peasants to the condition of serfs. There may be some surprise that this story shows the farmer getting into trouble, not because of a crop failure, but because of an overabundant harvest. A novelist would have chosen the former scenario. Although a complete crop failure may be a disaster, a partial failure can be a bonanza. In 1976, when fourteen months of unusually low rainfall in East Anglia had reduced the potato harvest dramatically, many potato farmers made fortunes. Yet when new insecticides increased fruit crops in the Vale of Evesham in the 1950s, a local producer was heard to say, *'There is a fortune awaiting the man who can make one apple grow where two do now.'*

Because of the need for farming always to aim at a surplus, the farmer is invariably in a weak position in the market. Realising this, most governments, even those which favour the principles of market economics, have decided that there are always exceptions to every rule, and that the farming industry has to be protected from the more extreme free market forces. This assessment is assuredly correct, but unfortunately the protection given is usually far too great.

The formal theory

To repeat the argument slightly differently, one says that the invention of credit must have preceded the invention of money for two reasons. The first is that money is created by the creation of debt. A system of giving credit and incurring debt must have existed long before someone found a way of measuring it in a common unit, or of making it transferable. The second is that by definition money is transferable debt, and the invention of money had to await the invention of legal processes for the assignment of debts, and for their enforcement. What the populace calls *money* is portable debt. In a modern society all money is just one form of transferable credit. The twin innovations of enforceable debt and portable debt completed the invention of money. They ensured that it had the three qualities which economists believe to be its essential features - a measure of value, a medium of exchange, and a store of wealth or value.

In a modern society, where precious metals are not used as a medium of exchange, it is easy to perceive the identity of *money* and *transferable (or assignable) debt*, but currencies made of precious metals seem to confuse the concept of money as debt. It is time to root out that confusion. As the above account has shown, the invention of metallic currencies was merely an early way of making debt assignable and portable. By convention, that is by an unspoken common agreement, everyone who held gold or silver, or any other form of portable money, was held to be a creditor of society for goods and services to a value based on the value given by consensus or decree to those metals. Gold itself is a fairly useless commodity, being needed for filling teeth, plating electrical terminals, durable ornamentation and little else. It became more useful, and therefore more valuable, by substituting, especially in an illiterate society, for transferable debts.

Gold gave way to banking when the bankers invented bills of exchange and cheques as instruments for assigning debts. The spread of literacy aided their popularity. It is undoubtedly significant that the adoption of simple Arabic arithmetic, the invention of workable accountancy and banking, the circumvention of usury laws, the invention of printing and the spread of literacy, all of which happened around the fifteenth century, appear to have laid the foundation of modern mercantile, and then industrial society.

Classifying the credit supply

If it is accepted that the credit supply is more significant than the money supply alone, let us make some suggestions for its classification. Credit deserves scientific study, and since Aristotle an essential feature of scientific study has been the process of classification: it helps to elucidate the truth.

We have already seen that credit falls into two important broad classes, intermediated and disintermediated (or 'non-intermediated'). If we use 'C' for credit, in the same way that economists use 'M' for money, we can name three classes of credit, C^{int}, C^{disint}, for the intermediated and disintermediated categories, and C^{total} for the total of all credit. But there is a further breakdown of credit which gives a second classification.

C0 could, for instance, be the counterpart of M0. It consists of the investments held by the Issue Department of the Bank of England. *(See page 55 for a list of the monetary aggregates.)*

C4 would be the counterpart of M4. C4 consists of the investments which originate from the lending of all bank deposits, including of course those of the building societies, but also the loans which represent the investment of the banks' capital bases. So C4 is slightly larger than M4, but there is a correspondence between M4 and C4.

There are no corresponding Cs for M1, or M2, but there is one for the no longer popular M3.

Before further Cs are allocated for other classes of credit a general discussion of the subject among economists would be desirable. One question to be answered is whether it is possible, or desirable, to make all the other possible Cs cumulative in the way that the Ms are cumulative up to the final one, which currently is M4, (the former M5 and M6 having been abandoned). There are many more Cs than Ms, and there may be no benefit from progressively cumulating them together before one gets to C^{total}. Further Cs may therefore be individual. They will be needed for the following categories, at the very least:-

(i)   Shareholders' funds of all incorporated businesses.

(ii) All bond issues. Bonds can also be subcategorised, possibly by the level of security, and also by maturity.

(iii) All trade credit. This will be a very large category.

(iv) All government borrowing, whether central or local.

(v) All lending abroad.

There are many possible and useful subcategories, the figures for some of which are already published by the Central Statistical Office, but which have never been given identifying numbers by economists as have the categories of money. The C.S.O. gives all its statistical categories identifying codes, each being a group of letters. One cannot, however, expect that these codes will become popular identifiers among students of monetary theory as they are not mnemonics.

Finally we would need to identify the total of all forms of credit which are readily transferable, and can therefore serve as a medium of exchange. Perhaps in this class we shall arrive at a far more useful figure for true money than is given presently by M4, for many of the components of M4 are not readily assignable. A Treasury bill (not included in M4), for instance, is much more readily transferable than some items which are included in M4, such as a fixed term deposit in a building society or a bank. A subcategory, if not, indeed, a separate category, would be those investments or deposits which are readily liquidated because of the existence of an efficient secondary capital market.

An essential step

The more one thinks about the classification of the components of the credit supply, the less satisfactory is the emphasis hitherto given by economists to the liabilities side of the balance sheets of the lending institutions, that is to their deposits. The change of viewpoint to the assets side reveals in very sharp focus the importance for the economy of the total credit supply (C^{total}). How could economists go on so long without any knowledge of C^{total}, or any apparent wish to know it? Why was C4 not calculated until 1990? No figures are published for C4 before 1985 even now. How could anyone construct any computerised emulation of the working of the economy without access to such important figures?

It seems absurd that monetary theorists who had belittled the importance of major elements of the credit supply were awarded the very highest academic honours. Earlier understanding of the significance of the total credit supply was simply forgotten. How could the British government throw away the Borrowing (Control and Guarantees) Act of 1946, which contained the legislative authority for supervising the credit supply?

A hundred-headed monster

Control of the entire credit supply should be the very essence of true monetarism. The arguments put forward in this book have surely shown that the government must seek to supervise and control the whole credit supply in all its many forms. That is the way to true monetarism, which we define as understanding the relationship of the credit supply to the functioning of the economic system and to economic growth.

True monetarism also acknowledges that the word *money* is not strictly definable; it is not a scientific term. One might perhaps replace the word monetarism by creditism, but the term is unacceptably ugly. In this book the term *monetarism* has therefore been retained, but has been redefined.

So many are the forms of credit, the task of controlling the whole credit supply is one worthy of Hercules. Perhaps that is why the British government, among others, has gradually backed away from doing so since the death of Lord Keynes. The abandoned Borrowing (Control and Guarantees) Act was dated 12th July 1946, which is three months after Keynes' death. It must have been in draft before his death, and no doubt had his approval. Section one of the Act gave the Treasury full power over almost the whole credit supply, for the borrowing of any sum over £10,000 in any single year was subject to control. Trade credit was not exempted, but one must suspect that the draftsmen did not contemplate the exercise of restrictions over it. Trade credit can be very important, as is illustrated by the situation in Russia at the time of writing. Russia's hyperinflation in the early 1990s coincides with a phenomenal increase in inter-company debt.

One of Hercules' tasks was to slay the Hydra, a dog with nine serpent heads. When one head was cut off, two more grew in its place. The total credit supply is a hundred-headed Hydra. When one source of credit is suppressed, others are invented to take its place, or other existing sources are expanded. In Greek mythology the duplication of the Hydra's head could be prevented by cauterising the wound. Analogous measures to deal with the sources of credit would doubtless destroy the economy as effectively as Hercules destroyed the Hydra.

The powers given by the Act of 1946, and which were dispensed with in 1988, should be reinstated. They should however be used with the greatest possible discretion, equal to that with which the flowers of the foxglove were used to treat heart disease. Three flowers are a remedy, four are a poison.

Credit guidelines

Applying control to the growth of credit overall is a daunting task. One suspects that the attraction of the theories of the monetarists was that they appeared to provide an easy way out of the many difficulties. Lazy-mindedness is a widespread human failing, even among those with the brain to win first-class academic honours. It has been a characteristic of the twentieth century to look for easy ways of doing things. One can but hope that a characteristic of the twenty-first century will be recognition that economic causes and effects are not linked in a simple, unchanging mechanical way.

The economic situation shifts and changes with a myriad varying details making up the whole. Any one of a vast number of factors may be different from the last similar scenario, and yet quite a small variation may warrant a different decision from that in the last apparently similar situation. Consequently no firm rules can be promulgated as to what should be the automatic responses of the supervising authority to any future event. Only guidelines can be formulated, and even those must carry a health warning. Governments must also recognise that the course of economic events is changed not only by actions they deliberately initiate themselves. As earlier chapters have shown, the course of events can be transformed by apparently innocent little taxes, and by detailed tax regulations which look even less significant. One need only compare the provision of housing finance in Britain, Germany and the USA to see how small differences in regulation and practice can cause huge differences in the housing market. For everything they have said about small businesses, generations of British politicians would give Japanese-style trust banks, as the providers of capital to business, a very warm welcome. Yet attempts to foster trust banks would instinctively veer towards some cumbersome and impotent bureaucratic structure. The chances that Whitehall would ever examine the minutiae of its own corporation tax rules instead are unlikely in the extreme. Nor is every structure of credit shaped only by government action. The rules and conventions of auditors and accountants can also be a major influence; so can the fashions, requirements and practices of the Stockmarket.

One guideline might be that a supply of new credit should preferably expand the stock of real assets. One would be cautious about any provision of credit to finance a take-over or buy-out, especially if the price reflects an inflation of asset values above intrinsic cost. Any supply of credit which tends to inflate asset values should be restrained, or neutralised, and especially those which suddenly inflate house prices in the manner experienced in Britain in 1971, 1979, and 1989.

Recognising the full subtlety of the economic mechanism is long overdue: proper study of credit supply in all its manifestations would help force economists to do this. The way forward for monetarists is to study the effects of proposed guidelines, and refine them. The immense effort hitherto wasted on spurious computer emulations of the economy should be directed to these studies instead. A new generation of economists is needed who fully understand bookkeeping and, above all, cost-accounting. Better still they should have had real hands-on experience in industry. Number-crunching mathematical economists, inevitably remote from the real action, are dispensable.

The purpose

The primary purpose of credit control should be to iron out the trade cycle. An excessive supply of credit creates an unsustainable boom, which goes into reverse when the borrowers try to reduce their debts. The proper phasing of credit creation and credit destruction is the goal. Lacking the correct mechanisms, some people have abandoned all faith in the possibility of eliminating the trade cycle. An air of resignation seems to permeate finance ministries around the world. They even think that it has a mystical and inevitable regularity about it. There is a psychological element in the cycle with the result that the more lunatic trade-cycle theories are like fairies: they happen if you believe in them! The true monetarist will continue to strive to reduce the cycle. He will not accept that it is beyond human control. He will also observe that many measures, supposed to be anti-inflationary, have had the effect of deepening the troughs of the trade cycle.

Out of the frictions and uncertainties of the trade cycle springs unemployment, the cruellest of all economic faults. From 1939 until 1971 there was little apparent unemployment, and no real depression. One reason for this was the gentle inflation which reduced the burden of debt associated with boom conditions, and thereby avoided recessionary effects. The house-price boom of 1979 was not followed by bankruptcies or house-repossessions because the subsequent 50 per cent inflation kept the nominal value of houses stable, even though real values fell substantially. Inflation is the debtor's friend. That must never be forgotten. The adverse consequences of curing inflation can be far worse than the consequences of letting it continue. Bankruptcy has a domino effect, taking sound businessmen down with the unsound.

There are those who insist that unemployment is inevitable, a price we pay for technological advance. They say this despite the obvious need for more goods and services for the poor, the sick, and the aged. It is a feeble and defeatist philosophy. Eliminating the extremes of the trade cycle will be an important step forward, allowing economies to move towards a beneficent equilibrium over much longer periods of time. It is a starting point, but the solution of the unemployment problem in its entirety almost certainly embraces many other structures and habits in society. That challenge lies beyond the scope of this book, which seeks only to reveal and if possible remove some of the crass economic errors of present day governments. The employment problem is several times larger still. One powerful element is the willingness of people in different countries to do the same task for less money. As the techniques and knowledge of manufacturing industry spread around the globe to poor countries as well as the rich, the challenge to employment in rich countries grows larger. Global free trade, carried to its fullest extent, must ultimately eliminate global differences in standards of living. That is bad news for over-complacent Europeans.

Surely human ingenuity can find a way of marrying the need for work with the unsatisfied need for goods and services. This was the same problem that stirred the consciences of those whom Keynes called the *Brave Heretics*, such as Gesell, Douglas and Marx. They were muddled and wrong in their analyses, but their hearts were in the right place, so Keynes was kind to their ideas. But one must be wary: there are no more dangerous beings than well-meaning, but wrong-headed do-gooders. Karl Marx is no doubt the most notorious example, but there are legions of others alive and active.

The humanitarian dimension

We see them in the European Community which is a hotbed for humanitarian attitudes. It is still fundamentally socialist, in the better sense of that adjective. Unfortunately it is difficult for a Community with a social conscience to compete with systems in other countries which are ruthless sweat shops. Free movement of labour, of goods, and of capital cannot coexist with different standards of living. Some protection of the western economies is inevitable in order to negate the effect of loading high social costs on industry. Despite the fashionable liberal theory to the contrary, the philosophy of free competition will not make everyone rich and happy. If like is not competing with like, victory and riches go to the nations which are less tender-hearted, not to those with socialistic provisions for the protection of workers. That is a paradox of economics. The standard British view is that mercantilism, the protection of one's own industry by discrimination, is both immoral and, in the long run, prejudicial to the growth of one's own economy. Other countries of the European Community seem less convinced of its eternal truth. Nor can their enthusiasm for the so-called Social Chapter be reconciled with success in a competitive world. Socialist ideals are the Achilles' heel of an economic community's competitive strength.

Despite strong British opposition, the European Community's attitude to farming is wholly protectionist. The consequences for several European countries of a market economy in food are too horrifying for them to contemplate. Millions more would become unemployed to no good purpose, while a fortunate few might become richer. It is not a problem for Britain which exposed its farming to free competition in the days when farm-workers had no votes, and eventually found different employment for them in urban conditions which were condemned by Benjamin Disraeli a century and a half ago. A technological revolution in farming methods happened after the Second World War, but the further surplus of labour it created was too small in number to carry any political weight, and anyway the majority were readily able to find alternative work during the post-war boom.

A free market in food could be a bonanza to the eastern Europeans, some of whom now have a market economy in agriculture, and also have grossly undervalued currencies. One British commentator prophesied that with a market economy Russia and the Ukraine could produce enough cereals to supply themselves and the whole of western Europe, and still have an annual surplus of fifty million tonnes. As has been made clear earlier, efficiency cannot of itself enable one country to compete with another which has an undervalued currency. The exchange rate, not industrial efficiency is the dominant factor in international competition. Future historians, free of current prejudices, will recognise that monetarist policies which ignored the way high interest rates overpriced the currency were destructive in the extreme.

The problems which should concern economists quickly define themselves. If this book rescues them from their current preoccupation with inadequate theories and counterproductive techniques, some progress will have been made. Far greater questions involve the extent to which mercantilism should be pursued, not for the purpose of protecting inefficiency, but to protect basic social conditions.

The aetiology of British inflation

As inflation has been the constant subject of the attention of monetarists, it may be appropriate to repeat here some thoughts about the genesis of inflation. The following is therefore the outline aetiology for British inflation since 1950.

The event which played a vital part in encouraging inflation was the decision to raise interest rates. That took place on 8th November 1951, and the rates increased fairly steadily for twenty-five years until Bank Rate had increased to seven and a half times its 1950 level. The rise in interest rates raised all costs, and therefore nominal GDP, which is truly a total of costs. The purpose of the increase was a bit vague at the start, but it soon became a regular means of supporting the exchange rate, a highly damaging action. Later it was argued - contrary to all common-sense - that increasing interest rates restrained inflation.

Higher interest rates caused great losses for holders of dated or irredeemable fixed interest bonds. To avoid further losses which might follow more interest rate increases, most investors began to favour short-term monetary instruments. Short-term deposits mushroomed to the consternation of M3- and M4-watchers who failed to understand the cause. The form of short-term investment the general public favoured was building society deposits. These had tax advantages for personal investors. The liabilities of the societies were £2.2billion in 1957. In 1958 they were exempted from the Control of Borrowing legislation. In 1967 their liabilities were £7billion. By 1992 the liabilities had risen to £245billion, despite the exodus of Abbey National from the category.

The building societies were permitted to finance only the market for housing, no matter what proportion of savings they attracted or what proportion of credit they generated. Loans made for house purchase also enjoyed tax advantages which were further enhanced by the abolition of a property tax, called *Schedule A Tax*, in the early 1960s. The inevitable effect of this unbalanced financial system was to inflate the value of houses far beyond the general level of inflation. Home-owners creamed off some of the gain in the value of their houses by borrowing for other products, and thus inflation was spread to other assets. By 1981 the gross monthly cost of financing a twenty-year mortgage to purchase a three-bedroomed semi-detached house had risen to about 100 times the cost of financing the purchase of the same house in July 1939. By 1990 the increase in cost was about 265 times, a hyperinflationary level.

As was explained in Chapter Nine, a change in the method of taxing companies also had the effect of pushing up interest rates. Naturally the effect of such increases was to stimulate most strongly the pressure for wage increases, thereby generating wage inflation. The particularly severe boom in house prices of 1979 helped cause inflation of 50 per cent in the next four years. A later boom in 1989 brought somewhat less inflation because by then the pressure for wage increases had been much lessened, but by no means eliminated, by persistent unemployment, and by legislative measures to disarm trade unions. It is ironic that a government so determined to eliminate inflation should have tolerated, indeed accelerated, such inflationary pressures within the economy. The example of house price inflation serves also to illustrate the political difficulty of eliminating inflation: necessary measures would damage the social aim of owner-occupied housing and antagonise the very constituency the government was keen to nurture. That said, there are many more palatable techniques than simply scrapping tax relief on mortgage interest. Restoring the former limits on borrowing to a multiple of income would help keep house prices and income levels more in line. Treating building societies more as banks, and finding ways to encourage them to develop more balanced asset portfolios, would also help reduce the excessive flow of house mortgage finance.

Some monetarists have blamed inflation wholly on government deficit financing. The preceding aetiology makes no mention of it. Although any creation of credit, whether for the government or others, can assist the progress of inflation, paradoxically government borrowing can in certain circumstances help stall its progress. The reason for this is that British government borrowing has often served to mop up an extraordinarily high level of gross personal sector saving which was way in excess of gross real capital formation. But for the government borrowing, private sector asset values might have been bid up even higher by savers, and general inflation would have resulted. This argument is well worth serious study. The increase in inflation at the end of the 1980s when the government was running a surplus is evidence which strongly supports such a hypothesis.

The disaster of high interest rates

For the British economy the policy of using high interest rates as an economic weapon was an unqualified disaster. But for British society it was also a disaster. Some of the probable social consequences of the policy, even though they have yet to be fully evaluated, bear repeating.

The need for more cash to service large mortgages tempted married women out to work in larger numbers. A successful campaign to get their income taken into account for mortgage limits merely increased the amount of credit available for house purchase, and pushed up prices still further. From finding it conveniently profitable to go out to work, married women moved to the stage of finding it absolutely necessary to do so. Most married women were winning the marginal income of the family, and did not need such high pay as the traditional family man, who sought its core income. Many employers, especially those in the booming new service industries, found that, contrary to their prejudices, most women were better workers than men, they were easier to train, more obedient to company policy, and, above all, cheaper. In some industries the effects of this discovery were dramatic, and none was more affected than the banking industry. From being a well-paid, wholly male profession, it became a predominantly female profession, and, relative to the 1930s, more poorly paid. By such roundabout means, and by the more direct means of raising the price of capital relative to that of labour, the policy of high interest rates diminished the rewards for work.

The number of well-paid male jobs, of the sort which would enable a man to maintain a home and family by his own earnings alone, became proportionately fewer. As a direct result for very many married women work became an economic necessity. At a time when advancing technology was reducing the total employ-ment of the staple economy, financial pressures were forcing millions of women to enlarge the labour market. One must leave it to social scientists to discover whether this change was the cause of the growth of divorce, of single-parent families, of crime, and of many other alleged ills of the 1980s and 1990s. At first sight the connection appears to be positive. If there should be a connection, then the ability to effect sensible controls of the total credit supply acquires a paramount social importance also. It becomes not just a problem of achieving economic growth but of overall human happiness, without which economic growth is a waste of effort and of the world's resources.

The future

The aim of this book has been to redirect and even upturn some economic ideas. If it encourages professional economists to replace some much-loved misconceptions about credit and monetarism, about inflation and interest rates, about economic management and planning, it will have succeeded. If these new trains of thought lead to new forms of economic observation and research, so much the better. If an author is allowed to preach a little, then my sermon would be directed to the sins of *economic modelling* which this book has properly labelled *emulation*.

Few academic pursuits enjoy such immediate application in the practical world as economics. Tempting theories and new techniques derived from them are seized upon by politicians in the name of managing the economy. Some appalling damage has been done to Britain down the years, with the blame being heaped on the supposed greed, indolence, militancy, incompetence or short-sightedness of its people. The true perpetrators - wrong-headed economists and uncomprehending politicians - rarely if ever acccept that the primary blame belongs to them.

The political errors continue apace. Successive governments since the 1970s have repeatedly proclaimed their foremost task has been to end inflation. It has sounded like firmness of political purpose, and yet . . . Even a totally disinterested observer would surely observe how long it takes them to get anywhere. Periodically governments switch their *prime economic objective* to the exchange rate of Sterling as they seek to support it at a damagingly high and unsustainable level. At such times politicians are willing to subordinate everything else to the *defence of the pound*. At the time of writing the levers of economic management are about to be given another almighty wrench in pursuit of the latest political fetish, which is to redress the Government's budget imbalance as an end in itself. This fetish is the product of the monetarists' belief mentioned on page 234: that is they like to blame inflation wholly on government deficit financing, and they ignore the very different hypothesis that British government borrowing can serve to mop up high gross personal sector saving. Much of that saving is contractual, and therefore unchanging. Its level does not respond to the varying need for finance for real capital formation. When that need is low, the excess saving can bid up asset values and thereby precipitate higher general inflation. A clever government would use its borrowing to neutralise that damaging effect.

For over fifty years perceptive economists have known that excess government spending can sometimes be a benefit to the economy, and at other times cause damage. The time for them to speak out is before doctrinaire policies are applied, not after the damage has been done.

This book has shown that many of the customary weapons of economic management in recent decades have been ineffective, and some have even achieved results quite the opposite of those intended. Principal among the tools misused has been the setting of the level of interest rates. The next generation of applied economists, armed, one trusts, with a better understanding of practical matters such as cost accounting, will discover that higher interest rates mean higher costs, and, inevitably, higher prices.

A computerised emulation is not a *Deus ex machina*

Different management of economies will require different economists. One practice which richly deserves to be treated with scepticism is their worship of applied algebra in an attempt to model, or rather emulate, the workings of an entire economy. It helps breed a mechanistic approach to economic management which is wholly at odds with every observable human trait: Goodhart's famous law has many fresh applications yet. The true division in schools of economists is that between the practical observers, and the idealistic seekers of mechanical repeatability. By comparison the distinction between monetarists and Keynesians is a mere shading of emphasis: they are much more similar than they like to think.

Some monetary theorists have raised mere possibilities to the category of necessities. They have turned probabilities into compulsions. Their study of the infinitely complex science of economics has been made to deduce very simple, indeed simplistic, principles. To protect their intellectual status they have sought to make those principles part of an unchallengeable Law, no longer for consideration by the logical part of the human mind, but to be protected in that area of the brain which is not amenable to reason, the area ruled by man's obsessive neuroses. The mechanistic approach to economic planning which economic modelling encourages is a handicap to correct decision-making. This book has argued that it is the whole credit supply, not the money supply alone, which affects the progress of the economy, but it must be emphasised that this does not mean that there is any mechanistic, unaltering relationship between the credit supply and GDP which can be emulated in a computer program. The relationship will always be different at different times. The task of the economist is to observe carefully what the differences are, and in what ways they are important.

Future generations of economists may liken their twentieth-century predecessors to the alchemists of old who used pseudo-scientific techniques in vain pursuit of the philosophers' stone. The pestles and mortars of the alchemists were used wtih misdirected skill, and so were the computers of the mathematical economists. Another analogy of a profession which misled itself is the doctors whose leaches killed patients as effectively as the economists' high interest rates have killed businesses.

True economists will in future be more flexible, more clearly scientific, less dogmatic and mechanistic. They will also understand that they can expect no final truth in a human science such as economics. The search for *True Monetarism* will for ever be a continuing process. Therefore the title of this book begins modestly, but optimistically, with the word *Towards*.

ONE HUNDRED PRINCIPLES

'If you tell the truth you don't have to remember anything.'

MARK TWAIN

ONE HUNDRED significant principles which have been elucidated are listed below. Of the two numbers against most principles, the first is the chapter in which it is first discussed or implied, and the second is the serial number. Principles from 94 to 100 are more general and bear only a serial number.

1.1   The drawing down of a loan facility granted by a bank increases both the total of credit in use (the credit supply), and the total of deposits (the money supply).

1.2   Except in extraordinary circumstances a government can administer short-term interest rates.

1.3   A bank can lend money for which it has no balancing deposit in the sure expectation that one will become available.

1.4   A central bank can fix interest rates because it is in a position analogous to a valve in a hydraulic system: it can control the flow of money between banks.

1.5   The level of notes and coin required in an economy is decided by market forces. Any attempt to restrict the amount of currency in issue will cause the public to invent alternatives.

1.6   If interest rates are raised, the ability of a business to survive may depend more on its capital structure, and especially its level of gearing, than on its efficiency.

1.7   Charging taxes on unused (but usable) buildings during a recession causes the unnecessary destruction of industrial capacity. At such a time mothballing or set-aside should be facilitated. British manufacturing jobs which were lost in the 1980s cannot readily be replaced because capital investment in plant and machinery has vanished with them.

2.8   The capital base of the banks has determined the size of the intermediated credit supply and therefore the money supply. This principle has been highlighted by the implementation of the Basel Convention. Capital adequacy ratios are at last seen to be all-important in determining the intermediated credit supply.

2.9   The rate of growth of the total credit supply should be the prime concern of monetarists. The rate of growth of the traditional monetary indicators is therefore of lesser importance than, and is subordinate to, the growth of the total of all credit. Money represents only a small part of the total credit supply.

2.10   Money is created by the granting of credit. Credit therefore comes before money in the causal process.

2.11   All things used as money are transferable debts.

2.12   Savings equal borrowings. Savings are not equal to investment unless one redefines savings to mean something quite different from the normal meaning.

2.13   The credit supply should be under governmental control.

2.14   Falling prices, even though they are not deflationary in origin, can precipitate a deflationary spiral, especially if there is an overhang of existing debt.

2.15   An increase in the money supply can only arise from an increase in the level of debt.

2.16   Deflation of prices is the normal result of technical innovation and high investment. Unfortunately deflation can bring growth to a halt.

2.17   Economists must not abuse statistical techniques.

2.18   Rising prices and inflation are not always the same thing. Unavoidable real cost increases due to technical problems may raise prices. It may be preferable to restrict the term inflation to price rises resulting from the debasement of the currency.

2.19   Falling prices and deflation are not the same thing. A true reduction in costs achieved by investment leads to lower prices. One may prefer not to call this deflation, which could be defined as an appreciation in the currency which is not the result of technology.

3.20 An oversupply of credit assists the growth of inflation, but it is not normally a first cause except when it is used to inflate asset values.

3.21 Low long-term interest rates encourage investment which leads to lower costs and therefore lower prices.

3.22 High long-term interest rates discourage investment, and the consequent running down of the economy will lead to higher prices.

4.23 The expectation that high interest rates will discourage the demand for credit can be frustrated by marketing pressure by lenders.

4.24 Standard monetary theory fails to explain Gibson's Paradox, which correlates high interest rates with rising prices, and low interest rates with falling prices.

4.25 The credit supply and demand functions are not independent of one another.

4.26 The assumed capacity to service debt is the factor which is the ultimate limitation on the total credit supply.

5.27 A properly thought out system of reserve assets might be successful in controlling the intermediated credit supply. Such a system has never yet been invented or applied in Britain.

5.28 The practice of British financial institutions of mismatching the maturity of assets and liabilities should be discouraged.

5.29 In economic systems exogenous variables are as rare as the Hydra and the Yeti. The whole economic system of the world is subject to dynamic interactions. Even the weather has ceased to be a wholly exogenous factor since the proliferation of greenhouse gases from mankind's activities.

6.30 Special deposits do not restrict the intermediated credit supply; they merely transfer part of it to the central bank.

6.31 Special deposits can in certain circumstances assist the growth of inflation.

7.32 Overfunding makes possible the expansion of the overall credit supply. It therefore assists the growth of inflation, except when it is used to reduce government short-term borrowing which has been granted zero risk-weighting by the central bank.

In the latter case it is neutral in its effect.

7.33   Underfunding increases the supply of credit to the private sector only if there is also an increase in the capital base of the banks.

7.34   Unless all government borrowing from banks is zero risk-weighted, underfunding will squeeze out private sector borrowers and cause a credit crunch. They will be forced to resort to the dis-intermediated sector of the credit supply. Private companies and individuals will not find that easy.

8.35   High interest rates can only cure inflation by causing high unemployment. It does not always work as unemployment and high inflation can continue together.

8.36   If a currency is put into a fixed exchange system at an overvaluation, the deflation which must follow will have its effects amplified if there is a serious overhang of existing debt. A deflationary spiral and a deep recession will be the result.

8.37   An overvalued currency will eventually ruin the economy of a trading country, but it may take a long time to do so.

8.38   Deflation will not be cured by lowering the interest rate if there is no mechanism for applying a negative nominal interest rate. Deflation is self-perpetuating, in the absence of drastic remedial measures.

8.39   Deflation is the worst enemy of economic progress, and it is coupled with the worst social evil - unemployment.

8.40   Falling interest rates can reduce inflation by reducing costs throughout the economy.

8.41   The limitations of the science of economics must be fully recognised.

8.42   Although algebraic equations can be devised to illustrate functional relationships, it does not mean that any constant values can be substituted for the algebraic symbols in the equations. Economic forces are too numerous, too frequent in occurrence, too variable, and too erratic in motivation and application for any fully stable relationships to exist. Moreover the data variables on which the functions are supposed to operate are unstable, inconsistently observed, unreliable, or just inaccurate.

9.43   Rising interest rates increase bank profits which in turn attract capital. With the help of the increased capital base, the banks increase the intermediated credit supply.

9.44   Rising interest rates cause inflation in the short term, firstly because they increase costs, and secondly because they motivate wage claims.

9.45   A classical corporation tax system can be inflationary as it can cause long-term interest rates to rise.

9.46   A classical corporation tax system may encourage debt capitalisation beyond a prudent level.

9.47   By encouraging excessive borrowing, a classical corporation tax system will ensure that any subsequent recession is more damaging than it need be as companies are forced into liquidation at an earlier point than would be the case if they were entirely financed by equity capital.

9.48   Equity capitalisation should be encouraged, or at least not discouraged, by the tax system, as businesses financed by equity can more easily survive a recession.

9.49   The tax rate on profits of corporations must be the same as the standard rate of income tax.

9.50   If a profits tax is applied to company profits, it must relate to profits calculated *before* the charge for interest. This would keep the tax fiscally neutral in its effect on the choice of equity or loan capitalisation.

9.51   Capital taxation can destabilise securities markets and thereby damage the capital base of insurance companies.

10.52   The results of econometric studies can be interesting, but should not be readily accepted as persuasive unless the physical connection of cause and effect which underlies the functional relationships is totally apparent. This would bring the science of economics into line with other human sciences.

12.53   Taxation should be planned to be neutral. It should not be levied in ways which harm international competitiveness.

12.54   Direct controls are necessary to limit credit expansion satisfactorily. (But the controls will doubtless be misapplied!)

12.55   Credit created to finance the purchase of existing assets, such as houses, will inflate their value, and then, through the multiplier, will cause general inflation.

12.56   The trade cycle is caused by the overexpansion of credit followed by an attempt to reduce it.

12.57   Attempts to repay an overhang of existing debt will cause a recessionary spiral. (See also 8.36)

12.58   Mild inflation is the least painful cure for an overhang of debt. It acts as an arbitrary form of wealth redistribution, taking from those with monetary assets for the benefit of those with monetary liabilities.

12.59   To raise interest rates after a credit explosion is economic vandalism.

12.60   Foreign banks must be made to observe the same prudence and capital ratios as domestic banks.

12.61   Credit institutions should be discouraged from overspecialisation in lending or there will be distortions in the supply of credit to differing sectors of the economy.

12.62   Particular care should be taken to make sure that the housing market is not oversupplied with credit. The warning sign is when the price of the site rises to more than about 15 per cent of the price of the finished house. High land prices constitute a form of taxation of the young for the benefit not of the state, but of the landowner.

12.63   Any shortage of intermediated credit especially injures the small business sector because it has no access to the alternative, the disintermediated credit supply.

12.64   Anti-inflationary measures have done more damage to the British economy (and others) than inflation itself.

12.65   High interest rates transfer buying power from the young, the have-nots, to the elderly, the haves.

12.66   Take-overs and management buy-outs of companies must not be allowed to cause asset price inflation, or to increase imprudently the proportion of loan capitalisation of industry.

12.67   Take-overs and management buy-outs paid for with borrowed cash must be limited, possibly eliminated. A management which thinks that it can do better than another should offer shares as the consideration for the acquisition of another company.

12.68 The decision to make or accept a take-over bid must be agreed at a general meeting. The hope is that this might prevent individual shareholders in target companies being picked off separately.

13.69 It is impossible to tax capital except in specie. Capital taxes are normally taxes on the nation's income which have been computed by reference to capital values.

13.70 The only logical definition of capital is that it is the surviving product of past economic activity.

13.71 Income is equal to the product of current economic activity during a prescribed period of time.

13.72 Thrift and debt are two faces of the same thing. Neither can exist without the other. Let all moralists, as well as economists, note and understand that one man's saving is another man's debt. Moralists who preach both the virtue of saving and the evil of usury are wholly illogical. (That does not mean that debt should be encouraged!)

13.73 Net negative saving (which means the repayment of debt from savings) is deflationary. Net positive saving need not be in any way deflationary.

13.74 Saving assists real capital formation only if it goes into the primary capital market.

13.75 Saving fed to the secondary capital market finances an equivalent dissaving, and nothing else.

13.76 The absolute limit on capital taxation (taxation by reference to capital values) is the aggregate net annual saving of the personal sector of the economy. It is unlikely that such a limit could ever be approached. A collapse in all asset values is the consequence of trying to approach or exceed that limit.

14.77 Money does not have a constant frequency of circulation.

14.78 The Fisher Equation (MV=PT) is a useless concept.

15.79 Money cannot be transferred from one country to another unless there is a concomitant flow of goods and services in the same direction. The laws of double entry bookkeeping ensure that any flow which is not so accompanied has to be balanced by a transfer of money in the opposite direction.

15.80   An entrepreneur cannot ignore nominal rates of interest and observe only real rates of interest.

15.81   Nominal interest rate expectations are probably more influential than inflationary expectations.

15.82   The true real rate of interest experienced by an entrepreneur is specific to his business; it may differ wildly from the average real rate of interest.

15.83   The R.P.I. is not a significant index for the businessman. There are other more appropriate deflators.

15.84   Different individuals in the community experience very different rates of retail price inflation.

15.85   An inflation of house prices mostly affects young workers.

15.86   The Third World debt problem would not have become so bad if banks in developed countries had *paid* lower interest rates.

15.87   A trade deficit can create the illusion of reduced unemployment by causing the creation of jobs in distribution.

15.88   The foreign business of United Kingdom banks, both deposit taking and loan granting, should be hived off to subsidiaries, and no bank may assume the liabilities of a defaulting subsidiary without the consent of the supervising authority. This is a reversal of existing policy.

16.89   Attempts to regulate an economy will always be counteracted, at least in part, by the public's response.

16.90   A market economy has no fourth dimension; it cannot plan forward to any worthwhile extent. Only planning can have the necessary fourth dimension.

16.91   Market forces cannot control the money supply.

16.92   Market economics should be allowed as much scope as possible, despite the obvious deficiencies.

17.93   Market economics can never be allowed full control over the farming industry. It is a special case because it cannot control its production closely enough, nor can it be allowed to produce less than the minimum needs of the people.

94   As high interest rates precipitate firstly credit creation

sprees, and then credit crunches, and as very low interest rates may stifle economic growth, the proper rates of interest are likely to be the low to intermediate ones; 5-7% may be achievable for industries' borrowing.

95   The historic real rate of interest paid by the British government has tended to be 3 per cent. Perhaps that can be achieved again.

96   Moderate inflation is not wholly evil. Like the poison digitalis it can have a curative effect in small quantities.

97   The need for governments to use inflation as a crude method of taxation may diminish as more and more state enterprises, and their capital funding, are transferred to the private sector. The root of the problem hitherto has been the near impossibility of setting tax rates at such a level as will finance all public expenditure, and yet not damage private initiative. If the public wants high spending it must be prepared to tolerate inflation, hopefully at a modest rate.

98   A study team should be sent abroad to examine central banking and capital systems and to see what we can copy and improve upon. Special attention should be given to any system which provides small businesses with capital in the form they want: that is for a guaranteed and lengthy period, and at a sensible and stable rate of interest.

99   The accumulation of wealth cannot be prevented, but if those with money spend, rather than save, those with lesser resources can thereby earn the money with which to purchase what they desire, and will not have the same need to borrow. A reduction in interest rates, by reducing the propensity to hold deposits, encourages depositors to spend their money. A multiplier effect follows.

100   Laws of economics are rarely, if ever, absolute. One must be prepared to recognise exceptions in specific circumstances.

BIBLIOGRAPHY

T HE PRACTICE of studying economic theory wholly on its own is a cause of great misgiving. It should be preceded by the acquisition of some important basic skills. The preliminary skills currently expected of a student of economics are simple arithmetic and basic statistical techniques. That is not enough, and to them should be added bookkeeping and accounts, the principles of cost accounting, the principles of inflation accounting, law of property (real and personal) and law of contract, company law, banking services, and the law and practice of taxation of all kinds.

The best books on these topics will be those recommended by the professional institutes which examine in them, especially the chartered bodies. For lists of all the currently recommended textbooks to be read by students reference should be made to those bodies.

Some specific suggestions:-

Accounting Theory and Practice, by M.W.E.Glautier and B.Underdown: Pitman. This seems to be the current successor to Pitman's great book on accountancy, Parker's Advanced Accounts.

Butterworths U.K. Tax Guide, consultant editor Professor John Tiley.

Butterworths Company Law Handbook, consultant editor Keith Walmsley.

Financial Accounting, by A.R.Jennings: D.P.Publications.

Costing, by T.Lucey: D.P.Publications.

Money and Banking in the UK: A History, by Michael Collins: Beckenham Croom Helm, 1988.

Inflation Accounting, 1975: H.M.S.O. The report of the Inflation Accounting Committee, chaired by F. E. P. Sandilands. Inflation accounting has given rise to much argument. The argument was intensified by the publication of this report. In it the basic problems are well discussed, but the recommendations are not the last word on the subject; there was at least one serious error. The discussion was continued by the Morpeth Committee. The leading accountancy firms published excellent booklets on the subject for the guidance of clients. As the Statement of Standard Accounting Practice on inflation accounting is currently in abeyance, presumably these booklets are no longer issued. Old copies should therefore be treasured, for this is a subject that will not go away, however much many practising accountants would like it to do so.

Public Finance in Theory and Practice, by A. R. Prest, revised by N. A. Barr: 7th Edition 1985: Weidenfeld and Nicholson. This has long been the standard textbook on fiscal theory. It is a comprehensive academic study.

The Structure and Reform of Direct Taxation, 1978: Institute of Fiscal Studies. Report of a Committee chaired by Professor J. E. Meade. One must read this report. Meade's scholarship is impeccable, but one must have some doubt about the practicality of his conclusions. The Meade Committee was not composed wholly of academics as it included two chartered accountants, a solicitor and a retired deputy chairman of the Board of Inland Revenue. Two of the academics were accountancy experts, not economists. One of the economists was John S. Flemming, one-time advocate of wealth tax and economics adviser to the Bank of England.

The Institute of Fiscal Studies would have preferred the Committee to cover the whole system of taxation, direct and indirect, but the task proved too great. This is a pity, because the tax system should be looked at as a whole, not in bits.

Macroeconomics, by Professor Wynne Godley and Francis Cripps: Fontana Paperbacks, 1983. Macroeconomic computer models may work no better than inspired guesswork, and may be subject to *the Butterfly Effect* or *Lorenz Attractors* of Chaos Theory, but it is important to understand what functional relationships are significant, and how they work, even if it is an act of optimism to try to put numbers in the functions.

A Textbook of Economics, by J. L. Hanson: Pitman. This is a good basic textbook.

A Dictionary of Economics and Commerce, by J. L. Hanson: Pitman have published this excellent little dictionary as a companion to the author's textbook.

Economics, by Michael Parker and David King: Addison Wesley. This is a current textbook which looks comprehensive. In this book the process of money creation by banks is described with singular clarity and brevity.

Monetary Economics, by B. Kettel: Graham and Trotman, 1985. A competent foundation textbook, written for banking students.

Monetarist Economics by Professor Milton Friedman: Institute of Economic Affairs, 1991. This is a collection of lectures and papers by Friedman. His destructive criticism of the command economy and of state interference is excellent. His monetary theory is not correct on all points, as *Towards True Monetarism* has tried to show.

Money in Britain, Michael Artis and Mervyn Lewis: Philip Alan, 1991. A critical review of monetary policy. There is an extensive list of references for those who require them.

The Economic Consequences of Mr. Churchill, J. M. Keynes: originally published by the Hogarth Press, 1925, but sadly now only in print in an expensive volume of Keynes' collected works published by Macmillan. Essential reading. Keynes is on top form in this book. He should have kept up the standard!

The Treatise on Money, J. M. Keynes: Macmillan, 1930. As in all Keynes' writings there are brilliant passages and ideas, but there are sections which are best forgotten. It is not worth the current price of £90. It is in two volumes of *The Collected Writings of John Maynard Keynes*, published by Macmillan and sponsored by the Institute of Economic Affairs.

The General Theory of Employment Interest and Money, J. M. Keynes: Macmillan, 1936. This may still be available in paperback. Everybody talks about this book as if it were the Bible of economics. Much of it is not easy reading. There are, as is usual with Keynes, some brilliant, well-written, and even entertaining passages. As is also usual with him he is not always writing up previously worked out ideas: he appears to be thinking while he is writing. There must be doubt as to whether the General Theory was intended to sustain the edifice which has since been built upon it by the so-called *Keynesians,* who should perhaps be called *Post-Keynesians.* Can one believe that a man of Keynes' intelligence was seriously advocating econometric modelling? If he was, then why did he say that economics had turned *'sour and silly'*?

Monetarist Perspectives, Professor David Laidler: Philip Allan, 1982. This book provides the opportunity to assess the monetarist creed as Laidler is the guru of the cult. One reviewer described him as a *'lucid surveyor of monetary economics'.* His theories are based on a premise which is not proven. The index ignores credit!

Money Information and Uncertainty, 2nd Edition 1989, C. A. E. Goodhart: Macmillan, and *Monetary Theory and Practice,* 1984, C. A. E. Goodhart: Macmillan. Professor C. A. E. Goodhart is professor of Banking and Finance at the London School of Economics. These books reveal a great deal. They show monetary theory put into practice by the Bank of England itself. One notes with some concern that these books were printed in Hong Kong. No doubt British printers had been rendered uncompetitive by the high interest policy which the Treasury supported.

For those who read German there are two useful foundation books on money by Hans Hoffmann. The first is a history of the Swiss National Bank, *75 Jahre Schweizerische Nationalbank,* (1982) and the second is *Mehr Wissen über das Geld und seiner Funktion* (1984: Liberalsozialistischen Partei, Bern.) The latter describes itself as an easily understood introduction, which it most certainly is, and it is a great pity that it is not available in English. The book sets out the Swiss, the German, and the Austrian systems of central banking and monetary control. Silvio Gesell features prominently in both books. They were published by the Swiss Liberal Socialist Party.

Sybil: or The Two Nations, Benjamin Disraeli, 1845. Disraeli's masterpiece may be entertaining romantic fiction, but it is also a source book for social conditions in an unplanned economy. The dramatic evocations of social and industrial conditions were based on official reports. His horrifying *Hell-house Wodgate* was in real life Willenhall in Staffordshire, the home of the lock-making industry. The subtitle, *The Two Nations,* has probably been more often quoted by leader writers than any other novel's title. The two nations are, of course, *The Rich* and *The Poor.*

INDEX

(Numerals in bold face indicate a chapter/section devoted to the subject entry.)